JERSEY TOUGH

My Wild Ride from Outlaw Biker to Undercover Cop

WAYNE "BIG CHUCK" BRADSHAW

WITH DOUGLAS P. LOVE

For Pearl and Barb,
to feel goodness glowing inside, where love and loyalty meet.

To the men and women on the thin blue line:
keep the faith. Better days are coming.

CONTENTS

Invictus

"Out of the night that covers me,
Black as the pit from pole to pole
I thank whatever gods may be
For my unconquerable soul.

In the fell clutch of circumstance
I have not winced nor cried aloud.

Under the bludgeonings of chance
My head is bloody, but unbowed.

Beyond the place of wrath and tears
Looms the Horror of the shade,
And yet the menace of the years
Finds, and shall find, me unafraid.

It matters not how strait the gate,
How charged with punishments the scroll,
I am the master of my fate:
I am the captain of my soul."

—William Ernest Henley

FOREWORD
By Renzo Gracie

My chosen profession has provided me with the opportunity to meet a staggering number of people, including Middle Eastern royalty, famous actors, other sports stars and many more. Occasionally I meet extraordinary people known only to their friends—remarkable individuals with amazing stories to tell. Wayne "Big Chuck" Bradshaw is one of those individuals. His life story is almost unbelievable.

Big Chuck is the only person in America to have gone from being an enforcer in one of the most feared motorcycle gangs to becoming a sworn police officer and decorated undercover narcotics detective. What makes his story even harder to believe is that he made many arrests and took down drug dealers on the same Jersey Shore turf where he once rode as an outlaw biker with the Pagans. If he wasn't a close personal friend and confidant, I wouldn't believe it to be true.

I consider myself an avid reader and was honored when Big Chuck asked me to write the foreword for his book. Although I thought I knew this gentle giant, I couldn't put the book down as I read of his difficult time in the U.S. Army, his wild days with the Pagans and then his distinguished 20-year police career.

Wayne Bradshaw is most assuredly unique. I dubbed him "Big Chuck" because of his physical size. After we became friends I came to realize he was bigger than life in ways other than his muscular 250-pound frame.

Big Chuck managed to cram several lifetimes of experiences into one action-packed existence.

Big Chuck grew up in a sheltered suburban community in Middletown, New Jersey. He dreamed of proudly serving his country and volunteered for the U.S. Army Infantry near the end of the Vietnam conflict. He trained as a rifleman and planned on going into the Special Forces someday. But the army instead sent him to Germany, where he became involved in a series of violent situations that shook him to the core. In the First Infantry Division he learned to meet violence with violence. His years in the army forever changed him.

Jersey Tough traces the amazing course of Big Chuck's life. It describes his youth and his decision to enlist in the army at the age of 18, when some teens were fleeing to Canada or finding other ways to avoid going to Vietnam. It takes us through his rough three years in the army, his return to the States, and his descent into the dangerous and unpredictable world of outlaw motorcycle gangs. His strength, his size and the violent skills he learned in the army brought him to the attention of the feared Pagans Motorcycle Club, which is believed to be the most dangerous and violent motorcycle gang in the country. Big Chuck describes the constant turf wars with other one-percent motorcycle clubs, including the ferocious Hells Angels and the Breed. He was made an officer in the club, an enforcer and a sergeant-at-arms in the Sandy Hook chapter of the Pagans, which ruled the Jersey Shore. I still have trouble seeing this gentle, hulking, intellectual man in such a role.

Incredibly, he survived two years with the Pagans and managed to leave the gang alive, with no physical scars and no criminal record. Although he was once arrested by the Middletown Police Department, he was never found guilty of a crime and moved on to become a sworn police officer in the very same department. The hard-earned street skills he learned with the Pagans MC gave him unique skills as an undercover narcotics detective. He made arrests at an astonishing rate.

The Big Chuck I befriended and personally taught Brazilian Jiu Jitsu to is a humble, deeply intelligent man, who rarely if ever talks about his violence-filled stint in the army and his time riding with the Pagans. We talked about his work as a police officer and Patrolmen's Benevolent Association leader who fearlessly stood up for his men time and again. I know him as a loyal and accomplished Jiu Jitsu student and someone who always went out of his way for my family and friends.

From a tumultuous criminal lifestyle to a career as an undercover narcotics detective, Big Chuck has seen life from many angles. Big Chuck Bradshaw is my American brother.

CHAPTER ONE
GOING UNDERCOVER

Glenn Frey's "Smuggler's Blues" was getting serious airtime, and New Jersey was at the very peak of the powdered cocaine revolution, when I reported to the Monmouth County Narcotics Task Force (MCNTF) in the spring of 1985. Like many other task force members, I was on loan from one of the local police departments operating within Monmouth County, the Middletown PD.

The MCNTF was a busy agency, with jurisdiction in some of the roughest places in the state, including Asbury Park. The city that was once a vacation spot for the rich and famous had fallen on some serious hard times, and drug dealing, street crime and even murders were routine.

In the '80s Asbury Park had all the charm of a war-ravaged city— gritty, dark streets punctuated by the occasional boarded-up building, real estate "for sale" signs that looked like they'd been hanging for years, and gutters littered with trash. It was a great place to live, if you were a rat. During the summer, tourists would still gravitate to the famous boardwalk, which was adjacent to the old Convention Hall, Paramount Theatre and arcade—massive structures from the 1920s and '30s that had fallen into disrepair decades earlier.

At night, locals and tourists alike packed dimly lit nightclubs to listen to up-and-coming artists, including Bruce Springsteen, a regular at the Stone Pony, the famous nightclub one block from the Atlantic Ocean. A few blocks away, other aspiring stars played at the Wonder Bar, with its weird smiling clown logo. Springsteen's "Born to Run" ruled the land, and perhaps the nearby boardwalk, too. The Boss sang dark and resonant themes about the Jersey Shore and breathed life into the dying city, at least for the summer.

Asbury Park's residential area, barely a mile away from the boardwalk and the nightclubs, was ignored by the tourists, for good reason. The landscape there was punctuated by burned-out buildings, rusting junk cars and streetlights that hadn't worked in years. That was the part of town where I'd be spending my time with the MCNTF.

What set me apart from most of the other undercovers was my years with the outlaw Pagans Motorcycle Club, which counted Asbury Park among its territories. We had ruled the bars and nightclubs there with an iron hand and would rain down a serious beating on any other motorcycle club that dared to come into the city. As a Pagan, I used to hang out on those very streets where the drug deals occurred, engage in wild bar fights as needed and pick up chicks who found it sexy to be riding with a bad-boy biker on a chopped Harley.

Now I was going back to some of the same places I used to ride in as a Pagan, only this time with a badge and a gun. It felt weird for me, because just seven years had passed since I'd left the Pagans. No doubt it felt weird, too, for some of the other task force members who knew about my days as an outlaw biker, a one-percenter.

The task force had money, an array of confiscated undercover, or UC, vehicles and access to skilled prosecuting attorneys. It was a happening operation. Still, my world was quite unlike that of "Sonny" Crocket and "Rico" Tubbs in *Miami Vice*, which was all over the tube at the time. There were no Ferraris, yachts or "go-fast" boats for us.

In order to get diverse (and hopefully talented) undercover operatives, local police agencies were asked to "loan" officers to the requesting task force. While on assignment, the "loaners" would continue to be paid by the department that employed them. When they completed their assignments, they would return to their departments—bringing their undercover experience, and contacts, with them. It was one of those rare things in the police world, a plan that really worked. Oftentimes, loaners couldn't function as undercover operatives. Loaners who couldn't cut it would sometimes recognize the problem themselves and volunteer to return to their agencies. Sometimes they wound up doing low-key surveillance duties or desk work.

Most loaners were good street cops from within the county. We worked crazy shift hours and often had to face confrontations late at night and alone. We dealt with all manner of situations, usually weary from the lack of sleep. And we frequently dealt with investigators from the prosecutor's office. Sometimes they had similar experience and had transferred to the prosecutor's office. But mostly they did not—and were there because of some political connection. Some of these men and women had no concept of what a real cop did on the street. Joining the task force, they suddenly became detectives and perceived themselves as cool. They had not paid their dues, and it showed. There was a rivalry between the men who came up through the ranks in the police department and those who had been assigned from the prosecutor's office. Some of those prosecutors had also investigated police brutality claims, adding even more tension.

My team included some very tough and skilled undercovers. The real leader was Rick Coutu—another police department loaner who was on temporary assignment to the task force. A couple of the guys were members of the Monmouth County Prosecutor's Office, where we were based. The police department loaners like Rick and I didn't care for them, and they didn't much like us. Still, we had each other's backs; you couldn't survive on the street any other way. In most cases, the county investigators were good and ambitious cops. But a handful were not of the same caliber, either untrained or uncaring, or both. Some of them you just wanted to strangle.

Rick Coutu, who was from Red Bank, was exceptionally street-smart, hard-core tough and a total adrenaline junkie. He was of average height and build but very fit. His thick, wavy hair and intense eyes commanded everyone's attention. Very little happened in Red Bank—a two-square-mile community on the banks of the Navesink River—that Rick didn't know about. Ultimately, the team trusted him—I trusted him—because he was incapable of letting people down. He had focus and nerves of steel. I was willing to follow that guy anywhere, even if that meant going into hostile territory unarmed.

Getting caught with a handgun in New Jersey at the time would land you in more serious trouble than any street-level drug bust. Prosecutors routinely sought stiff sentences for criminals caught with both hard drugs and a gun—and judges were more than willing to hand down those rulings. Just about the only people carrying guns were the cops; if you were working an undercover operation and trying to keep a low profile, you went in unarmed.

Loaners drifted in and out of the MCNTF, usually sent by a local police chief to sharpen up an up-and-comer for his detective bureau. Some PDS sent their problem children because they hated the Monmouth County Prosecutor's Office and creating conflict was just part of the game for them.

Mike Panchak, aka "Pancakes," from the Eatontown Police Department, and Rick and I were in it for the rush. We made our own hours, and there was certainly no reason to be in the office before noon. Everyone on the task force dressed down, and most guys sported beards and earrings. I didn't like how my beard grew out, so I stayed clean-shaven and went with a basic blue-collar look.

Like the rest of the new guys, I had to work out an undercover persona for myself—an image that would be believable to people on the street, and one that I could maintain under any circumstances. How would I dress, and how would I act during undercover operations? I knew that I wanted something simple, an easy façade that I could slip into whenever needed. Undercovers have to maintain focus at all times—getting drug buys done, for example, while keeping detailed mental notes about what's happening around them. Everything done while undercover would eventually have to be written up in case reports. UCs are often interrogated by the dealer, and there's no margin for error in responses.

The undercover persona I selected came naturally; I based it on my years as a sergeant-at-arms for the Pagans Motorcycle Club, based in Atlantic Highlands on the Jersey Shore. I knew that drill because I'd lived it. I would wear the same clothes I'd worn in the past: cutoff T-shirts, black jeans and engineer boots. And I'd stick with the same Jersey tough attitude I already had.

My clothes, attitude and tattoos allowed me to fit in seamlessly. I was the UC operative who didn't need much training, outside the usual administrative briefings.

Two years earlier, when I'd first joined the Middletown Police Department as a cop, I was very wary during my first night on the street. I had no idea at the time if the guys would back me up or not, because of my history with the Pagans. At the MCNTF, I had a new worry: the group had access to the FBI's files on Pagan members. That meant my file in the MCNTF was thick and not altogether favorable.

Working with the MCNTF often involved policing the notoriously crime-ridden area around Springwood Avenue in Asbury Park, just a mile and a half from the oceanfront boardwalk. The area was so bad it was actually featured on *Ripley's Believe It Or Not!* as the most crime-infested block in the U.S. ever. No one, not even armed cops on patrol, felt safe there.

Local officials were so troubled that they renamed Springwood "Lake Avenue" for a while, hoping it might make a difference in how it was perceived. The name change didn't make a damned bit of difference for the people who lived there—or the cops who tried to keep order. The task force was charged with going in and cracking down on some of the many drug dealers who had managed to operate with impunity for years.

The neighborhood was almost entirely African-American, which meant white guys like me looked distinctly out of place. If you were white, there could be only three reasons for being there: (1) you were a cop; (2) you were seriously lost and potentially in more danger than you could ever dream; (3) you were buying drugs.

The Asbury Park Police were ever-present, but it would have taken a full company of officers to clean up the place. Periodically, we'd send an undercover cop and an informant down there to buy some heroin—typically just a couple of dime bags, which sold for $10 apiece and were usually in glassine or cellophane packages stamped with names like "Murder" and "Hot Shot."

The undercover would then try to persuade the target to let him come back alone for more product, a practice we called "doubling." Repeat buys of small amounts of drugs confirmed that the dealer was in play without financially crippling the unit. We got to the big dogs by bagging the up-and-comers, then flipping our targets into informants after they were arrested.

One hot and humid June day, one of our UCs, Rob Uribe, attempted to buy a dime bag from a dealer, only to get ripped off. When Uribe went to make the buy, the dealer grabbed the bill and ripped it in half, leaving him with a torn $10 bill—and no drugs. When the UC arrived at our prearranged meeting place, all he had to show for his efforts was half of a $10 bill; the dealer still had the other half.

"Fuck them," Rick Coutu shouted. "If we let them rip us off, we might as well pack it in. We've got to hit back."

In one sense, the rip-off was no big deal. The unit hadn't invested much time in the investigation, and there hadn't been a financial loss, either. But it didn't bode well for our ability to work the neighborhood, and that was enough to infuriate Coutu and some of the other guys.

Rick argued that if we let a single dealer in this neighborhood get away with ripping off one of the undercovers, we'd be plagued by people trying to rip us off for the balance of the summer. Our effectiveness as a unit would be compromised, and that had him pissed off.

"I say we go back in—but this time in force," Coutu continued. "We drive right up to the crowd, take out clubs and threaten them wholesale for ripping us off. We'll act like we're crazy motherfuckers and see what gives. We want them to think that they fucked with the wrong people."

Rick's plan was insane. Six members of the task force would hit Lake Avenue, two each in three undercover vehicles. The area was mostly residential, with run-down two-story wood-frame houses on narrow pieces of property surrounded by rusty chain-link fences and a handful of storefronts—liquor stores, barbershops and restaurants that sold cheap fried chicken and pizza. We'd be carrying props—40-ounce bottles of malt liquor and bottles of cheap wine, all wrapped in brown paper bags.

Once at the location, we'd jump out of our cars, clubs in hand, and challenge the crowd, threatening them loudly and angrily for not making good on the earlier drug deal. Before things got too out of control, plainclothes detective Rusty Swanick would pull up in one of the unmarked police units to bust us. The six undercovers would scatter, dispersing through the crowd and down side streets—making it impossible for the detective to grab more than one of us.

The only question that remained was who was going to get taken down and roughed up by the plainclothes cop. I was the unlucky one picked by Swanick. The two of us had never clicked, and now he was going to have some fun at my expense. In fairness to Swanick, he was a good, tough cop. He knew his neighborhood and was respected on the street. He was a stocky six-footer with what at the time was called a singles-bar mustache. In this not-so-well-conceived plan, he would have to get it right or my partners and I could be in real danger.

I didn't breathe a word of dissent to this "plan" but knew it was madness. The Lake Avenue crowd was a large and dangerous one to be messing with under any circumstances—and we were deliberately going to swoop in to incite the guys who hung around there, armed only with wooden clubs and baseball bats. We would be vastly outnumbered, and we had no idea how the crowd would react. Only one of us—Swanick—would be carrying a firearm.

I couldn't believe that someone as level-headed as Rick would even think of such a thing. It was a true barometer of how really charismatic Coutu was. If anyone else had suggested a plan like this, they would have been laughed at. How flawed and wild was this scheme? My mind was racing. What if we jump out and get shot? What if Swanick crashes his car and doesn't get there when he's supposed to? What if the scattering undercover officers walk into a group of hood rats who want to have some fun with the Caucasian outsiders? What if I really have to hit someone with the tree branch and wind up facing an internal affairs investigation? What if we hit someone with our vehicles when we drive into the crowd, or if an undercover or two suddenly go missing?

There was no doubt that Rick's plan would convince even the most jaded street dealer to believe we were street thugs, not cops. Cops follow rules, and they run operations that give them a clear tactical advantage. They don't send in a half dozen guys with clubs to threaten three hundred hardened street thugs. Only a crazy-assed bunch of drugged-up criminal white boys act like that.

There was another major risk factor, too: we knew that the area we were headed to was teeming with Five Percenters, a street gang with a noted history of violent assault and murder, and little regard for handgun laws. Five Percenters were often under 18 and didn't fear the legal system. If you got shot down here, the first suspects were the Five Percenters. And if one of them carried a piece, he was a dangerous hombre.

The Five Percenters group was formed in Harlem by Clarence Smith, aka "the Father," or "Clarence 13X," in 1963. Asbury Park's

African-American youth had been targeted by the gang, and anyone who elected not to join was guaranteed a daily beat-down. The gang had a bizarre philosophy, and some of us wondered why anyone would buy in. Still, the threat of certain retribution kept the group's numbers up. The gang made serious cash through the drug trade, and its members were a dangerous force to be reckoned with. In the crowd we intended to threaten, I was sure there would be at least 20 or so Five Percenters.

★   ★   ★

It was about 4 p.m. that June day when we launched our operation and headed toward Lake Avenue. The sun was sinking, but the temperature was still about 90, and everyone in Asbury Park seemed to be outside in an effort to beat the heat and humidity. I was driving a ratty, old two-door Ford Thunderbird, with Tom Perez, an undercover from the prosecutor's office, riding shotgun. Like some other military veterans, I had been a serious student of Sun Tzu's classic book, *The Art of War*. Coutu's punitive expedition, or at least the charade of it, violated every tenant of the Chinese general's rules of engagement. Those who ignore the art of war usually pay for it dearly. This was in my head during the breakneck ride with Perez that afternoon.

The corner of Lake and Ridge Avenues was swarming with people when we arrived, with dozens of locals hanging around the fried chicken place and a handful of other stores nearby. All three of our cars screeched to a stop in the heart of the strip. Some corner-dwellers had to jump out of the way to avoid getting hit.

We all got out of our vehicles, absolutely skied on pure adrenaline. Wielding clubs, we demanded to know who'd ripped off our buddy. The crowd parted and we briefly held the upper hand. But it didn't take long for the street toughs to realize that we were vastly outnumbered, and some serious smack talk started to come back at us.

As I waded into the group to see who was talking shit, a man of about 50 years old, wearing a white button-down short-sleeved shirt, quietly walked up to me. He cocked his head to one side and said, "You white boys is crazy, but you gonna be dead soon if you don't get out. Someone be comin' for you right now, ya hear?" He chuckled to himself, turned, and disappeared into the crowd.

My gut told me that this guy was serious and I had better watch my back. It was also clear that our ruse was working: we weren't cops to these cats, but invading thugs. We were in deep, perhaps too deep. One thing was certain: there would be no witnesses here to whatever level of violence was headed our way.

I didn't have time to react before I spotted Swanick's unmarked sedan racing up the flat, two-lane street and braking to a stop at the corner, just a few yards away from me. Perez melted into the crowd. The other UCs piled into two cars and sped away. Swanick had a freebie here, a person he could jack up to the delight of the many bystanders: me.

Stone-faced, the detective grabbed me and shoved me up against a painted cement-block wall outside a barbershop, punching me repeatedly and leaving me with bruised ribs and a bloody lip. Then he pushed me face-down onto the pavement and ordered me to stay spread-eagled there, which I did. I cursed at him as he tossed the inside of my Thunderbird on the pretense of looking for drugs.

The detective walked back to me and yanked me up onto my feet. Staring at me, and still showing no sign that we knew each other, he threatened to take me down if he ever saw me again. He shoved me into the driver's seat and ordered me out of town.

I swung a quick right turn off Lake Avenue onto Ridge Avenue, only to find it choked with cars.

A black male, wearing a white T-shirt and about 19 years of age, approached my car. He was average in size and had shaved his unusually round head. His demeanor was casual, and I knew that I had seen him, or at least a picture of him, somewhere. I just couldn't recall the circumstances.

"You still looking for something?" he asked.

"Yeah, jump in," I said, watching as he opened the passenger side door, pulled the passenger seatback forward and hopped into the back of the Thunderbird, where he wouldn't be seen. His decision to sit behind me provided him with a huge tactical advantage and put me in immediate danger. I had no idea if he was armed, and I immediately started wondering if I'd just allowed a hitter from the Five Percenters to get into my car. I couldn't see his hands from my position, and I tried to recall if I'd seen any telltale bulges under his shirt. Suddenly, everything I said and did became critical to my survival.

A cold shiver traveled up my spine. Because of the adrenaline rush I was on, I'd made a catastrophic tactical error by allowing a potential assassin to get behind me. I pictured him pulling out a blade and carving me up. I certainly wasn't a cop to him. I was some lowlife who was likely carrying cash. My thoughts ran wild. I had to be able to document every move I made for the police report that I'd be filling out—if I survived. This was no time to panic. I had never seen this guy before. But for some reason, I got the sense that he liked me, or at least was willing to take my buy money. Maybe he'd seen Swanick trying to reshape my face and rib cage and decided we had something in common.

Still wondering about my passenger's intentions, I looked down the street and observed a man and woman walking toward me, between the parked cars along Ridge. The woman was pushing a baby carriage with a young child in it. The dude was very muscular and tough-looking, in his mid- to late 20s, with a comb pushed into his long, bushy hair. He was wearing blue jeans and a sleeveless white undershirt.

Without missing a step, he reached under the baby carriage, pulled out a large-caliber pistol and walked toward my car. Standing next to the driver's door, no more than three feet away, he pointed the gun at my chest. Nearby, the baby started to cry. Still seated and unable to react, I tried to maintain my composure.

"The fuck you doing here. I don't fucking know you," he said.

Keeping my hands where he could see them, I said, "I came to do business. I am here for the summer. You do me, you can take me off, but if you want to do business I am here for a couple of months more."

This guy was solid with the weapon. He wasn't a shaker. When an untested street thug pulls a pistol on you, he is jerky and usually loud. They try to intimidate, and yelling helps them calm their own fears. But this guy wasn't like that.

I wondered if this could be the guy the old man was trying to warn me about. This shooter was considering his options and trying to decide if he should pull the trigger. I was clearly in serious danger and had no apparent backup. I was alone. It would have been profoundly easy for him to shoot me and escape. Even if there was a witness other than the woman pushing the baby carriage, no one in this neighborhood would ever finger this guy.

My no-name passenger got out of the car's back seat and walked around to the driver's-side window. He put one hand on the rearview mirror and leaned in through the open window. "You motherfuckers really is crazy, you know that? Can't believe you ain't been capped yet." Then he walked off to talk with the shooter.

They were too far away for me to hear their conversation, but I didn't dare move a muscle. I could see that my back-seat passenger didn't have a gun under his T-shirt. But I couldn't tell if he was carrying a knife or not. One thing was clear: I was deeply relieved to have him out of my car. I swore to myself that I would try to avoid a repeat of that scenario.

Nodding to the teen with the shaved, round head, the dealer said, "He say you looking for a quarter. You got cash to show me?"

I pulled out a rolled wad.

The dealer weighed his options for what felt like an endless period of time. All I could do was sit still and maintain a distant look. Without a word, he lowered the gun and then put it back in the stroller. He seemed not to notice the baby, who continued to cry. The woman paid no attention to the child, either.

"Can I get a quarter ounce, or an eightball at least?" I asked the man with the stroller.

"Wait here," he said.

I watched as the shooter walked to the other side of the street and disappeared. While I waited for him to come back, I tried to figure why this other cat seemed so familiar. Because of the round shape of his head, I tagged him "Cannonball Head."

Seconds later, the gunman came back with a plastic baggie full of white powder—what looked like a solid quarter-ounce of coke. We briefly negotiated the price, and I gave him cash. He turned around and walked down the street, his girlfriend pushing the stroller behind him.

Cannonball Head had little to say, other than to tell me to look for him the next time around. "Be careful with that shit, boy," he said mockingly.

I sat silent for a few seconds, deeply thankful that I had survived. I also tried to memorize what the two men looked like and how they were dressed. I knew I had reports to write and mug shots to review. I wanted to make 100 percent sure that I correctly identified the men who were responsible—and ensure that the court case was solid. I also knew that there'd be a defense attorney looking to embarrass me on the witness stand.

I thought back to Rick Coutu's plan and how things had gone down. One thing was certain: the plan had worked but had morphed in its own direction. That was the thing about UC work. No matter what plan someone crafted beforehand, the bad guys on the street seemed to have a habit of changing things up. UC work was all about dealing with unexpected situations. It was a great scene for adrenalin junkies—for a while. Later, I'd realize that the stress from encounters like that takes its toll on a person. If the physical encounters don't kill you, the emotional stress will.

My UC partner, Tom Perez, appeared out of nowhere and jumped into my vehicle. I wondered how long he'd been nearby and if he'd watched what had just gone down with Cannonball Head. I said little as we drove back to an industrial park about a mile away for a prearranged meeting with Rick and the other UCs.

I wanted to do a field test on the powder I'd bought from the gunman. All undercovers carry in their surveillance vehicles small test kits designed to evaluate product in the field—to reveal if a drug is real or counterfeit—and, if it is real, its relative potency. The cocaine test kits were about half the size of a pack of cigarettes. Each one contained two small capsules of chemicals and a thick plastic bag for mixing the suspected drug and the chemicals. When the chemical comes into contact with high-grade cocaine, the mixture turns a deep blue.

With Perez looking over my shoulder, I took a small amount of the powder I'd bought on the street and placed it into the test kit, carefully breaking open the glass-like capsules one at a time. The mixture immediately turned cobalt blue. This meant to me that the gunman was a solid cocaine dealer.

We had succeeded in our mission, and miraculously no one on either side had got hurt. The target I'd made the buy from could be taken down at any time: he was a real player, and there was no informant to protect. By then, it was late on a Friday afternoon. We had the weekend off, and the case work would resume on Monday morning. Though it sounds strange, task force members rarely worked weekends, since that meant overtime, which the brass wanted to avoid.

Monday morning, back in our headquarters at the Monmouth County Prosecutor's Office, I walked past a "Top 10 Most Wanted" poster and immediately realized why Cannonball Head had looked familiar. His face was on it: he was wanted for murder, as a hit-man for the Five Percent street gang. During our encounter, I'd known that I was in serious danger, but it wasn't until that moment in the hallway that I realized how close I'd come to death. I had been lucky as shit.

Cannonball Head became our top priority, and all efforts were focused on bringing him in. The one solid connection we had, and the man who could potentially lead us to Cannonball, was the guy I'd bought the coke from, the man who'd hidden the gun in the stroller. We decided to take him down immediately.

Based on my information, the MCNTF obtained an arrest warrant for the dealer, whom we'd now identified as a guy named Jerome Minter. To protect the identities of the task force members, local police were asked to pick him up, take him to the Monmouth County jail for processing and then bring him to the task force's headquarters for questioning.

A uniformed officer walked Minter into an interrogation room containing two chairs and a desk, and handcuffed him to a steel rail that was bolted to the wall.

"Fuck you, you goddamned fucking asshole," he shouted as I walked in the door.

"You don't have to like me," I told him. "But you should hear me out. After that, I walk."

His look softened slightly but he said nothing.

"You see your charge sheet? See anything about a piece being shoved into my face? See anything about endangering a minor by putting a piece in a stroller?

"No, you don't," I continued. "You just see the drug charge that you and I know is legit. I could burn you on the piece. But to do that I would have to fuck over your woman. I take this up with DYFS [New Jersey's Department of Youth and Family Services], they'll take your woman's kid away. But you don't see that charge, do you? You know why? Because I may be the one fucking person in your fucked world who gives a fuck about that kid. Now let's get this straight. I forget, forever, all the shit about the piece, the kid and his mom. And you give me Cannonball Head's location. No one will know you gave him up. You have my word. He set you up with me anyway. How the fuck you want to play it?"

Minter looked at me from the corner of his eye and sat silently, considering my offer. Then he gave me what I needed. There was no further conversation between us. But his eyes silently telegraphed two words: "Thank you."

Outside the interrogation room, I passed on the location to the prosecutor's office, which handled Cannonball Head's takedown. It felt good to get the killer off the street.

CHAPTER TWO

BLOWING THE SHOT

The Monmouth County Narcotics Task Force operated out of a non-descript three-story office building down the street from the massive Superior Court building in Freehold. Our sprawling offices—nothing more than cubicles for each investigator, separated by rows of chest-high dividers, were on the second floor and directly below the County Prosecutor's offices.

One afternoon in June, Tom Perez, Rick Coutu and I were working on some paperwork when the receptionist walked in and said there was a white guy out front named Mike Hanson who claimed to have information about an African-American drug dealer in Asbury Park. Perez asked the receptionist to bring him upstairs.

It sounds odd to have someone walk in off the street and offer up information about a drug dealer. But the truth was that it happened on a fairly consistent basis. Sometimes you'd see someone trying to offer up information on criminal activity as a way to get a reduced sentence or obtain a "get out of jail free" card in some unrelated court case. Other times, guys would find themselves in a dispute and try to rat the other individuals out.

While the receptionist walked Hanson upstairs, one of the detectives ran a quick computer check on him for "wants and warrants." He came up clean. Tom met privately with Hanson and quickly decided that this guy had the potential to become a serious informant. He brought him back to where Coutu and I, along with a couple of the other guys, were working.

Hanson introduced himself to the four of us and shook our hands; there was no bravado in his tone or mannerisms. Judging from his clothes and the multiple tattoos on both arms, Hanson was a hard-core biker. Wearing jeans, black T-shirt and construction boots, he stood about six foot one and weighed about 180 to 190 pounds. He had long, thick brown hair and a neatly trimmed beard.

The biker told us he was there to talk about "Mr. Brown," an African-American drug dealer who worked the streets in Asbury Park. We knew exactly who he was talking about; we'd been trying to take down this guy for a while because he seemed to move a lot of product. But we hadn't been able to get close to him.

Hanson sat across the table and looked at the four of us. He seemed to focus on me, in part because I, too, was dressed like a biker and had multiple tats. All of us were wearing casual clothes to help us fit in during undercover operations; elsewhere on the floor, detectives wore jackets and ties. Perez said little but gave me a nod; whatever developed, Hanson was going to be my new confidential informant, or CI.

Hanson described how he wanted to help us take down his drug dealer—who coincidentally happened to be a good friend of his. The biker explained that he'd gotten hooked on heroin as a result of being with Mr. Brown, and he was convinced that the only way to kick his habit was to get his dealer off the street—for a long time.

Hanson's story was hard to believe, and I told him so.

"We have no charges against you," I said. "Is this a revenge thing? If it is we have to move very carefully. These things become ambushes way too easily."

"It isn't like that at all," Hanson said. "If I don't take this guy off the street, I will never give up my habit.'

"Are you so tight with him that you can make me fit in?"

"Yeah, but we have to fix up in the room in front of him," he said, meaning that both of us would have to cook and shoot a load of heroin into our veins in front of the dealer.

Hanson assured me that if we passed Mr. Brown's test, we could buy some real weight from him—like a "bundle," for starters. A bundle is equal to 10 glassine bags of heroin.

"I respect you for doing this, man, but if you think I am putting a spike in my veins you got it wrong," I told him. "I want this fucker gone. He is the real deal. But I am not going to shoot anything into my veins."

"Then he'll never go for it," my new CI said. His look telegraphed defeat. It was clear that there was no other way to do a buy with Mr. Brown.

"Where would this likely go down?" I asked.

"A motel room," he said. "It'll be a room in some motel in Asbury Park."

I asked Hanson if he wanted a cup of coffee. The two of us walked over to a lunch room with round white tables, chairs, a coffee machine, microwave and refrigerator. We chatted casually. I needed to know that I would be able to work with Hanson out on the street; I also needed to know that I could control him, no matter what the circumstances.

My mind was racing. This was too good to be true; I wanted to take down Mr. Brown, but there was no way I was going to shoot up heroin, no matter what kind of bust I could make. As I talked to him, I realized that Hanson was agenda-free; he really did just want his dealer friend off the street so that he could get off drugs.

"Hey, bro. What if we cook up and blow the shot?" I asked. "I had friends in the army shoot dope, I know the drill. I know how to cook it up, and I know how to draw the syringe. We just turn our back. Once the works are filled, he ain't gonna have to see the last act. How about that? Can you hack it? Can you blow the shot? Because if you don't, this case is shit. You are getting named in a police report. I cannot bullshit you; I think you are a stand-up guy."

"I can hack it," Hanson said. "I'll blow the shot. It won't be the hardest thing I've ever done."

Over the next couple of weeks, the team kept Mr. Brown under surveillance from a distance, and I continued to meet with my CI. He was cold as ice, and I believed I could trust him when the buy went down.

Hanson made contact with the dealer on a Thursday and arranged for a meeting in a run-down two-story motel that offered hourly rates—along with dingy rooms, dim lighting and filthy patterned carpeting. Late that night, we parked in the lot and took one of the exterior wrought-iron staircases up to the second-floor room where Mr. Brown was supposed to be waiting.

My CI knocked on a wood door with peeling red enamel. The room's curtains were drawn, but the lights were on and we could hear muffled voices inside. The dealer, dressed in dyed black jeans and an unbuttoned black sport shirt, opened the door a few inches and stared out at Hanson and me with dark-colored, uncaring eyes. There was another guy in the room, sitting in a threadbare chair in a corner.

The seediness and squalor were appalling. The smell of the burned junk, the way this seemingly innocuous powder can hollow out a man, struck me. My informant had thick black tracks hideously marking his skin. If he wore a short-sleeved shirt, anyone would be disgusted. What woman would love him? He had the demeanor of a schoolteacher but the scars of a craven addict. How scarred were the souls involved in this *danse macabre*?

Showing no hint of concern, Hanson made the brief introductions and said that each of us would be buying a bundle—but that I would be paying for both of us. Mr. Brown seemed okay with that. It didn't make much difference to him where the money was coming from.

I asked if we could fix up a little—just a taste—to keep Mr. Jones away, and Mr. Brown insisted that I shoot up in front of him. There was drug paraphernalia on the round table, including needles, syringes and cotton.

Hanson and I both tensed up when there was a knock on the door.

It was Mr. Brown's girlfriend, a woman in her early 20s, wearing a tight top, shorts, high heels and lots of gold jewelry. She gave him a kiss, walked over to the bed and leaned back on the headboard. She was hot as a pistol and clearly distracted the dealer.

I handed over cash for the two decks we were buying and gave Hanson two bags of smack. We each emptied the contents of two envelopes into a spoon, and used the syringe to add a small amount of water. Next we held the spoons over lighters and carefully heated the mixture. We stirred the heroin into the water, using the plastic top of the syringe. When the mixture started to bubble, we knew it was done, or "cooked."

Hanson and I grabbed small bits of cotton off the table, rolled them between our fingers until we had tiny round balls, and dropped them into the liquid mixture. We poked the needles into the centers of the cotton balls and pulled back on the plungers to suck all the heroin into the syringes.

Taking pieces of yellowing surgical tubing from the table, we tied off our upper arms to make the veins more apparent. We put one end of the tubing between our teeth, held the other end with our right hand, and pulled until we started to cut off circulation. I looked over at Mr. Brown for a second and saw that his attention was focused more on his girlfriend than on us.

Thank God for the bombshell, whoever the hell she was.

Hanson and I sat on the foot of the bed, ready to do the shot. My CI successfully blew his shot, allowing the heroin to run harmlessly down his forearm and onto the already stained bedspread. Mr. Brown seemed unconcerned about my CI, whom he knew to be a junkie; he was more interested in my actions.

But as I casually turned my back to Mr. Brown, I inadvertently stabbed myself in the arm—exactly what I didn't want to do.

My mind raced, and I wondered who else had used the dirty needle that was now stuck in my arm. For all the insane risks I ever took, this was the most extreme. I was potentially under attack from something microscopic in size but every bit as deadly as a razor or knife.

Fuck, fuck, fuck, I silently screamed. *I have a dirty goddamned needle in my arm.* I would have preferred a knife fight or a shootout. I felt as if a white-hot poker was stabbing me in the gut.

I quietly pulled the needle out and shot the junk onto the floor. Mr. Brown had looked away just long enough for me to cover my actions. He saw the blood on my arm from where the needle had gone in and took that as proof positive that I'd done the shot.

Getting stuck with that needle was skeevy, and it freaked me out. I understood the risks, and I'd volunteered for this job. But this was insidious and creepy. Fuck. Blood-borne pathogens. Would I contract hepatitis, herpes or some other sexually-transmitted disease? If I did get sick, what then? Wild thoughts raced through my brain.

My CI and I left Mr. Brown's hotel room with 16 bags of heroin. Hanson told me not to worry too much about the needle, because he thought they were clean. But it was very tough indeed to trust a junkie biker's word that I was safe from infection. AIDS, thank God, hadn't yet reached the heroin crowd in Asbury Park. It was only a few short years later that AIDS became rampant there.

Hours later, I was back at headquarters, checking in the drugs as evidence. My plan was to go back and "double up" Mr. Brown, buying twice the quantity of drugs to further bolster my case against him. Fixing up in his presence was no longer necessary; I had passed the test. But I never got a chance to do another buy from Mr. Brown, who was believed to be the biggest heroin dealer in Asbury Park. The next day, Middletown Police Chief Joe McCarthy ordered me to leave the task force and return to the police department. He knew I loved my work with the undercover unit, but he was ordering me off, effective immediately, for reasons that had nothing to do with me.

Even before I got the news that I was done with the case, something felt off in the task force offices. Some of the senior officers weren't there, and that was unusual.

Captain Harry Valentine called me into his office and asked me to shut the door.

"Bradshaw, I'm sorry to have to tell you, but Chief McCarthy wants you back in Middletown," the captain said. "Gather your personal items, do what you need to do and then get out of here. You're not to return. Understand?"

"Captain, what the hell. What's going on?" I asked.

Valentine had little to say. But apparently the Monmouth County Prosecutor's Office had put together a series of indictments against three Middletown Police Department detectives—Steve Xanthos, Kevin McCauley and Pat Greeves—for violently assaulting a couple of meth dealers while on a drug raid. Xanthos was known for making heavy-duty arrests, but his tactics weren't always the cleanest. McCauley and I had been friends for years, and I was surprised to hear about him. No doubt, Chief McCarthy was pissed. His force was now down by three detectives, and he had a major public relations problem on his hands. The chief wanted nothing to do with the Monmouth County prosecutor, and that meant that I couldn't continue on the MCNTF.

Now I realized why the task force offices had seemed so quiet. A number of the guys had apparently taken some time off to avoid having to tell me about Chief McCarthy's decision. Valentine was the low man on the totem pole, and so he'd been stuck with the task. I tried calling headquarters in Middletown to find out what the chief had in mind for me. But oddly, it seemed that some of the commanding officers there had also left early. I wasn't going to learn anything more about my next assignment tonight. I literally had no idea what my next assignment was going to be.

What a roller-coaster I was on! I'm on the verge of really smacking some home runs, then the pinch hitter takes my spot in the lineup. What did this say about my personality, that no one in the brass wanted to look me in the eye? Did they think I was deranged, a risk to flip out? If so, they needn't have worried. It had been a hell of a summer. A real blast. I was in no position to even make a case with Chief McCarthy—he valued loyalty, and I wouldn't have the job if it weren't for him sticking his neck out. I'd heard there was an opening in a new, smaller undercover operation. I would shoot for that and enjoy the remainder of the summer. Besides, my friend was one of the indicted detectives. And lest I forget, McCauley had invited me along on the ill-fated narcotics raid that resulted in his arrest. Lucky for me, I had been busy that night in Asbury Park.

My MCNTF partners wasted no time taking me out for a proper farewell celebration, complete with a visit to a strip club in Eatontown that I could have done without, an elaborate steak dinner and some sorrowful goodbyes early the following morning.

On Monday morning, I reported for work at the Middletown Police Department. There, the chief saw me and called me into his office for a quick conversation.

"I know you liked it out there and were kicking ass. But there's no way in the world we can have a guy like you helping those motherfuckers," McCarthy said.

I had no choice but to agree—and truthfully, I was worried about my buddy McCauley.

The chief pulled one of the lieutenants into the conversation. "Hey, Danny, you know that three weeks of vacation you've got for Bradshaw, right? You've got that in the books, right?

The lieutenant gave me a quick glance. It was clear he had no idea what the chief was talking about. But it was the chief.

"Yeah, absolutely!" the lieutenant responded.

"Great," the chief said before turning to me. "Okay, then take three weeks off and when you get back, the next opening at the Bayshore Narcotics Task Force is yours."

I couldn't complain. I suddenly had much of August off.

CHAPTER THREE

THE POLITICS OF CONTRABAND

One month later, I started work with another undercover unit—the Bayshore Narcotics Task Force, responsible for driving down illicit drug activity in the northern section of Monmouth County. I was excited to be part of the group, even though it was a tiny, low-budget operation.

A group of local police departments had teamed up to form the BNTF, with each one providing staff on a rotating basis. There were only three of us in the unit when it started. John McCabe, a detective lieutenant from Hazlet, was the group's supervisor; he brought John "Jack" Mullins with him from Hazlet. I was the only one who had any undercover experience, with three months' worth under my belt, but all of us had spent some time on the streets and knew the area and its residents well. Other officers had already nicknamed Detective Lieutenant McCabe "Father John" because he had an uncanny ability to be able to get suspects to confess to just about anything without using excessive force. Soon the Keansburg Police Department sent over another officer, Armand "Armie" Ertle, and the Union Beach PD sent over Alton Bennett, giving us a total of five.

We worked out of the Holmdel Police Department, which—like many small municipal police forces—was housed in the town hall. The two-story V-shaped building was just five years old; it had a light-colored stone façade and dark shingled roof. It was located on Crawfords Corner

Road, not far from the Garden State Parkway, which made it easier for us to move around the area. The task force operated out of a room in the basement, across the hall from the police gym.

Holmdel had an upscale population of about 16 thousand and a low crime rate—which made the police headquarters a great place for us, since we didn't need to worry as much about low-level criminals seeing us and later identifying us as cops. Most of our operations and arrests would take place miles away, in the communities of Middletown, Keansburg and Union Beach.

The transfer energized me. We were like a special-ops team, with very loose supervision. It was all about the character of the undercover operatives, their mutual trust—and, as always, results. I was on cloud nine. I had gone from an outlaw motorcycle culture, with jail always hanging over my head like a Sword of Damocles, to law enforcement with a nice amount of heady danger associated with it. I sincerely liked and respected my co-workers, and they returned the sentiment. We were determined to make this task force the highlight of our careers. I felt like I was born to it.

On my first day there, I met the supervisor, McCabe. He wouldn't be part of the task force's everyday operations but would have full authority over the unit. McCabe was average in both height and weight, with a very mild personality. I got the sense that he could be a quiet but strong leader. He and I talked for a bit in the office and came up with the idea of going undercover as members of an outlaw biker gang—which would be easy for me. It wasn't long before he suggested that Jack Mullins and I go out for a drink in Hazlet. We'd be working together closely, relying on each other, so it made sense for us to get to know each other.

Though Jack had no prior undercover experience, I was sure he'd quickly get up to speed and make a superb undercover. He was street-smart, a born raconteur and had prior military experience with a top-notch outfit in the Philippines. He also looked like a perfect fit as an outlaw biker.

Jack and I headed for a quiet, out-of-the-way bar for lunch and a couple of drinks. We grabbed two bar stools, ordered pizzas and draft beers and watched a little of the baseball game that was playing on the TV. We were having a great time, telling war stories and laughing like hell. Jack could put away multiple drinks without it showing. We spent half the afternoon at the bar, sipping brews together.

Suddenly Jack looked me straight in the eye and said, "I'm feeling like I should kick your fucking ass. I've fucking heard about you, all your fucking stories, and I'm fucking done with it."

"I know you're fucking around, man," I said.

"I'm not fucking around at all. You need a beating, and I am the perfect person to do it," Jack said. "It'll get things started out right."

"You're fucking serious?"

"Fucking right I am," he shot back. "I will beat you out to the parking lot, you motherfucker."

There was no way I was going to let this go, cop or no cop. I stood, walked out of the bar and headed to the parking lot around back—ready to pound him into the pavement.

Jack came at me with fists held high. Just before he got within striking distance, he stopped and burst out laughing. "You thought I was serious?" he asked. "Everyone knows about you, you're the last person I would ever want to fight. You're killing me, man."

McCabe had been right to send the two of us out that day.

I can only imagine the stories Jack must have been told about me. Police agencies are a bit like beauty parlors, places where gossip is told and retold—and often embellished at every step. As a former member of an outlaw motorcycle gang who rode through town on a custom Harley, got into bar fights on a regular basis and otherwise wreaked havoc on the Jersey Shore, I was no doubt real fodder for coffee break meetings in the field. The fact that I was a black belt martial artist also added to my tough guy image. Inevitably, the myth is much bigger than the man. I knew that going into the game, so I played things as low-key as I could.

I rarely attended police-related drunk-fests and avoided confrontations with co-workers.

The following day, the Bayshore Narcotics Task Force began its work in the field. As awesome as the whole assignment was, we needed to show real results or our credibility would be compromised. We also needed to make allies of every police chief, patrolman and detective we came into contact with. We needed these guys to want to turn over low-level criminals to us so that we could use them as confidential informants. The only way we could do that was to be liked and respected—and treat our word as our bond. The unit had a lot of spirit, but not much in the way of equipment. We had one crappy old sedan and an old blue full-sized Chevrolet van—the sort used by tradespeople, with two seats up front and a large open cargo area. Like the MCNTF, we had no electronic surveillance equipment.

I felt that our best disguise was as bikers, and so we went with the idea that we were a chapter of the Norsemen Motorcycle Club. The guys were cool with the idea, but there was one obvious element missing: we had no motorcycles, and the powers that be weren't willing to provide us with any. Somehow we managed to wing it. The van helped a lot, because motorcycle clubs always rode with a cargo van just in case one of the expensive custom bikes broke down. There was nothing worse than seeing a hand-painted and chromed motorcycle on the back of a tow truck.

Jack and I soon made our first bust using that van. We were driving down a highway near Union Beach in the Chevy when we saw two guys in their early 20s hitchhiking. We stopped to pick them up and headed down toward their destination, Keansburg.

"Hey, you got any dope?" I asked.

"As a matter of fact, I do," one of the guys said, reaching into his pants pocket and pulling out a very large bag of marijuana. Jack and I were stunned. We sat quietly while the guy pulled out rolling papers and made a joint. Maybe we were too quiet, because they immediately became suspicious.

"They're cops," one of the guys whispered.

"Fucking right," I said. I hit the brakes and brought the van to a quick stop on the side of the highway. One of the guys hopped out of the back and tried to make a run for it, but I caught him, tackled him and brought him back to the van in handcuffs. Jack had the other guy in handcuffs, too. Both men had been unarmed.

As we headed over to the Keansburg Police Department to book them, Jack and I gave each other a quiet look. We were worried that these guys might be locals, able to describe us and our van to their buddies. But we had no problem maintaining our cover. The hitchhikers were from another part of the state, and there was no way they would be back here anytime soon. They were soon processed for felony-weight possession of a controlled substance.

In my biker days, I couldn't have cared less if someone was carrying some weed. Even as a cop, carrying a small amount of marijuana was no big deal to me. But this case was different because of the quantity they were carrying and the casual manner they demonstrated. I was struck by their sheer stupidity.

Big Bad John Jankowski, a known drug dealer who had long avoided arrest, was target number one for the BNTF.

Jankowski was a major-league cocaine dealer, and his coke was always of high quality. He was a huge guy—a brutal one, too, and skilled with a shotgun. He lived in Union Beach, in northern Monmouth County, and had a brother, Stan Jankowski, who was a cop with the Middletown Police Department. The word on the street was that Stan fed his brother inside info to stay ahead of the law. But I knew Stan, and I knew that the word on the street was 100 percent bullshit. What kept the police away from Big John's door was his reputation for violence and his excellent street sense.

No one would give up Big John, no matter how much jail time was at stake. They all knew that this bad actor liked shotguns and wasn't afraid to use them. The trick was coming up with a plan to take him down without getting any of us shot or killed. I was also determined that the BNTF was going to take Big John down without any help—or knowledge—from the MCNTF. Though the two agencies had the same goals, there was considerable interagency competition; I didn't want my former task force involved, and no one else did, either.

Big John had a modus operandi that was tough to penetrate as well. He sold virtually everything himself, right out of his house. Unless you were a close and trusted personal friend, you couldn't score from him. The only way he'd deal with someone new was if the buyer brought his girlfriend or wife with him. If the cops were surveilling his house, the drug buys would always appear innocent enough; he was just having a couple of people over for a visit. But the woman was there for another, more sinister reason, too—satisfying Big John's sexual desires.

After a buyer made a few scores with Big John, they'd realize that he had the best product and the best prices in town. They'd also see that he was reliable, with a solid supply of drugs. Buyers knew a good thing when they saw it, so they would keep coming back. Once Big John knew that a buyer was even slightly dependent on him, he'd change the rules of the game.

"Just have your girl come," Big John would tell the buyer. "I don't want you near my house. It's too hot. If I see you instead of her alone, you got a real problem with me."

And no one wanted a problem with Big John.

When the wife or girlfriend visited, Jankowski would demand that they give him oral sex—or there'd be no deal. The dealer would lay out a nice railroad-track line of coke on his living room table and tell the girl that she had a choice: snort the coke and give him head or leave empty-handed. Most girls wound up doing the deal John's way; most of them were too afraid to ever tell their husbands and boyfriends what had happened, for fear that someone would end up dead.

That Big John used women in such a demeaning way was galling to all of us. I had multiple channels of information that corroborated his quasi-rape MO. We all possessed a deep appreciation for dark, and I mean real dark, humor. But there were no jokes about Big John's method of sexual fulfillment. It made taking him down an almost sacred obligation. Some cops felt that these women put themselves in harm's way by getting involved with serious dope dealers. Don't buy cocaine and Big John won't rape you, they argued. That was one view, but it wasn't universal. Most saw John as the ultimate bully and abuser of the vulnerable. These girls may have been wrong, or weak, but they didn't deserve the treatment they were getting from this asshole.

Jack Mullins and I spent weeks brainstorming and working our CIs, trying to get one of them to give us something on Big John. We were determined to get the dealer, no matter how long it took.

Then, in the spring of 1986, we heard about Steve Zukka, who went by the street name of "Shoes" because of his bizarre habit of stealing people's footwear. He insisted that he'd known Big John for years and was adamant that he could help us take down the dealer—if we could get him a girl to take with him on the drug buy. Shoes was 140 pounds, about five foot eight, with long, greasy hair and several missing front teeth. He was related to organized crime thug Vinnie Calabro and would often sleep in Calabro's low-budget pool house. Otherwise, Shoes had no real home, and he rarely showered. The guy was largely invisible in Union Beach.

Sitting in the task force's modest office, Mullins and I tossed around different ideas for coming up with a female companion for Shoes—a tough task indeed. We had no access to female undercover officers in the BNTF, and we knew that my former unit, the MCNTF, wouldn't supply us with one unless they assumed full control over the operation.

Mullins and I hit on the idea of using a dispatcher for the Holmdel Police Department who also happened to be a "special" police officer, meaning that she could work as a uniformed officer during peak summer periods, when the department was at its busiest. Essentially, the "specials" were part-time police officers, with less training than full-fledged officers, and often belittled as "rent-a-cops."

The Holmdel dispatcher, Kerri Adams, was slender, with long, straight hair and a decent figure. To be sure, hanging with Shoes would be difficult for anyone to stomach, but she would get the chance to work a major undercover drug case. Maybe we could convince our superiors to green-light using Adams for this operation.

A couple of other elements had to be factored into the equation, too. First, Kerri was too pretty, too "normal," to play Shoes's girlfriend. I worried that Big John wouldn't believe that Kerri and Shoes were actually a couple. Why would a girl like Kerri ever spend time with a guy like Shoes—much less sleep with him? In addition, rumors were circulating that Kerri was involved with a high-ranking member of the department. If true, how would that play into the equation?

I took the dispatcher aside and asked if she'd be willing to work with us, which she was. It was the kind of willingness that comes from seeing how cool UC work looked in the movies and on TV. She was blissfully unaware of how down and dirty this game could get, and I was hesitant to tell her. She had the nerve to do two very difficult things: be seen as Shoes's girlfriend and buy coke from a genuine bad guy.

We took the plan to McCabe, the task force's leader, whose response was lukewarm at best because of the dispatcher's minimal training and lack of experience in the field. Still, he agreed to take the plan to Holmdel Chief of Police Bruce Phillips.

Chief Phillips agreed to go along with the plan and promised to take the heat if something went wrong. We all knew that it was a risky move and that we'd be putting a police dispatcher in harm's way. If it went bad and Big John swatted Shoes like a fly and raped our UC, there was going to be hell to pay.

Still, Mullins and I intended to be there every step of the way, ready to step in if Jankowski, or Shoes, did anything unexpected. There was an upside to this case, too. McCabe and Phillips wanted to take Jankowski down in a big way, and they knew that we wouldn't get many opportunities.

With close surveillance from Mullins and me, Shoes took his "girl-friend" to Big John's house in Union Beach one Thursday evening. It was a large, comfortable two-story house with a wraparound porch, set close to the street. Shoes was clearly in love with his newfound friend, while Kerri did her best not to projectile vomit when she was close to him. It was hard to tell what bothered her more—his odor or his appearance. Mullins and I watched from a distance. It was a quiet evening, and both of us listened intently for any indication that the buy was not going down as planned.

After about 15 minutes, Shoes walked out with Kerri at his side. The two of them hopped into her car—a ratty old Honda Civic that we used for undercover work—and drove to our prearranged meeting spot behind a quiet commercial complex on Florence Avenue. Mullins and I followed in our UC vehicle, another nondescript sedan.

"We fucking did it!" Shoes said as I watched Kerri get out of the car and walk over at a slower, more controlled pace. She looked happy at having made the drug buy, too. Or maybe it was that she'd put a few feet between her and our ripe-smelling CI. She held up an eightball—an eighth-ounce of high quality coke.

"Oh, man, that's beautiful," I told Kerri as Jack listened to Shoes's rapid-paced version of what had happened.

Big John was going down. I was sure we'd be able to do a second buy.

The four of us started making plans for Shoes and Kerri to make a return visit to Big John's a few days later. Within hours, Jack and I had the coke safely locked away in an evidence locker and the written reports completed—with some help from Kerri.

Later that night, I went over the evening's events in my head. I was pretty sure Big John wasn't buying that Shoes and Kerri were boyfriend and girlfriend. The combination was just too odd. I had a hunch that he was thinking ahead to the day when he was going to tell Shoes to take a hike and insist that Kerri make a buy on her own. Kerri was attractive, and Big John was no doubt going to go back to his usual modus operandi. She would do one more buy from the dealer, and no more.

The next night, a Friday, Big John held a poker game in his house. It would prove to be his last night alive.

He had invited over a small group of his friends, including Ricky Jefferson, an up-and-coming white boxer who could hit like a mule and never seemed to bleed. Jefferson was there with his black transgender girlfriend. Jefferson's reputation in the ring ensured that no one ever dared talk to him about his sexual orientation.

After a few hours, the other guys left—but Jefferson and his girlfriend stuck around for few more lines and drinks. At some point, someone picked up a ball-peen hammer and caved in Big John's head.

It was around dinnertime Saturday night that Mullins called me to say that Big John had been murdered.

"We know who killed him," Mullins said to me during the call.

An involuntary shiver ran through me, and I wondered if he could be right.

I reflected on the bizarre conversation I'd had with Shoes Thursday night, about an hour after he and Kerri made the buy from Big John. Shoes suggested that he and I rip off Big John's sizeable drug stash.

"I did good, didn't I, man?" Shoes said to me.

"Fucking right, man. You even set it up for next week," I said. Shoes had stunned Mullins and me by arranging for him and Kerri to go back to Big John's house to "double up" and make a second buy. "Gotta hand it to you, Shoes. No one can ever say you ain't got balls the size of boulders," I continued. "Anything else you want to talk about?"

"Yeah, but just between you and me," he said.

We ducked behind a parked commercial van to get away from Kerri, Mullins and our backup team. Mullins shot me a glance as if to ask, "What the fuck is Shoes up to now?"

"Man, I just know Big John is sitting on two kilos of blow as we speak. He keeps it in the kitchen, inside a cupboard," Shoes told me.

"Is that right? How the fuck you know where he keeps it?" I asked. "I know he didn't show you. Also, how can you be so sure how much weight he's sitting on? If you think we are going to rip the house on a search warrant, guessing he's holding weight, you gotta stop going to the movies, man."

"It ain't like that," Shoes said, gesturing with his hands as he continued his rant. "I got a friend, he fills me in. No, fuck no, no warrants. I want to sneak in and steal the whole load. You and me. I can move it. Make some serious cash. You know you can trust me to be straight with you. We been through so much. John thinks no one got the balls to do him like that. But I do. I got the balls and I won't get caught by that fuck. A 4 a.m. in-and-out. We can be set, big-time."

God help this stupid man. Shoes had no plan and even less of a chance of surviving if Big John even got a hint that he was thinking about ripping him off. Still, I wanted to hear more about the supposed stash.

"Okay, you go in and take him off," I said. "What the fuck you need me for? Some kinda wheelman?"

"It's not gonna happen, but that asshole might wake up at the wrong time, to take a shit or some bullshit like that," Shoes said. "You gotta whack that bitch out. I don't know anyone else could handle it. He could use an ass-kicking anyway. You're the perfect person to give it to him."

"Well, no shit. I don't know whether I should be flattered or pissed," I said, shaking my head at the absurdity of this conversation. I wondered what Mullins's reaction would be.

"Shoes, I ain't selling my badge for that scumbag's yayho. No fucking way. Don't ever fucking talk to me about it again. You got balls; start using your brains."

My crazy CI looked deflated. I reached over and put my hand on his shoulder.

"Man, I . . ."

"Shoes, we are still good. We all get carried away in this shitty business," I said. "Next week, we double the cocksucker. When we take him down we'll set it up so you can see him going down, he just can't see you."

Shoes walked away, but he was a simple read. He wanted to rip off Big John, and he was convinced that he could get away with it. Later I related the conversation to Mullins. Both of us thought he was nuts. Within a week, we'd double Big John and get him off the street. Shoes's plan would become history.

With Big John dead, Mullins was now convinced that Shoes was to blame. The CI had gone ahead with his half-assed plan on his own, the dealer had discovered him and things had gone bad. Mullins and I agreed that we had to go pick up Shoes for questioning—and we had to get him now. Mullins said he'd swing by my place in Keansburg in a half hour or so to pick me up. I glanced at my watch. It was 8:30 p.m.

I was in my garage working out when Mullins called. The detached garage sat about 50 feet away from the two-story house that I shared with my wife, Jane, a tall, Nordic blonde who worked as a hostess in a nearby restaurant, and with my 125-pound dog, an Akita named Bushi. I'd converted the structure into a gym, and I routinely worked out in there—mostly doing weights and practicing my Korean Karate. The concrete floor was covered with mats. On this night, I'd been working on some karate kicks and other moves as the dog relaxed in the corner and kept one eye on me.

After a while, I headed inside to get cleaned up and put on some jeans and a black T-shirt. In the kitchen, I scribbled a note to Jane that I was going out working and likely wouldn't be home for a while. Working late at night and occasionally on weekends was all part of my undercover work with the BNTF, and she knew it. Perhaps more importantly, Jane and I weren't all that close anymore.

Mullins swung by my house to pick me up, and we headed over to Vinnie Calabro's house, a big, glitzy bi-level in a large development. We were amped up, and the more we talked, the more we liked Shoes for the murder. He had the motivation and the opportunity.

A Virgin Mary statue was on the lawn in front of Calabro's house, something that I always found amusing, given his involvement with organized crime. Shoes slept in the pool house, which was part storage shed and part lounge for those enjoying the big in-ground pool. The structure held a sofa, a couple of chairs, a coffee table, and a bathroom and shower that Shoes somehow seemed to ignore. Vinnie put up with his degenerate nephew living out there only because he was family; the less he saw of Shoes, the better. Mullins and I had never once seen Shoes inside the main house.

Mullins pulled our van into the driveway, threw it into park and shut off the engine and lights. We walked around the right side of the house and into the backyard like we owned the place. Calabro had never once complained about Mullins and me—two thuggish-looking bikers—wandering around his property; he wasn't scared of us. And besides, he had his own legal battles to contend with.

Shoes was just walking out of the pool house when Mullins and I turned the corner. We immediately hijacked our 140-pound CI and tossed him in the back of the van.

"What the fuck is going on?" I asked him. "Big John is dead—his head was caved in. You got any idea how that may have fucking happened? You went into his house without me, didn't you?"

Mullins seemed certain that Shoes was to blame, and he jumped in before the guy had a chance to react to my questions. There was no doubt in Mullins's tone or line of questioning. "We know you fucking killed him," he said without any trace of emotion. "We want to know how and when you did it."

Shoes came unglued but said nothing for a few seconds. His face told the story. He'd had no idea what had happened to Big John. Mullins and I knew immediately that he hadn't done it. He also gave us a very credible alibi.

"I didn't touch the guy. I swear! What, you think I'm crazy?" Shoes said. He was adamant, saying that he never got near Big John's house, that he had nothing to do with the murder and that he couldn't believe we were looking at him for the crime.

People who are guilty of something act different than someone falsely accused. Very few people are clever enough actors to feign innocence. Trained interrogators often know right away because of the "tells" people give upon accusation. Shoes passed our test, and it was clear that someone else out there was responsible for taking out Big John.

I was deeply relieved that Shoes wasn't involved. To be sure, bagging Big John's killer had its allure. But God knows what Shoes would have said if he'd been arrested. Any chance of keeping a lid on the admittedly shaky decision to use Kerri on this assignment would have been blown in a big way. I also hadn't been relishing the idea of having to explain to a prosecuting attorney how Shoes had invited me to become his accomplice in knocking off a drug dealer. How could a CI see an undercover cop as the perfect partner for a drug theft and possible drug-related murder?

★　　★　　★

Because of our involvement in the undercover buy, Mullins and I had to stay away from the investigation into Big John's murder; we needed to ensure that no one outside of the investigating officers knew anything about Shoes's involvement in our drug buy—or the involvement of our special police officer, Kerri. We were very concerned about reporters covering the murder. If word got out that Shoes had worked with cops on the drug buy, his life could easily be placed in jeopardy. The Union Beach Police Department, which had jurisdiction, turned over the investigation to the major crimes unit within the Monmouth County Prosecutor's Office.

Union Beach's McCabe gave the prosecutor's office the full case file on our investigation into Big John, including the intel we'd developed through our CI, surveillance photos and more. He also told them about our use of the special officer in the drug buy; he laid it all out for them. The unit used our files as the basis for its murder investigation, and things seemed to be going well for a while. But then there was a major screw-up that put our CI's life in danger.

As the media began probing Big John's murder, Monmouth County Prosecutor John Kaye disclosed to a reporter for the *Asbury Park Press* that his narcotics officers had already made a drug buy from the dealer. The investigation was supposed to have been kept confidential.

Steve Zukka, aka Shoes, had told people that he was among the last to have seen Big John alive. It wouldn't take an FBI investigator to put two and two together and start asking if Shoes had been a participant in the drug buy that Kaye had described.

We complained, loudly, up the chain of command. But the damage had been done, and Shoes was in danger. There wasn't much we could do for him; our task force didn't have the monetary resources or manpower to relocate him and give him a new identity. Shoes was pretty much on his own. He was meat on the street.

Somehow, Shoes was able to lie low and escape death. And Mullins and I were able to breathe a sigh of relief.

Pretty quickly, the major crimes unit determined that Big John and Ricky Jefferson had gotten into a heated argument over some bullshit thing that *seemed* important after a shitload of coke and booze had been ingested by the two men. The boxer took a hammer to the dealer's head and literally beat his brains out.

Jefferson pleaded not guilty, setting the stage for a salacious murder trial complete with testimony from his transgender girlfriend, who enjoyed using a range of fingernail polish colors throughout the course of the trial. She vamped for the media while Jefferson remained stoic. But Jefferson went down hard, found guilty of premeditated first-degree murder.

CHAPTER FOUR

CLOWNS TO THE LEFT, JOKERS TO THE RIGHT

After the Big John takedown, we had a lull. We were partly dependent on street cops for some of our leads, and there just wasn't much happening. When we had a "hot" CI, someone who was providing solid information to the task force, we'd work around the clock. Sometimes we wouldn't sleep for three days. Now we had no hot CIs, and Mullins and I were getting impatient. Mullins decided to hit the phone.

Armed with literally dozens of reports on drug arrests from nearby towns, Mullins would track down the targets and cold-call them, not unlike someone working in a boiler room operation selling penny stocks. Each time, he'd tell the individual that he was a trucker who was continually on the road and needed to make a score. Most of the people he reached would simply hang up or tell him to go fuck himself— clearly the prudent thing to do, given that they were already facing drug charges. But he didn't care, and he'd keep calling them back for weeks. He used the same story each and every time; he was one of the most tenacious individuals I knew.

One day, Mullins's continued cold calls paid off. Hunched over his loose-leaf binder full of arrest records and fooling with a pen in one hand, he was on the line again, with a streetwise white kid named Tom Mason, who'd been picked up by local law enforcement for selling LSD.

Mason lived with his mother in Aberdeen, and it was the mother who always picked up the phone.

Suddenly, Mullins's tone changed, and he stopped twirling his pen. He shot me a glance, and I instantly knew that Mason had agreed to a meet. The target was ready to do a deal for a substantial amount of LSD. It was clear that Mason didn't want anything to do with the stranger on the other end of the phone, but my partner's smooth-talking and Mason's greed were just too good a match. Better yet, there was no informant to protect in this case. If the deal went down, we could make an arrest as soon as we wanted; there would be no need for a cooling-down period. I high-fived Mullins and asked him to fill me in on the call.

Mason had agreed to a meet the following night, a Thursday, in the parking lot of an elementary school in Aberdeen. It was late June 1986, and the school was closed for summer break. The plan was for Mullins to meet Mason in the far corner of the school's parking lot, which wasn't visible from the road. We would get the kid into the back of our cargo van and have him sit on the folding chair we had back there.

We were psyched about the meet because we knew that the sale of a significant quantity of LSD could bring a heavy jail sentence. We could paint a grim picture for Mason of the jail time he was facing and then flip him, giving us a way to bring down his supplier. Unbeknownst to us at the time, the enhanced penalties for selling drugs at the school were in effect at the time—even though school was closed and no kids were around. We would never have done the deal there had school been open.

Mullins and I needed a cover story for the meet, and we opted to be bikers again. We would tell the kid that Mullins was, indeed, a long-distance trucker—but that he was also the vice president of the Norsemen Motorcycle Club, and I was its president. We needed a large quantity of drugs for a major biker bash that was going down the following weekend in East Keansburg. The key was keeping Mullins silent. Although he convincingly looked like a biker, he could not talk the talk.

As we headed over to the school for the meeting the next day, I told Mullins, "Keep your fucking mouth shut. Just grunt, and I'll fill in the blanks."

He grunted roughly in response.

I pulled the van into the lot adjacent to Strathmore Elementary School on Church Street and drove to the secluded area in the back. Mullins and I both scoped out the school grounds to make sure there were no kids hanging out in the playground or ball fields. But it was after dark and no one was around. The two of us sat in the van and waited.

Mason drove into the lot about 20 minutes later and parked a couple of spaces away from our van. He slowly got out of the late-model Mercedes-Benz E-Class and scoped out the area before walking in our direction. I assumed he was driving one of his parents' cars. He was in his early 20s, with straight, very long dark-brown hair. Mullins got out and slid the rear door open, showing Mason the folding chair.

"I have to fucking get over one hundred bikes into a fucking park, keep the motherfucking pigs off our ass and get these crazy fuckers high. You have any fucking idea how much of a bitch this is?" I asked Mason, who'd never seen me before and had no idea who I was.

Mullins grunted in agreement.

The expression on my target's face told me all I needed to know. He was interested in making some quick money off me and didn't really care who I was.

"Man, you want to make some serious money? Let's get these fuckers smashed," I said. You gotta come in on at least a hundred hits. Bare fucking minimum. These fuckers are sick. You know, man, some guys just drink and howl at the moon, but some got to get out there."

Mason had no difficulty with the quantity; price was his issue. Rule number one for undercovers is to always haggle over the price. No one agrees to pay the price first proposed by a dealer. After some negotiating, we had a deal.

"This fucker's alright, isn't he?" I said to Mullins.

"Fucking A," he grunted back.

Everything was going smoothly. Mullins was doing what I'd asked of him and keeping quiet. And Mason seemed ready to do a deal. But the deal wasn't done yet, and I hoped that we could wrap this operation up quickly. The dealer did not look like a Don Juan, and I wondered if I could close the deal by offering him sex with a biker chick.

"Hey man, Juicy Lucy gonna be hot out there. Why don't you come? I'll have her show you a good time," I said.

Turning to Mullins, I continued, "That fucking chick is flat out wild. Whatcha say, bro, this cat and Juicy Lucy?"

"Fucking A," he grunted.

Suddenly, I sneezed.

Mullins looked my way and said, "God bless you."

Mason looked like he'd been punched in the face. His eyes opened wide, and he looked at Mullins and then at me. Would a bad-ass outlaw biker say "God bless you" to another biker? There was only one answer: no.

I was sure it was only a matter of milliseconds before Mason bolted out of our van.

I smashed Mullins in the right shoulder with my left fist. "God bless me? You motherfucker, when has God ever blessed me?"

Before our target had a chance to react, I turned to him and said: "Are we good? If you're bullshit, a lot of bikers are gonna be on me. That means I'm on you. But if we're square, Juicy Lucy will be there with her fucking tongue out."

"We're square," Mason said.

We set up another meeting for late in the afternoon the following day. Mason jumped out of the van, got in his car and drove away, leaving Mullins and me sitting in the dark van, cursing at each other. I was still pissed at the "God bless you." And he continued to find the humor in it. He was also pissed that I was angry at him—because in the end we'd been successful.

The truth was, I thought Mullins's slip of the tongue was funny, too. But I also knew that Mason could have easily realized that we were undercover cops and pulled a weapon on us. We were lucky—this time.

The following day, a Friday, we met Mason behind a local supermarket. Both of us were dressed as bikers. I was wearing my black leather jacket with the sleeves cut off and a grimy T-shirt underneath. Mullins was wearing jeans, a black T-shirt and black leather engineer boots.

Right on time, our target pulled into the parking lot in the Mercedes—and rolled into the spot next to our van.

Mason threw the van's sliding door open and flopped into the folding chair. He pulled a vial out of his pocket containing more than 150 LSD tabs and asked if Lucy was still coming to our party.

I pulled out my gun and put it in his face.

"We're cops, you stupid asshole," I said, as Mullins pulled out his badge.

Mason's face went ashen and his eyes briefly darted toward the door handle, which was beyond his reach. He opted to stay in his seat.

Mullins hopped out of the van, opened the sliding door and pulled Mason out while I kept the gun pointed in the target's direction. Mason was in handcuffs within seconds. Turning this guy would be no problem, provided he had someone of real substance to give up.

My partner explained to Mason that he would be behind bars at the Monmouth County jail through the weekend—and not in some quiet holding cell at the nearby Aberdeen Police Department. A judge likely wouldn't arraign him or set bail on such heavy charges until Monday. Mason would no doubt make great entertainment for gangbangers.

"I've heard of guys similar to you going queer in one night, and you have at least three nights," I told Mason. "But maybe you can fight that shit off. What do you think?"

"I can't go to jail, man," he pleaded.

"Okay, maybe you do go to jail down the road," I said. "It's likely. Judges see LSD on a sheet and they picture their darling daughter grinning insanely and jumping out a window. But that's light years away, and we aren't gonna look for blood if you help us."

"We will see to it you go home tonight," I continued. "No heavy bail, on my word. No county jail, but you gotta give me some very good reason to save your virgin ass. Now is not the time to protect someone who would never do the same for you."

Mason thought about it for a few seconds. "I can take you to the drug house right now," he said. "Just keep me out of County, okay?"

"I give you my word. If you come through for me, you can sit next to me when I call the judge for bail."

With Mason sitting in the back, we drove off to the drug house, which was located in a middle-class neighborhood in Marlboro and supposedly contained a cornucopia of cocaine, LSD and marijuana. Mullins and I knew we were taking a calculated risk; we had no intelligence on the owners of the house, or the people who may be inside, other than what Mason was telling us. Still, we knew the guy was scared, and his only way out of his predicament was to feed us good intel.

We pulled up in front of a sprawling, well-maintained two-story colonial on a tree-lined street. The house was set back about 40 feet from the road, and several late-model cars were parked in the driveway. It looked like a small party was going on. A typical drug house was so filthy that you had to beat the cockroaches away even during the middle of the day. Clearly that wouldn't be the case tonight.

Mullins turned around and warned Mason that he was fucked if anything went wrong. He was going to introduce us and then keep his mouth shut.

Mason only nodded in response. He turned, grabbed the door handle, and slid the van's side door open.

"Get back here," Mullins quietly hissed at me.

"Fuck you! I'm getting my head straight," I replied. Like other undercovers, I spent a minute or two getting focused before heading into any kind of a meet, in much the same way an actor would get into character before stepping on stage.

"Get the fuck back here now," he growled.

Furious that I'd lost my focus, I walked back to the van.

"What the fuck is it?"

"Hey, jerk-off, your handcuffs are hanging off your belt behind your back. Great undercover man you are," he said.

I reached back and felt the cold metal cuffs dangling over my belt. Fuck. Mullins was right. I couldn't believe my blunder. I tossed the cuffs to Mullins, who put them in the front of the van.

Both of us laughed nervously. We were now even for the "God bless you" moment. I took a moment to get my focus back and somehow felt more confident than I'd been before.

Mason walked me in, quickly introduced us to his supplier—a guy in his early twenties with long, disheveled hair—and let me take the lead while he headed into the kitchen to get a drink. Judging from the home's décor and the pictures on the tables, the place was owned by the guy's parents. While they were away, the son was using his parents' place to party and make some cash for himself.

About a half dozen men and a couple of women were in the living room, none of whom I'd ever seen before. There was some coke on the coffee table, and the supplier made it clear that he had loads of both coke and LSD.

I launched into biker mode, telling the group how I had a bunch of boys coming into town for the weekend and how they were all "in real need." I played it tough, made suggestive comments to the girls and looked hard at their stoned boyfriends, who made no effort to confront me or otherwise get me to back off.

"Hey, this looks like a great place to party. I look forward to coming back, boys."

My comments drew no response, but it was clear from the looks I was getting that they didn't want me back, under any circumstances. Maybe they objected to me wearing a black Harley-Davidson baseball cap or drinking their beer. I headed for the door, tossing an arm around Mason's shoulder as we left.

The three of us headed back to the Holmdel Police headquarters to process Mason, place the confiscated drugs in the evidence vault and figure out our next steps in taking down the supplier. Mason's bail was low, so he was soon released from custody—just as we'd promised.

New Jersey's undercovers rarely worked on Saturdays or Sundays, and Mullins had some personal business that he needed to attend to; I didn't ask what it was, and didn't want to know. We huddled with our supervisor, McCabe, and agreed that I would go back and hit the house with Armand "Armie" Ertle.

"Armie, we are going to give a gift to our long-suffering taxpayers," I said. "There's no need for drug-buy money this time. It's time for the Norsemen Motorcycle Club to collect."

The next night, a Saturday, Armie and I rolled on the house in Marlboro. Just like before, we were dressed like bikers and using our UC van. But there was no Mason this time.

I knocked on the door and then let myself in, as if I was family, with Armie right behind. I knew Armie was loaded for bear and hoping for some action. But I was hoping that this was going to be a simple takedown, with no need for violence—more of a "scoop and run" operation.

About a half dozen people were hanging out in the living room, with drugs sitting in plain sight on the coffee table, just like I'd seen the previous evening. I spotted the dealer, flashed a Kansas City bankroll—a $100 bill wrapped around a wad of singles—and asked him to bring out a load of coke.

The dealer disappeared into another room and returned with a sizeable number of individually wrapped glassine envelopes of cocaine. He dumped them on the kitchen table and waited.

"Fuck it, give me all you have. I'll take it off your hands," I said, holding my bankroll at eye level.

The dealer glanced at one of his party guests.

"This isn't cool, man," the guy said.

The dealer hesitated.

"I fucking told you I would pay for it," I said. "Now let's get this fucking done before there's a problem. My friend is getting tired. He can be an asshole when he's tired."

The target turned and left the room again, returning a minute later with what appeared to be the rest of the stash of coke.

"Okay, let's load this up," I said to Armie.

Both of us promptly filled our pockets with coke. Armie said nothing. But the wide grin on his face said it all: he was psyched, and no one was going to get in our way.

The supplier took a couple of steps toward us and asked for payment.

"I ain't paying you shit, motherfucker. You take one more fucking step toward me—any of you fucks—and I'll fuck you all up and burn this shithole down. With you motherfuckers in it."

"Let's fuck them up anyway," my partner shouted.

No one moved. The supplier and his buddies were frozen in fear. Armie and I weren't even armed but were relying purely on our acting skills. It was a performance worthy of Bruce Willis, if only we could keep it going for another minute or two and make it out alive.

The supplier and his buddies did what they thought was the prudent thing: they allowed us to leave, carrying their coke in our pockets. I tucked my cash back into my pocket alongside the coke and followed Armie outside.

We walked with a slow but deliberate pace toward our van, which was parked on the street. Each of us took a glance or two back to make sure that no one was following us or coming out the front door with a shotgun. The supplier and the others stayed inside, and we left without incident.

Armie and I gave each other a high-five when we were safely away from the house and headed back to BNTF headquarters to log in the drugs. The following day, uniformed officers returned to the house to arrest the supplier on felony drug sale charges. He was subsequently convicted.

Later that night, Armie and I treated ourselves to steak and good Scotch. It wasn't until the first burn of Scotch hit us that we realized what a crazy and dangerous stunt we'd pulled. We'd known nothing about the supplier and the other men in the house before we walked through the front door. Like the Bible says, "Be ye wise as serpents and harmless as doves."

As I sat there, twirling the ice in my Scotch, I thought back to my days in the Pagans Motorcycle Club, some nine years earlier. If I was fearless tonight and able to pull off my undercover persona as a member of the Norsemen Motorcycle Club, it was because I'd learned how to act like—and be—a tough guy while riding with the Pagans. I wasn't acting the part so much as simply reverting back to deeply ingrained behavior that I'd learned at an earlier age.

I could tell, looking at Armie as he hammered back one Scotch after another, that he was relieved to have survived the drug buy. Both of us were fearful that night. But there was a difference between us in the way we handled it.

My time in the Pagans, and my years in the army, had hardened me. I knew fear. But now I recognized the emotion and controlled it. My response in dangerous situations was measured. Fear heightened my senses and sped up my reaction times. I knew exactly what I'd do if someone pulled a buck knife or a gun on me, because I'd confronted those situations in the past. And if someone pushed me far enough, I could kill.

CHAPTER FIVE
GROWING UP CHUCK

Sometimes I wonder what my dad, Herbert "Bud" Bradshaw, expected me to be when I grew up. Pro sports is a pretty good bet—at least judging from what he enjoyed watching on TV at home in Middletown, New Jersey. I'm pretty sure that he was royally pissed with me when I was riding with the Pagans. And I guess he was pleased to see me turn things around and become a cop. But he never had all that much to say to me one way or the other. My brother Mike and I were expected to find our own way forward, for better or worse. Growing up, I thought I had an idyllic childhood in Middle America. But maybe, just maybe, my upbringing had some flaws that I didn't recognize at the time.

My dad, who was born in nearby Fair Haven, had wanted to name me after John Wayne—which explains where my first name comes from. But my mother wanted to name me after my father's father, Charles Bradshaw. At least on paper, my dad won the battle over what my name was going to be. But my mom, Pearl, won out at home—which was perhaps more important. Growing up, I was known as Chuck.

Bud Bradshaw ran a milk delivery business until the first 24-hour convenience stores put a stranglehold on competitive costs and he was forced to shut it down. He later ran for, and was elected, tax collector for the Town of Middletown. He would go on to become the town administrator—quite an accomplishment for a quiet guy who kept to

My brother, Mike, left, and me with
the family dog, Toughy, around 1962.

himself and never attended college. Pearl stayed at home, taking care of me and Mike, who is a year and a half older than I am. Mom—who was also born nearby, in Rumson—spent much of her time trying to keep Mike and me from killing each other during the fights that broke out with some regularity.

My dad's heritage was English and Irish, two groups that have been fighting each other for centuries. My mother's heritage was German and Russian—the two of which have also been fighting each other for centuries.

The family home was in a fairly isolated part of town that was dotted with small farms back in the 1950s. It wasn't uncommon to find a horseshoe while digging to plant a shrub or replace one of the many posts that held up the split rail fence out front. Our three-bedroom home was adjacent to the street; in the back was the small warehouse and cold storage that my dad needed for the milk business.

We had few neighbors, and aside from Little League baseball and Pop Warner football, I was mostly a loner as a kid. My brother, more socially adept, made friends with the few kids our age in the area. Somehow, I was frozen out of opportunities to hang out with any of Mike's friends. To this day, I don't know what he told our peers about me, perhaps that I was adopted from a gang of feral dwarves or that I was growing a reptilian tail. But as the Cold War continued between the United States and Russia, Mike and I were engaged in our very own cold war.

During the summer, we took turns working on the truck with my dad as he delivered fresh bottled milk to homes around Middletown— carrying four quarts at a time in one of those open wire baskets that haven't been made in decades—and leaving the ice-cold bottles in small insulated metal containers outside his customers' front doors. My dad's milk delivery truck was small, with room only for the driver and one passenger. It was either Mike or me, not both. It wasn't as if either one of us was going to fight for the opportunity to ride along with Dad on his early morning runs. The Marxist principal of no pay for work was strictly enforced.

Mike and I were both left alone to deal with breakfast on our respective workdays. My mother would be damned if she was getting up that early—around 5 a.m.—to see to it that we got a nourishing breakfast. Indeed, given the number of fights that she broke up between the two of us, it's amazing that she even got out of bed sober and stayed that way during the day. Valium hadn't been invented yet, and the notion of going to a therapist for counseling to deal with your day-to-day challenges was unheard of.

Evenings were often spent with the family, sitting in the living room, watching TV. During the summer, watching Yankee games was our routine. My father had first dibs on what was watched on the black-and-white TV in the living room, and that meant every televised New York Yankees game in its entirety. After 1964, the Yankees sucked but Bud was undeterred. He just ramped up the swearing at the tube. My father wanted second baseman Horace Clarke tarred, feathered and run out of town on a rail. Those were among his more gentle thoughts about that study in baseball mediocrity.

My mom was unfazed by all the Yankee games. She quietly and

My brother, Mike; Mom; Dad; and me at my parents' 50th wedding anniversary.

serenely devoured books like a Benedictine monk devoured scripture. She could converse on any number of subjects, at any depth. She was considered wise. I suppose that was the one thing I coveted in my mother. Without ever saying anything to me, and strictly leading by example, she got me hooked on books. It was during my youth that my intense thirst for the written word was born.

In those innocent days, my mom would take me to Woolworth's, the local five-and-dime store, where I would buy Classics Illustrated Comics. They weren't comic books per se but more graphic novels that were suitable for young readers. I read the Classics Comic version of Cooper's *The Last of the Mohicans* until it crumbled away in my hands. As soon as the Middletown school librarian approved, I read the unabridged version. I still remember reading it while the sporting world was rendered breathless by Cassius Clay knocking out Sonny Liston in Maine. It was a damn tough read. But in my mind's eye I was in a war canoe paddling at the foot of Glens Falls, and there was nothing better for me than being transported to a faraway place like that.

As a kid, I often spent time playing solitary games or going for walks with my dog, Snoopy, a brown-and-white beagle. I doubt if anyone from the neighborhood even owned a leash for their dog, much less used it. I learned how to enjoy quiet time alone; I was the one person that I trusted the most.

One day, I took Snoopy on a walk through the fields and woods near my house. As I emerged from the woods, I crossed paths with John Mangione, who was a couple of years older than I was and already an accomplished house burglar at the age of 13. He was also the first child I ever heard say to his mother (or any adult for that matter), "Go fuck yourself." Papillon's life in the notorious French penal colony on Devil's Island would have been akin to living in paradise compared to what I'd experience if I ever said anything of the sort to my mother.

On that particular day, Mangione was carrying a 12-gauge shotgun when he confronted me. I knew that the shotgun had been a gift from his father, and it struck me as odd that his dad would have given him any kind of firearm, much less a shotgun. The teen jacked a shell into the chamber and pointed the barrel at my chest, with his finger on the trigger. I innocently told him he should never point a loaded gun at anyone.

Mangione raised the gun so that he could sight along its long barrel.

When I looked like I was going to shit in my pants, the kid lowered the weapon and laughingly meandered into the woods, much to the chagrin of the animals who lived there.

With the exception of my early run-in with my shotgun-carrying neighbor, there is little doubt that growing up in the '60s was both idyllic and innocent. We practiced nuclear air raid drills in elementary school, crawling under desks or sitting next to a cement block wall in a hallway with our hands over our ears—as if that could have done anything to save our lives.

Hell, this was the time of MAD (Mutually Assured Destruction), when both the U.S. and the Soviets had aircraft with nuclear payloads airborne 24/7, 365. There was little to no dissent about it, either; the threat of a nuclear World War III was very much on the minds of the Americans living in the 1960s. We believed that America was the land of the free and the home of the brave; it was a nation that was all about mom and apple pie and, of course, baseball. The fact that the heathen communists in Russia didn't even play baseball was reason enough to exterminate them, as far as I was concerned.

But the new medium of black-and-white television gave us a much more frightening scenario to scare us into wanting all things Soviet to be no more. There beyond the fuzzy reception and horizontal lines on our heavy wood-wrapped consoles, we observed the face of the enemy. Nikita Khrushchev, fat, bald and intimidating, banged his shoe on the wooden podium of the United Nations, shouting at America, "We will bury you."

We took his words to heart. I knew deep down that when I was of age, I would be training to kill Russians. Those of us growing up in the era of the Beatles on *The Ed Sullivan Show* spent our waking hours with a radioactive nuclear background music "blowing in the wind."

One day in November 1963, I remember feigning illness to stay home from school. I must have put on a first-rate act, because second-rate performances held unpleasant disciplinary consequences. While my father was napping that afternoon, the front door burst open and our neighbor Mr. Stobo came running in to say the president had been shot. The world stopped for a few days and Walter Cronkite took over the airwaves. Then Jack Ruby amazingly sauntered in and killed Lee Harvey Oswald. Even at my tender age, it was very apparent something had gone terribly wrong, and that life in the U.S. was going to be different for everyone.

As my brother and I got a bit older, we found new ways to amuse ourselves—often at the expense of those around us, including my dad. Once, Mike and I found a way to remove the device that controlled the flow of gas in the oversized globe-shaped cigarette lighter that our father used. Removing the "governor" on the lighter ensured that the flame would be far larger than ever needed. When we were done with our modifications, we placed the lighter near my father's easy chair and waited out of sight to see what would happen next.

Dad reached for the lighter and used it to light up one of the many Winstons he needed to calm his nerves from sharing his home with Mike and me. The lighter sent out a truly prodigious flame, nearly igniting my father's hair. My brother and I fell to the floor, laughing uncontrollably. Our pleasure was short-lived; we were both confined to our rooms for a week.

Much of how we spent our time was left to our active and untamed imaginations. Once, we created our own day of the living dead, using nothing more than ketchup. Mike generously applied it to my face and limbs and then helped position me on the side of the road. It didn't take long for a middle-aged couple to pull over and check on what looked like a child lying in a bloody heap. As they bent down over me, I jumped up, screaming maniacally, my "bloody" limbs flailing. Leaving the Good Samaritans frozen in shock, I ran into the woods, laughing so hard that I choked.

Our "good fun" led to some unanticipated and near-tragic consequences for our neighbors the Kluins. Somehow, in the intellectually barren dark days prior to video games and the internet, Mike and I got instructions to build a UFO. Using clothes hangers to construct the base, plastic dry cleaner's bags for the hot air balloon sections, lighter fluid and some other odds and ends, we created our contraption. We launched it one Saturday night in the middle of summer and were shocked to see that it was actually capable of flight—uncontrolled flight, that is.

"Shit, Mike, this thing is going to burn the Kluins' house down," I shouted as our UFO crashed onto the roof. The gasoline-soaked cotton rags used to "power" the craft's flight continued to burn majestically. We had a choice: run and warn the Kluins that we'd just set the roof of their house on fire, or stand where we were and contemplate the potential risk we were in. We stood there and watched, wondering what the food would be like in reform school.

Someone was watching over us that evening, as a gust of wind suddenly blew the burning remains of our craft onto a vacant lot next door. Mike and I stayed mum in the following weeks as the Kluins and our parents speculated about what might have caused that large and unsettling scorch mark on those roof shingles.

When I turned 17, I followed in my brother's footsteps and obtained a driver's license. What my parents didn't know is that I had been preparing myself for the occasion for months, "borrowing" my mom's car and using it to make beer runs for myself and my friends. The drinking age in New Jersey at the time was 21, but it was easy enough to get over that hurdle. We would simply drive to nearby Red Bank, about five miles away, find a drunk on the street and negotiate with him to make a buy for us—he'd be rewarded with a cheap bottle of Mad Dog 20/20 or Ripple.

Middletown High School was so overcrowded those days that the administration ran two shifts, one in the early morning and another that began at 12:10. I attended the second session, and it wasn't unusual for me to imbibe just before showing up for class.

Around the same time, I had my first real girlfriend, Gina, a semi-hot Italian girl who went to the same high school. Gina taught me the night moves as I gallantly laid her down on my black leather jacket in a secluded area called Dutch Neck.

My pursuit of scholarly perfection aside, I needed money. In those formative years, I learned that money doesn't talk, it screams. Gina, bless her heart, could not be asked to *walk* to our den of assignation. I needed wheels. I needed a job. I sought and found one as a dishwasher at a local pizzeria, Luigi's in Red Bank, saved up some cash and bought a used Ford Maverick.

At least I was mobile, and outside of a bad case of dishpan hands, life was good. But my days of working in Luigi's kitchen soon came to an abrupt halt. There was other work for me.

Maria, the very tough widowed owner of Luigi's, called me into a meeting one night; her boyfriend, the bartender, was also there. Maria explained that the neighborhood around the pizza place had become something of a jungle, a high-crime area where her delivery boys were often beaten up and robbed because of the cash they carried. But the area was also lucrative, and she wanted to continue making deliveries there.

"Chuck, what's your height and weight?" Maria asked.

"Six foot one, 225 pounds," I said.

"You boxed Golden Gloves."

"Yeah, well, I didn't bring home the crown, but I learned to mix it up."

"I heard you want to buy a motorcycle, be some kinda Hells Angel or something," Maria continued.

"I'll start with getting a bike first, but yeah, I do like that kinda shit."

"I know. So stay away from my niece, she's a nice, proper Italian girl."

"You mean me, try to deflower the little princess? I wouldn't think of it."

"You are 'promoted' to pizza delivery as of now. Bring me some of those hoods, I mean friends, of yours, and they are hired, too," Maria continued. "If some toes get stepped on or heads bloodied, I won't be crying about it. But I will not stand for another delivery guy getting slapped around and giving up my money. Do what you got to do; I can watch your back. I know some people in town hall."

My boss viewed me as some kind of biker thug—and, oddly, an asset to her business.

I promptly called two guys—one a friend named Mike who'd managed to grow a full beard by the time he was 16, and the other an acquaintance, Billy. Like me, Mike was into motorcycles, beer and girls of lesser morals. He loved to fight. I mean, this cat reveled in it. Lean and not too tall, he made up for what he lacked in size with sheer violence. He had major balls and was loyal to a fault. Maria hired him on the spot.

Billy was another story. He was bigger than me, older by a couple of years and his past suggested a familiarity with gray prison bars. There was no question that he was a thug, and there was no need to worry about whether he'd be beaten or robbed while doing his deliveries. It was more of a question of how much he'd come back with and how much he'd keep for himself. I made my misgivings about Billy clear to Maria.

"I think I know who this Billy guy is," she told me. "There is no doubt in my mind he is gonna steal from me. But you and Mike won't, and it will take some time before he starts taking enough that I have to sack him. He won't mind being fired. He never did a job he wasn't fired from. By the time Billy's reign of terror ends, it will be years before anyone even dreams of robbing one of my guys. It will make the job that much easier for you and Mike."

When Luigi ran the pizza place, no one in their right mind would have ever dared steal from him. He had a fiery temper and a colorful background, from what I could learn. No one dared touch or say a bad word about Maria while he was alive, either.

Mike, Billy and I went to work with a different attitude that night. Billy supplied us with his "combat" weapon of choice, a thin, semi-flexible piece of BX armored electrical cable wrapped in black electrical tape.

"Be careful you don't kill someone with this, huh?" Billy said. "My conscience will bother me for about three seconds."

When making deliveries to the shakier parts of town, we carried our weapons in plain sight. Not one of us got robbed.

Drunk customers were sometimes inclined to make disparaging remarks about our mothers or ethnicity. The three of us looked forward to those moments, and their aftermath. We'd normally use some of our hard-earned cash to have a few drinks after work. Then we'd drive over to the offending party's house and throw a brick through their picture window or break their car windshield. The picture window was a favorite target during the bitter cold winter months. We would drive by the next day to see cardboard or plywood where the glass window had been, providing the inhabitants with minimal protection from Jack Frost.

Billy was bored and was dying to smack someone, anyone, with his wire cord while on the job. On at least five different occasions, I walked into what felt like ambush scenarios. But each time it happened, my potential attackers thought twice and opted to leave me alone. Suddenly it wasn't Caspar Milquetoast delivering pizza anymore; I was something much more powerful. I had respect on the street, and it felt good. I wanted more.

Just as Maria had predicted, Billy started stealing increasing amounts of money from her. Eventually, she grew tired of the losses and sacked him as promised. Mike, handsome, witty and fearless, began a new career as a bricklayer. That lasted until he became a heroin junkie and was ultimately done in by a one-inch-long needle housing essence of opium.

CHAPTER SIX
LIFE DURING WARTIME

I captained the freshman football team for the Middletown Lions when I was 15 and still in junior high school. Because of overcrowding in the growing bedroom community, junior high was spread out among the Middletown School District's seventh-, eighth- and ninth-grade schools. Mirroring the 48-square-mile community, the school district was a vast melting pot, with students who were rich and poor, African-American and white. Characterwise, I was still a very straight and seemingly well-adjusted teenager who was interested in girls, football and my grades, in that order. But my ability to play football, which I loved and which defined my life, was in the process of being derailed.

I injured my cervical spine in the Pop Warner league, and as early as freshman year, in 1968, it was causing me pain. I was also aware that at the high school, butt blocking and butt tackling was how it was done. This meant sticking your face mask into your opponent's chest on every block or tackle—a practice that was banned just a few years later due to the vast number of spinal injuries. I wondered how long I'd last.

The Vietnam War was raging at the time, but it was distant to me, both in miles and in relevance. I knew I'd have to register for the draft soon, but registering was the furthest thing from my mind. Southeast Asia came into increasing focus for me one evening in a banquet hall in Middletown, where an awards assembly was being held for the high

school football team. The Middletown Lions had won the state championship, and everyone in town wanted to celebrate. As a member of the
freshman team, I had never had any real contact with the varsity team.
They were the stuff of legends, larger than life. I was trying to pump up
my mojo, because over the next three years, I would have to attempt
to live up to their legacy. Elected officials from Middletown, who had a
real sense of community and genuinely cared about the town, were at
the event in force.

One award recipient, who was going to West Point Military
Academy, was roundly applauded by the audience. Then a town councilman took the podium, holding a wrinkled paper in his hand. He said
it was a letter from a former football player who had recently been killed
in action in Vietnam; he wanted to read it to the crowd.

In the letter, the soldier described the men he fought against as cowards who often used women and children as shields. He wrote that the
enemy didn't have the courage to fight and that the war was winna-
ble—if U.S. forces would be allowed to take it to the enemy. He spoke
of how much he loved his country and how proud he was to be fighting
alongside such good and decent men.

Suddenly we heard the sound of a woman openly weeping. It was the
mother of the slain soldier, sitting in the audience with her husband and
younger children. Her husband was attempting to comfort her and had
one arm around her shoulder as he held her hand.

"Okay, I think we've heard enough," the husband said.

"No, I don't think we have heard enough," the councilman said as
he lifted the letter up and continued to read to the astonished crowd.
Finally, he seemed to catch the collective atmosphere in the room and
stopped. With a puzzled and confused demeanor, he surrendered the
microphone and walked away from the podium.

When I entered Middletown High School in 1969, marijuana, LSD, long hair, loud music and defiance of authority were the order of the day. Bruce Springsteen, who was born just a few miles away in Long Branch, was a key player in a riot involving the Middletown Police as well as a bunch of students from my hometown. Springsteen and his newly formed band, Steel Mill, flew into a rage when the Middletown Police ordered them to stop playing at 10 p.m. Springsteen started throwing things on the stage, and the crowd started rioting. From what I've heard, Springsteen is still pissed about that night at the Clearwater Swim Club and won't let any members of the Middletown Police Department moonlight as security for him.

Meanwhile, my football career as offensive tackle was about as well coordinated as Dick Nixon's last administration, and between the neck smashing, the butt blocking and the abusive, loud and foulmouthed coach, I soon found myself thinking about leaving the team. By that point, each butt block sent tingling electrical shocks from my neck through my arms and down to my wrists. I was worried, but the coach wasn't.

"You're just not tough enough," he shouted at me.

Well, the coach was right. I wasn't tough enough. I had this sickening love of my cervical spine, and I wanted to reach the age of 21 able to walk and use all four limbs. Fuck it. I quit. The coach was furious that I would leave the team. A 225-pound high school lineman was rare in those days. I was out, and there was no going back.

I was heartbroken, and my father—who was well known in town and proud of his son's position on the Middletown Lions football team—was crushed. For reasons that I may never fully understand, he took my decision to leave the team personally; our already brittle relationship was now on a razor's edge. I got the feeling that he thought I was, well, a pussy for quitting.

My dad seemed unapproachable on any subject not sports-related. He was universally quiet, and I sensed he was angry and somehow

*The Bradshaw family home in Middletown has been
vacant and abandoned in recent years. Bud Bradshaw ran his milk
delivery business from a building behind the house.*

unhappy. His mood impacted my brother and my mom as well. I knew
that people in town considered my mom a noted beauty. But somehow
he was never able to show any sort of appreciation to her, despite her
round-the-clock housework. I can't remember a single moment growing
up when he thanked her for making dinner or cleaning the house or
making sure that his two sons had clean clothes to wear. And he was
mostly a hostile critic of his sons. Despite his gruff exterior, I knew that
he loved us—he just would never take the simple step of saying so. Like
so many men of his generation, Bud Bradshaw was completely unable to
demonstrate love to either his wife or children. I can't even remember
him talking during our family dinners; he would only express displeasure

when something wasn't to his liking. I suppose a lot of men his age acted the same way; I didn't think much of it at the time.

With football gone and my dad uninterested and remote, I became acquainted with a crowd from another part of the large town I grew up in—the blue-collar, hard-drinking brawlers. In my eyes, the older guys in this crowd were almost legendary tough guys. Some rode chopped Harleys, some drove pickup trucks and they all loved to drink keg beer, eat thick steaks and brawl. The opposite of bullies, they sought out only tough opponents.

In the summer, parties began in the afternoon. Eight-ounce boxing gloves were handed out, and—amid flowing beer, marijuana smoke and the latest from the Allman Brothers—we beat the crap out of each other. When we weren't fighting, the girls kept the food flowing as the guys talked about their landscaping and construction jobs, how much somebody could bench press and, of course, the new Model 74 Harley.

Halfway through my senior year, in January 1973, I turned 18 and was able to legally start drinking (the state had lowered the drinking age from 21). School suddenly became more fun, as I could now enjoy a few beers before heading off to the afternoon session. I became a creature without controls. Large and muscular from weightlifting, I had a battered motorcycle to ride and some money in my pocket. Life was a drunken blur.

I drank when delivering pizza and drank after boxing at parties. My brother was off to college, and my parents (well-meaning as they were) could not stem the tide of wild rage that coursed through my veins. My father was forever taciturn, obsessed with golf and watching the Yankees. My mother desperately sought to keep me on some kind of path toward happiness and a white-collar job. Somehow, both were reduced to being bystanders in my race toward . . . something. I knew only that the race had to be wild, dangerous and unpredictable.

Then I was sick with the flu. Lying around my parents' house, I found a copy of Norman Mailer's *The Naked and the Dead*. It all but burned my brain. The central character was Sam Croft, a cold-blooded killer who looked death and hardship straight in the eye and overcame them. Croft was a staff sergeant in the U.S. Army Infantry. I all but memorized the parts of the book that involved Croft. It fired my imagination, and nothing could stop me from entering the Army Infantry. The administration at Middletown High was only too happy to provide me with a diploma; it only required the teachers to sign off on my passing their courses. My parents seemed pleased, too. Maybe they knew I was an accident waiting to happen, and hoped the army would help straighten me out.

By the end of March, I was beginning basic training in Fort Knox, Kentucky, home of the Seventh Calvary and perhaps best known as the location of the United States Bullion Depository. The 109-thousand-acre base covers parts of Bullitt, Hardin and Meade Counties and for decades was the home of the U.S. Army Armor Center, where the army and marine corps trained on tanks.

There was no backslapping or high-fives as I enlisted. The Vietnam War was still on, though winding down. The overwhelming mood of the country was either weary of our lack of success or completely opposed to the war. When I opted for infantry, in the face of aptitude scores that were very highly regarded, I cannot recall a single person—including my recruiter—who thought I was making a sound decision. My grand plan was to complete the required infantry school, apply for airborne, then try out for Special Forces. At the time, you needed to be at least a buck sergeant (the lowest grade) to even apply.

Though full of bravado, I was aware that I had a real learning curve ahead of me. I had read Robin Moore's *The Green Berets* and was well aware that more than a little seasoning was needed to make the grade— one of only a handful of accurate personal assessments I made in those days. In my limited understanding, Special Forces seemed the best route to being a Sam Croft sort of soldier. But much more than that, Green Berets seemed free. I know that may appear to be odd, but in their elite unconventionality, they were outside the paradigm and, in my mind, able to express themselves quite differently than conventional soldiers. But these proved to be nothing more than intellectual ramblings when confronted with the harsh realities that defined the American army as the Vietnam conflict ground to its brutal conclusion.

CHAPTER SEVEN

WELCOME TO THE MACHINE

The army recruiter picked me up at my house early on the morning of my induction ceremony. I gave my mom a small hug and said "See you later" to Dad. The recruiter watched from a few feet away.

"What's up with your father?" he asked a while later.

"Nothing," I said.

"You didn't see it, but your dad put his hand out for you to shake, then pulled it back."

The recruiter and I headed to Newark for the swearing-in. Next stop was Newark Airport to catch a plane to some city in Kentucky, followed by a bus ride to the base. It was the first time I'd ever even been on a plane.

I had entered a completely alien world, and I was utterly alone. Things were exactly the way I wanted them, or so I thought at the time. Most of the men in my training company were from Detroit and the surrounding suburbs, anxious to get away from a city that had a grand history but seemed headed for higher unemployment rates. Suddenly I was being referred to as "the big white boy" from New Jersey.

At Fort Knox, I didn't stand out or fall short. I was simply another green recruit, and I started to realize just how inconsequential a human being I was; in the army, I was truly just a number, and nobody much cared what happened to me. I didn't suffer the fate of Cordell O'Keefe,

*My first day in the U.S. Army,
at Fort Knox, Kentucky, during
the spring of 1973.*

who was ridiculed for being obese and nicknamed "Hog Head" by a drill sergeant. The drill instructor's Southern twang made it sound more like "Hoeg Head." Nor did I stand out as one of those macho guys who would constantly pester certain trainees into buying or using grass. By and large, basic training was a positive experience. I was starting to get comfortable with the idea of soldiering.

As new recruits, we were instructed to avoid the Patton Club, a nightclub on the base for enlisted men, named after the famous general. But one of my new friends and I opted to go despite the restriction— and we promptly got pulled into a fight. Black/white tensions ran higher in the club than they did on the base. I had offered to buy a beer for an African-American soldier, but the offer was not viewed kindly, and my buddy and I retreated to another part of the club. Things continued to go downhill as a white solider was attacked after he asked an African-American soldier to stop groping his wife.

Break time during training
at Fort Polk, Louisiana,
during the summer of 1973.

My buddy and I decided to leave before we got hauled in by military police. But we couldn't get out the door before soldiers from another training company exchanged words with the two of us. Though it wasn't racial in nature this time, it was still a wild and verbal free-for-all. Minutes later the MPs arrived, and soldiers scattered in all directions.

The next stop for me, along with hundreds of other trainees, was Fort Polk, Louisiana, and we were "lucky" enough to be there in the middle of a Southern summer. It was ridiculously fucking hot and humid. The base, which covers almost two hundred thousand acres, is about 10 miles east of Leesville, Louisiana, and some 17 miles north of De Ridder, in Beauregard Parish. We boarded buses and headed for Tiger Land, deep in the heart of old Dixie. "Fort Puke Lousyana," as we called it, boasted wooden barracks dating back to World War II, snakes and some of the world's largest cockroaches.

For some reason, I got there a couple of days before most of the other recruits. I was given a bunk in an ancient shack-like dorm with the most immaculately shined wooden floor. Two steps down, in the rear of the building, was a primitive latrine and shower area, with no walls or partitions between any of the stalls. Worse still, there were two inches of green and smelly water covering the floor. There was no way to avoid the green flood when you were using the john; you just had to deal with it.

When the training company was finally at full strength, equipment was drawn and we waited for what we were sure would be two very hot and challenging months of training, starting at the end of June and continuing through the end of August. The men were a diverse lot from all parts of the country, roughly 60 percent Hispanic and black, and 40 percent white.

I look back at those two months in Southern hell as some of the happiest days of my life. We were being trained for combat in hot places, and the conditions could not have been more realistic. We speed marched, patrolled, shot every conceivable weapon, rarely slept and became razor-sharp. My 225-pound weight dropped by more than 40 pounds, leaving me hardened steel at 182 pounds. Before you could even eat chow, you needed to complete a circuit on a rusty set of parallel bars. This was the army I had dreamt of: hard-core and run by combat veterans who commanded respect by their every action.

In retrospect, "Fort Puke" training seems a real no-bullshit time in my army career. We were learning the craft of light infantry tactics and survival, setting up L-shaped ambushes and navigating by topographical map and compass by night—all while removing the chiggers that burrowed into our feet and ankles, and avoiding the venomous snakes and scorpions.

When the training ended in late August, we were dispersed and given 10 days' leave before heading to the bases we'd been assigned to. My parents were set to pick me up at Newark Airport. I patiently watched them meander through the crowd in my direction. My mother headed right toward me, then walked by as if I wasn't even there. Though I'd been gone only five months, I was lean and tanned and 182 pounds, and she couldn't even recognize her own son.

The 10 days' leave was a blur. My friends seemed dull, and in my mind I was headed for great adventure. They were headed for boring white-collar jobs in the suburbs, the next generation of Ward and June Cleaver in *Leave it to Beaver*. I never expressed it, but I felt an odd sense of contempt for my friends. They were working, making money and learning trades. They had girlfriends and seemed to have purposeful futures. I, on the other hand, was leaving behind everything I knew. I didn't expect to ever even come back to New Jersey, except maybe to visit, and I liked the soldiering. The spit-and-polish barracks stuff sucked, but creeping around a forest at night, hunting a dangerous enemy—that rocked. It seemed like a perfect kicking-off point for whatever the rest of my life had in store.

Two sets of papers arrived for me during my leave—the first promoted me to private first class, and the second assigned me to Mechanized Infantry, First Infantry Division Forward, Cooke Barracks, in Göppingen, West Germany.

Soon I was hopping on another plane out of Newark, this time headed about eight hours east to Frankfurt for processing, and then on a train south to my new "home" in Göppingen (pronounced *Gerpinggen*), some 20 or 30 miles east of Stuttgart. As I rode south on the train, I was struck by the orderly, green countryside. Göppingen seemed clean and inviting, though Cooke Barracks wasn't much of a step up from Fort Polk.

Soon after I arrived, Specialist Fourth Rondell "Rodney" Black introduced me to the Old Man, Captain Harry Timpson. Timpson looked more like your local pharmacist than someone whose troops may have to fight against a Russian rifle company. But his looks were deceiving, and he was a tough guy worthy of our respect—just like most of the other officers in the company. Platoon Lieutenant Edgar was six foot six, wiry and muscular, a West Point graduate and as tough, intelligent and fair as anyone I have ever met. The other platoon lieutenants were comparable to him and equally capable. But my platoon sergeant, Max Koncha, was one of the most interesting men in the U.S. Army. He was respected by all the men, for all the right reasons.

Koncha didn't talk about himself all that much, and none of us had a clue where he was born. There was speculation that he was from either Germany or the USSR. What I quickly learned from my new buddies was that he'd fought in World War II on both sides of the Eastern Front. He was with the Russians at Kursk for the largest tank battle in history of warfare. He was in Indochina with the French Foreign Legion long before the region was called Vietnam, and then he was with the U.S. Army Infantry during the Vietnam War. Sergeant Koncha, the mad Russian.

The drab light-brown building housing our company would have fit quite well into any run-down urban tenement block. The three-story structure held four platoons, each cordoned off by chest-high dividers like those found between office cubicles. Six-foot-tall gray steel lockers and steel-framed cots were laid out in rows. The lockers contained everything we owned—clothes, personal belongings, books and boots. Behind the barracks was our low, rectangular mess hall.

The rank-and-file soldiers were compartmentalized—not by the officers but by societal peer pressure. Many of those in the unit were returning veterans from Vietnam who brought their drug- and alcohol-abuse problems with them. Some of the veterans were hardened men who'd served time in the country's rice paddies and jungles. The rest were mostly young men who'd joined the army under threat of incarceration from local police. There were a few, like me, who thought that the army was a route to excitement and adventure. Again, Hispanic and African-American soldiers outnumbered whites. Until I went to Germany, I never even knew what a Chicano was. Many of the Puerto Ricans were from New York City. Over time, I came to respect the Hispanics. With few exceptions, they were loyal to each other, tough as nails and never backed down from a fight, even if their opponent was much bigger.

Unlike the African-Americans, the Hispanics weren't under any pressure from their peers to avoid contact with white soldiers.

Many of my fellow white recruits were drug-heads, heavy users of hashish, speed and heroin. Some, from the South, were derogatorily labeled as rednecks, goat ropers or hicks. Other whites were labeled either as "white boys" or "rabbits," meaning those who were cowards and did not like to fight whenever the odds were less than advantageous. Mostly, the guys within these groups had each other's backs. Since I did not fit any of these groups, my back was exposed.

Not surprisingly, the showers and toilets at Cooke Barracks were quite basic. Sometimes they were violent places as well. There were several open toilet stalls, which offered no privacy, and a handful of closed stalls. The shower room had about eight spigots, reminiscent of those found in a high school locker room. Since each group of soldiers had its own musical preferences, battling boom boxes were the order of the day. Control over the music was usually settled by a good beat-down from whichever group outnumbered the others. Soul music won out most often.

My second night in the barracks, I was awakened by someone trying to break into my locker. It was Toby Jeffries, a meek white soldier. When I grabbed him and shouted at him to stop pulling at my lock, he babbled almost incoherently that I should let him go because he was looking for his girlfriend. Ultimately, Jeffries collapsed onto his bunk. The next day, I asked one of the other guys what was going on with Jeffries.

"Take a look at his hand," he said.

I quickly realized that Jeffries was missing the trigger finger on his right hand. From what I could learn, the soldier had cut off his own finger with a buck knife, hoping to get a medical discharge. But his plan failed miserably; he was given an Article 15 disciplinary proceeding for destruction of government property and ordered to shoot with his middle finger.

How the fuck, I wondered, could this guy deal with the pain of self-amputation? Guys in my platoon explained that he'd bought the strong barbiturate methaqualone, which was sold in Germany as Mandrax. The drug is both a sedative and hypnotic; it acts as a central nervous system depressant. Mixed with beer, it turns you into a staggering zombie, oblivious to pain. Jeffries simply popped a couple of pills, downed a couple of beers and chopped off his finger. The other men did nothing to stop the guy, of course, because they wanted to see if he was going to go through with it.

Jeffries was far from the only Mandrax zombie prowling around Cooke Barracks; he was just one of the more colorful ones. Eventually, he was cashiered out on a dishonorable discharge for drug use.

I wondered how such a situation could be allowed to continue. How could credible and experienced officers allow this festering situation to go seemingly unnoticed, especially when they knew they'd have to depend on soldiers like Jeffries in the field? For one thing, the senior NCOs and officers weren't around the barracks at night; they retired to their more comfortable and quieter housing. Sure, there was an NCO stationed at the entrance to the barracks—the "charge of quarters," or CQ, who was theoretically responsible for our welfare. Officers tended to come by a couple of times a night to check on the CQ. It all sounded like an ideal system that would keep everyone safe.

But there were roving gangs of inebriated soldiers, some of whom had reputations for "fragging," or rolling grenades in the direction of their superior officers. Others were known for serious brutality. Either case could render a CQ deaf, dumb and blind—at least for the length of his shift. No one wanted to be publicly associated with incidents of racial violence or drunken behavior, because it could mean disciplinary action or worse. So people hid the problems and did their best to ensure that others didn't see them as well.

My promotion to private first class had pushed my pay to more than $300 a month. But the promotion came at a price. Since I didn't mix with any of the white groups on the base, and I obviously wasn't black or

Hispanic, I had to be a rat, an informant to the Criminal Investigative Division, or CID. At least, that was the fiction created by one of my squad mates who was trying to find a way to bolster his own credibility. The guy claimed that he found a piece of paper from CID that had fallen out of my pocket. The fictional piece of paper "got lost," but other guys in the platoon still believed his story, and I was seriously frozen out. In a way, it didn't bother me, since I just wanted to be a soldier anyway. Still, I was always wary of being ambushed by men who worried about me ratting them out.

Each morning, we had our Physical Training (PT) calisthenics and a four-mile run, followed by breakfast. Then the entire company gathered on a grassy open area adjacent to the barracks. The First Sergeant—whom we referred to simply as "Top"—oversaw muster and delivered the orders of the day. He typically ended the formation by naming those individuals who had to report for urinalysis or drug-related issues. This did not affect those whose alcohol problems were so severe (sadly, most NCOs) that they looked like they were one step ahead of downing a Sterno can by the railroad tracks. Most of the white NCOs had faces severely lined by years of alcohol abuse, thin, stick-like arms, and paunches. When PT ended, they huffed cigarettes and looked very close to death. The African-American and Hispanic NCOs seemed to fare better, but some were classic drunks as well. Three things quickly became evident: alcohol abuse was not a sin, drug use was and there was a hell of a lot of both.

Although the African-American and Hispanic soldiers had their share of drug burnouts, alcohol was clearly the drug of choice. That it tended to make violence more palatable seemed all the better. A large percentage of the white soldiers, however, were totally immersed in the drug culture. They were not even trying to play the game. They had tuned in, turned on and dropped out. They were obvious in their preference, and fell out to formation, to use one First Sergeant's words, dressed like "Joe Shit the Rag Man."

★　　★　　★

José Presca was a Mexican-American drug dealer and gangbanger who joined the army to escape a jail sentence. He was large in build, usually high as a kite, and very clever and calculating. His buck knife was said to have found its way into many a rival dealer's stomach. He knew I was no informant. And since I actually liked soldiering, I was beyond suspicion in terms of drug involvement.

"Let's go do a mission," Presca said one evening, using code to signal his desire to go somewhere to smoke hash.

"Yeah, man, okay," I said, wondering what would happen next.

"These people here think you a lifer," he said. "But I know better, homes. You should come with me one weekend. I have this problem, you see. The Man knows I am doing business, so when I come in from off post they look at me. But I am not stupid. I can still bring in what I need. But these eyes are always looking at me, homes. They would never look at you. I am telling you, homes, they all thinking you a lifer. I can take you to meet my people, there are lots of women too. You can make *bookoo* [beaucoup] money. No one would fuck with you, if I put out the word you are my P." *P* was short for partner.

"Man, I don't know . . ."

"What's not to know? You way smarter than these people here. I know how to keep these things very cool. You would have to be way-out loco you turn this down, P."

"What are we talking about moving here, José?"

"P, it is not cool to talk of this if you are not in. But if you were in? Dope, homes. Could be some morphine, some gray and brown," Presca said, referring to heroin or smack. "You know, P, small, easy to hide. But *bookoo* bucks."

"You respect I got to think on this, right, José?"

"Yeah, I respect that. Just don't be thinking too long."

Presca and I walked side by side in the dark. "Yo, homes, let me tell you about me and my Ps back in the world. Some of the shit we did, homes."

"Where, L.A.?" I asked.

"East L.A.," he said.

"Don't know nothin' about that place, P."

"I know that," Presca continued. "You don't know nothin' about nothin', homes. So me and my Ps, we see this fine-looking bitch coming off the bus. She was going to walk to another bus. We surround her, P. We tellin' her she got to give it up to the group. P, we talkin' some fine pussy here. She starts cryin' and shit, she pregnant and all that."

"What the fuck, P. Man, this shit's heavy," I protested.

"We settle for her blowin' all of us. Part as friends, like," Presca said. "After she got on it, it was looking like she diggin' it, P."

"Sweet Mary's ass, man, I can't go there, no way. No disrespect to you, P."

"It's cool, P. It's just a thing, homes, just a thing," Presca said as we continued walking.

José Presca was one of the biggest dealers on the base and wanted me to move heroin and morphine. I realized that turning him down carried risks every bit as large as the ones facing me if I carried the dope. In some ways, it was a very tempting offer. Presca was a likable guy—if you could somehow compartmentalize and ignore the violence that was part of his life. There'd be no more worries of people targeting me on the base, and drugs and women would be plentiful. But was I ready to become a heroin trafficker? I had just gotten to this base a few weeks earlier, and already this crazy shit was happening. Would I get carved up like a Christmas turkey if I refused?

In time, I turned Presca's offer down. I was very concerned about the potential danger I was putting myself in, but still couldn't convince myself to become a drug trafficker. When he realized I wasn't interested, Presca simply smiled and explained that he could never understand why anyone would walk away from such an offer.

Presca wasn't the only dangerous character in my platoon. Big T, also known as "Troubleman," was easily the most feared man on the base. Terrence Williams stood six foot five and weighed 280. He was so nasty that his superiors had refused to promote him year after year; amazingly, he was still a private first class at age 28. Williams had done hard time prior to the army and was known to have fragged his Second Lieutenant in Vietnam. He was said to have a loaded .45-caliber pistol; soldiers weren't allowed to carry loaded weapons when they weren't doing specific types of weapon-related training.

In time, I came to believe all three things about him but could only prove that he did, indeed, carry a loaded pistol. Big T was the unchallenged and true leader of the African-American soldiers on base. He was militant, intelligent and very charismatic. He used his minions like pawns in a chess match. Sometimes he created violent dramas just for his own amusement. Other times he could be introspective and almost charming. His demeanor changed in a second, and letting your guard down with him could cost you big-time. Having him as a squad member was akin to swimming daily in a stream with a water moccasin.

Big T was so feared that Sergeant Koncha wouldn't even shake his bunk to wake him up for PT—and Koncha had been known to knock bunks over. Maybe German tanks at Kursk and Indochinese guerillas were easier to deal with than Troubleman.

When I wasn't dealing with the likes of Presca and Big T, I squeezed in time to play on the company's football team. Though it was called flag football, our games were played with nine-man formations and had more in common with the gladiator games in Rome than something played on the Great Lawn in New York's Central Park. At least the gladiators had shields. With me playing offensive center, our team won the base championship. I even managed a couple of touchdown catches, as centers were eligible in those games. You just had to see through the red stuff dripping down your face.

CHAPTER EIGHT

HEAR NO EVIL

In October, 1973, the First Infantry Division Forward participated in Operation Reforger (which stood for "Return of Forces to Germany"), a yearly joint military exercise utilizing American, German, Canadian and British forces. Thousands of men participated in this fast-moving month-long war game between 1969 and 1988, when the military started scaling it back. My entire company was to proceed by railhead to an undisclosed location in the countryside. We were scheduled to depart at around 1 a.m., using our armored personnel carriers for the short ride to the local train station. The APCs would be loaded onto large flatbed freight cars for the 12- to 15-hour ride to the area where the operations would be conducted. No one had a clue where we were headed.

By 10 p.m. that night, most of the men in my assigned squad were in our barracks, readying their gear for weeks in the field. Boom boxes were blaring, there was constant shouting among the men and some of the guys were dragging their asses back to the barracks weary and drunk. In the field, we wore drab olive fatigues, flack vests, canteens, boots, camo helmets and heavy coats to help keep out the cold. Each of us carried a parka for protection against the rain that was sure to fall, a sleeping bag, the all-important rubber inflatable mattress, C-rations and shelter halves—two men, each carrying a shelter half, would put them together to form a tent in the field. Most of the time I carried a brown wood-handled switchblade with a six-inch blade. Even though people could see the switchblade's outline in my pocket, no one challenged me about carrying it—at least when we were on base. But I couldn't carry the switchblade on Reforger or any field exercise like it, because the blade would have been confiscated, along with drugs and alcohol, during the stringent "health and welfare inspection."

None of us were armed while we were on post, nor were we allowed to carry any privately owned firearms. Only law enforcement and security personnel on the base were allowed to have weapons. We would pick up our weapons from the Arms Room right before we left for Reforger.

Big T and three members of his posse showed up at the barracks after midnight, drunk, loud and decidedly not funny. One of the men, Willie Kane, was determined to impress Big T at the expense of one of the other men in the squad, Private First Class Jimmy Woodson. Knowing Woodson was a soft target, Kane began beating the shit out of the kid with his fists. Woodson fell to the ground, whimpering and making no effort to fight back. Kane kicked the kid several times as Big T stood by with a bemused smile on his face. Dozens of men watched the beating take place, but none stepped in to stop Kane or defend Woodson. Eventually, an African-American NCO, Sergeant James Roland, walked in on the fight and intervened—drawing shouts and threats from both Big T and Kane.

Roland ignored the shouts and left the barracks without any indication that he intended to punish Kane for the beat-down he'd just witnessed. A few feet away, another soldier, Carlos Campeno, sat quietly on his bunk, shaking his head and looking disgusted. I wondered if he was pissed at Kane for beating Woodson or angry at Woodson for not even attempting to defend himself.

"What the fuck you looking at, Campeno? You want some?" Kane shouted.

"You trying to scare me, Kane? 'Cause I'm not going to lay down like him," Campeno said.

"Just letting you know," Kane said.

"We can get it on anytime you want, Kane," Campeno said. "Just so you know, you got your people, but I got my people, too."

Kane quieted down.

The Latinos had their people, the African-Americans had their people and I had no people. No matter. What was clear was that I'd be spending a good chunk of the next month inside a cramped APC with my four African-American squad members—Big T, Kane, Terry Brown and Demarco Percell, along with Woodson, Campeno and Frank Procter.

Individually, I got along well with all four men. Only T was bigger than me; Percell and Brown were comparable in size and Kane was slightly smaller. I will never forget Brown and Percell saying that they considered me their friend. I had to know that if any of the other "brothers" were around, they wouldn't be openly friendly toward me. They also said that they wouldn't fight every African-American guy on this base for me—prompting me to wonder what people had been saying.

When it was time to head out around 1 a.m., each squad crammed into a single APC. The squad sergeant stood in the command cupola, while the driver sat below him, maneuvering the vehicle on its tank-like treads. Though technically an armored vehicle, the M113 APC had a relatively thin and soft skin—not at all like the bulletproof troop transport vehicles used today. We knew that the vehicle could easily be penetrated by an enemy machine gun round, which would ricochet around and likely kill or maim several men. But riding on one of the rough metal benches in an APC certainly beat walking through the German wilderness, especially when the forecast called for miserably cold, wet weather.

We carried M16s, M16s fitted with M203 grenade launchers, M60 machine guns and the M79 grenade launcher—what's known as a "blooper gun" because of the popping sound it makes when fired.

On the ride to the train station, I took turns with Kane, Brown, Percell and Big T standing in the cargo hatch opening of the APC.

Woodson looked like shit, with a black eye and large bruises on his face. He'd limped into the vehicle and silently slumped into a seat.

True to his name, Troubleman was watching me. I was scared of him and the other guys but did my best not to show it. It wasn't long before he launched into another of his very hard-line militant diatribes against white people, and authority in general. If he thought I was going to take the bait, he was wrong. I was contemplating what my chances would be in a fight against Big T or one of his buddies. Even on my best day, I knew that both Big T and Percell could beat me in a straight fight. I knew I could make Percell suffer, but not enough. A fight between Brown and me would probably result in a stalemate. I knew that I could take Kane, and he knew it, too. Kane hated the fact that I was tougher and stronger than he was, and that likely made him the most dangerous one of the four.

The lumbering APC rolled into the rail yard, and we loaded onto the eastbound train. The train pulled out right on time and rolled through idyllic-looking small German towns and verdant green forests. We arrived and off-loaded along with thousands of other troops and pieces of equipment. Amazingly, given the size of the operation, the off-loading went smoothly.

My squad sergeant was Staff Sergeant Anders, who was tough as nails and had a Combat Infantry Badge—an award given to infantrymen and Special Forces soldiers who had personally fought in active ground combat. When drinking, he was one of Big T's cohorts and the only person who drank with the man and still dared to vehemently disagree with him. Anders was a complex man, an alcoholic who was quite well read. He was a militant African-American, but in a much more intellectual manner than Big T. He didn't stop the black power rhetoric that was rampant in the squad; nor did he foster it.

When Anders was around, things seemed to function more smoothly.

I liked him, and he went out of his way to praise me for any extra efforts I attempted. On the first night of the Reforger exercise, we set up a defensive perimeter. I suggested a placement of an M60 machine gun that was at odds with what Anders had proposed, and was surprised to see him agree with me and change the placement. It was a small gesture, but an important one for me. I would go all out for this guy, no matter what the circumstances. Sergeant Anders's skills in commanding his men seemed apparent to everyone around him; I suspected that he would have quickly moved up through the ranks if he wasn't an alcoholic.

Anders ordered Campeno and Procter to stay with the APC for maintenance and security while the rest of us went out on a lengthy patrol. Walking through the woods with weapons and packs built up a powerful thirst for more than the water in our canteens. It would only be a matter of time before we'd be moving frenetically from one point to another in our APCs and not doing as many foot patrols. If we wanted to get hammered, now was the time.

As with any field maneuvers, the first thing that took place at Reforger was a "health and welfare inspection" in which military police aggressively searched all the vehicles and men for booze and drugs. Any drugs or alcohol found in common areas—like our APC—were simply destroyed. There was never any investigation as to who may have stashed it. The vast majority of contraband found during these searches was beer, wine and hard liquor. Easily hidden items like speed or smack, of course, usually escaped detection. The checks were extremely thorough, and I was always amazed when several days later someone produced a bottle of Scotch. But most alcohol was found.

Anders led our squad in a search for booze, eventually finding a *Gasthaus*—a small inn with a restaurant, bar and a few hotel rooms for rent. These places were often patrolled by senior NCOs or regular officers to ensure that soldiers didn't get hammered while out on patrol. Ironically, the officers often enjoyed drinking at the bars while supposedly securing them.

Our sergeant successfully bribed the two drunk NCOs at our *Gasthaus*, buying a half dozen large bottles of cheap local wine. As we continued our patrol, the wine flowed freely for all of us except Woodson, who was still walking with a slight limp. Anders eventually realized that we might be lost—yet another reason to continue drinking. We were still drinking when a patrol walked past us headed in the opposite direction. The soldiers in that unit were all white, and sober.

"Hey, soldier, where the fuck are we?" Anders demanded, as he grabbed one of the men by his shoulder straps and pulled him closer.

Ignoring Anders's rank, the soldier slapped the topographic map out of his hand and pushed the sergeant away—causing his liter of wine to drop to the ground. Drunk and angry about the loss of the wine, I launched myself at the nearest member of the patrol, threw him to the ground and pummeled his face. Brown and Percell also went on the attack and had no trouble beating their opponents.

Big T and Sergeant Anders pulled me off my bloodied victim, and we went running up the path we'd seen the patrol come down. We were confident that the guys in the other patrol weren't going anywhere for a while, and radioing for help was out of the question. Somehow, the battery for their PRC-25 field radio had gone missing, along with the spare. The radio weighed some 24 pounds and consisted of two parts, metal boxes called "cans." The upper can held the battery while the lower one held the separate battery pack. Two metal clips held the cans together, making it quick and easy to remove the battery.

That night, we were allowed to skirt light discipline and build a fire. Big T was dispensing some of the wine we had left. It didn't take long for word of our stash to spread, and soon there were about 10 soldiers hanging around the fire; I was the lone white one. I held my canteen cup out for a drink, and T filled it, deliberately giving me more than some of the others.

"You see, not all white boys are the same," Big T said. "I been trying to tell you. Drink up, man, you got more coming."

There were no dissenters, and Anders sat there smiling.

T launched into one of his black power sermons and I headed off to my sleeping bag. I found his proselytizing vaguely comforting that night.

Early the next morning, the field operations began anew. Big T managed to stow the last bottle of wine in a safe location, just in case we had an opportunity to do some more drinking. As fate would have it, we were ordered to stand down for at least several hours in a clearing adjacent to a dirt road. With no foot patrols, our squad got out of the APC and opened the last bottle. Big T was still doing the honors, and Procter was drinking with us, as the sun started to sink closer to the horizon.

Hailing from Arizona and weighing in at about 150 pounds, Procter was generally a harmless, gregarious drunk. But he could become loud. Now, having missed the previous evening's revelry, he was making up for lost drinking time. Procter and Big T were seated next to each other on a bench inside the APC as others milled around outside, near the vehicle's cargo ramp. While Big T launched into another political lecture for the group, Procter filled and refilled the cup from his canteen. It wasn't long before he was lit.

"You're prejudiced man," Procter shouted at Big T, who was seated to Procter's left. He repeated the remark time and again as he pawed at Big T's shoulder—angering him more every time. It was growing difficult to see, because the sun had set and the only light we had was the soft glow from the APC's power source.

Big T suddenly erupted in anger and backhand-slapped Procter while they were still seated next to each other. Then he rose and began to smash the kid's face flat. I watched as Big T grabbed Procter by his hair and dragged him out of the APC.

Kane, sitting across from me on another bench, was clearly unnerved and fighting off a sense of shock. Slowly, he pushed the barrel of his M16 up to my chest and in a quivering voice said, "Don't do anything, man."

Sergeant Anders screamed for T to stop, but his plea was ignored.

T was in a zone, and anyone who dared intrude would be in imminent mortal danger.

T grabbed Procter by the hair and dragged him onto the forest floor, smashing the guy with his other fist as he went. Procter was gurgling blood but the beating continued.

Suddenly Big T looked up and stared at us. No one did or said anything.

Anders broke the silence to announce that we'd received orders to move out. Procter was left at the edge of the clearing while the sergeant set up a first-aid pickup. We all silently boarded the APC as T went back to his drunken speech. Anders did nothing but ordered all of us to stay seated in the cargo area.

A half hour later, Procter was picked up by medics and taken to the rear area for treatment. His wounds were serious enough that he could not return to Operation Reforger.

The unit knew there would be an inquiry into the man's severe beating. I knew that most of the men would immediately disavow any knowledge of the incident. Procter must have somehow fallen while out on patrol. The other black guys in the unit wouldn't think of ratting on Big T. The only person in question was me, and I'd already made up my mind. There was no way I would risk my life to tell anyone what happened that night.

After our patrols ended, we returned to base and piled out of the APC to bed down for a few hours of rest on our air mattresses. No one said anything about Procter, and no one came to investigate, either.

The next night, Big T came over to me and asked if he could see me back inside the vehicle. Kane was already there when the two of us climbed inside.

"You ever hear that rumor about me carrying a .45?" Big T asked, standing just inches away from me. Kane stood off to the side, his hands resting on his waist.

"Yeah, I've heard it," I said.

"What'd you see between me and Procter?" he asked.

"I saw an argument. Beyond that, nothing," I said.

T nodded his head, but Kane grinned. He knew that I was fucked and wouldn't get out alive if I even whispered to anyone about what happened. My only way to stay alive was to shut the fuck up and not say a word. I was furious with myself, with them and with the whole fucking army that night. I turned to stare at Kane.

"The reason I didn't see anything is because I don't give a fuck," I told Kane. "I don't give a fuck about you, about him or myself. Fuck Procter and fuck the army. And Kane, fuck you!"

I stormed out of the APC, walked into the forest and screamed an oath at the world.

The next morning, our unit saddled up and we resumed our war games.

After about a week of literally ripping up the German countryside with our APCs, tanks and other heavy vehicles, we were ordered to bring our vehicles back to base so they could be repainted. They had all been a deep forest green. Now, using patterns, we were quickly spray painting them for use in the desert. It was an emergency atmosphere: the 1973 Yom Kippur War was on, and we were preparing for deployment to the Middle East. But very little information trickled down, and the orders to redeploy never came.

While we waited for word from higher-ups, several German police vehicles came into the camp. Armed with warrants, the police arrested two of the men in our division, a slim Chicano who had a reputation for brutality and carried a knife, and his close friend, a white guy from California who was noted for his fighting prowess and was usually drunk. Every time the two of them were together, we'd usually wind up hearing some story about a person getting beaten or stomped into a jelly-like mass. Apparently the two men had savagely beaten a local man in a bar, and the authorities had successfully tracked them down. Later, we learned that they were both given 10-year jail sentences in German prisons. For me, the arrests meant there were two fewer violent individuals to deal with. But there were plenty of others in this shark tank.

One winter day, the entire unit was transported to Oberammergau, south of Munich and deep in the Bavarian Alps. The area's beautiful mountains, deep snow and quaint villages with expensive boutiques draw thousands of tourists every winter. The village was so beautiful, in fact, that the U.S. Army was forbidden from entering it except on direct orders. We were billeted at some sort of training base and began training for winter warfare. After we completed a small round of war games, we were told that we'd begin learning how to ski the following day. Some of us were excited to learn in this playground of the rich and the famous. But not everyone was so thrilled.

"Fuck that motherfucking shit. You won't see my ass skiing down no goddamn mountain," one of the men said.

We were driven to a resort with a bar, at the base of some very steep mountain slopes. After arguably the briefest class ever given in downhill skiing, we were taken to the mountaintop, and told to start.

A tough Chicano sergeant announced he would go first. "I ain't scared of this fucking shit," the sergeant announced as he pushed off on his ski poles.

The instructors had directed us to ski downhill in a series of turns to help keep our speed under control. But the sergeant ignored that concept and instead headed straight downhill, with his ski poles tucked firmly up into his armpits—much as one would see from world-class downhill skiers. His technique worked for a bit. Halfway down, he lost control and became airborne, his legs and arms flailing wildly before he hit the snow hard.

Others followed the sergeant, with similar results. My roommate, fearing that he, too, would crash on the way down, looked around for a trail that wasn't as steep. He found one, and had a good run going until he realized that the trail ended in a ski jump. We watched with morbid curiosity as he flew off the end of the ski jump and landed somewhere out of our view. We worried briefly if he was still alive. But our first priority was finding our own, and safe, way down the mountain.

I found a suitable slope and pushed off. Much like the sergeant who had gone first, I aimed straight down the mountain, poles tucked. I tried to turn once, only to wipe out in the snow and draw laughter from some of the other men.

Pissed off, I stood up, ignored the instructor's advice again, and headed straight down. As I rapidly gained speed, I started to rethink my decision—but it was too late. I was headed for the picture window at the lodge's bar and could make out the faces of people sitting there enjoying an after-ski drink. I had a decision to make: continue straight and go through the window or wipe out in front of everyone.

I crashed right outside the bar, landing hard in the packed snow. I felt an intense pain on my outer right thigh, and wondered if I'd broken a bone or worse. Gently patting the area, I discovered a can of C-rations in the thigh pocket of my fatigue pants. I pulled the crushed can out of my pocket and stared at it: pork and lima beans.

CHAPTER NINE
ROCKIN' ROBIN

After returning to base in Göppingen, we were told that new dormitory-type barracks would be ready in the spring. So we wintered in our old barracks amid battling boom boxes and Mandrax zombies. A lot of the men seemed anxious to move into the new quarters, but I had deep-seated concerns. Drawing a room with Big T, Kane or Brown would be a nightmare. These guys partied late all the time, and they were hooked up with some of the most violent and militant soldiers on the base.

There wasn't much I could do about the matter, and so amid the din from the boom boxes and shouts from the men, I immersed myself in the books that I kept stashed in the bottom of my locker: *The Dogs of War*, by Frederick Forsyth; *The Seven Minutes*, by Irving Wallace; *Uhuru* and *The Honey Badger*, both by Robert Ruark; and *Journey to Ixtlan: The Lessons of Don Juan*, by Carlos Castaneda.

Journey to Ixtlan was one of my favorites; it had been given to me by one of the guys I knew on the base, and it rocked me. Castaneda writes about his apprenticeship to a teacher named don Juan, whose age is impossible to know. Don Juan speaks of being a hunter and a warrior, and how a man's only real reason for life is to hunt power— power to make him stronger inside. He teaches that life is a beautiful and mysterious thing, and that it can be taken from you in an instant. So rather than lament its risks and dangers, a hunter lives as a warrior, strategically maneuvering through each moment and living life to its fullest. Being a true spiritual warrior is the only task worthy of our manhood. Toltec wisdom, in short: the creator left us with two options, and only two—misery or strength. You choose.

When the barracks were completed the following spring, we learned who we would be paired up with. I drew Brown as my roommate. The good news was that he was being sent back home to tend to a family issue, so I would be alone for a while.

The dorm scene played out to a different tune. Now the boom boxes were replaced by state-of-the-art stereo systems, played at high volume behind closed doors in semi-private rooms.

The newfound privacy also meant that the men didn't have to be inconvenienced any longer when shooting smack or smoking blocks of hash. Smoking hash was easy. All you needed to do was get a can of soda or beer from the dispenser, drink or pour out the liquid and then form the can into the shape of a canoe. Then you'd take the rank pin from your collar and poke holes in the can. Finally, you'd crumble a large chunk of morphine green or Turkish black hash onto the can, and begin your smoking pleasure. Spoons for cooking heroin were easily stolen from the mess hall during meal time.

We fell into a routine that blended field operations with hours upon hours of hanging around our barracks and almost invariably getting into trouble, either with drugs or fighting among ourselves. Our five-day work week of training was punctuated by guard duty stints and mini field exercises that would include two or three 10-mile walks and all-night patrols. Although I drank the hearty local beer, I was a very lean (for me) 195 pounds.

Full-scale field exercises were about a month in length and happened in May, October and February on sprawling American bases at Hohenfels and Grafenwöhr, which had large cement barracks where we could spend a couple of nights in before going back out into the woods. When we were out in our APCs, we used a sleeping bag along with an inflatable air mattress and our "shelter halves" to protect ourselves from the elements—if we were lucky enough to be able to sleep lying down. Other times, we grabbed a few hours' sleep inside our vehicles.

One night, we were out practicing an assault on a steep hill covered in pine trees. My new lieutenant, Robin Bailey—whom we referred to as "Rockin' Robin"—suddenly herded the entire platoon into APCs and roared off into the night, leaving me and a green new guy on the hilltop in pitch darkness.

"What now?" Private First Class Jerry Gormley asked as the sound of the rumbling APCs grew fainter.

The two of us pooled all our German marks and walked toward the nearest town, the lights barely visible in the distance. No one in our unit seemed interested in finding us, so we figured we would have to find our own way home.

After walking for an hour or so, we made it to a small *Gasthaus* serving beer to five or six local farmers in a bustling metropolis of about 30 residents. Though the inn's proprietors weren't particularly happy to have machine-gun-toting soldiers at their tables, the cash seemed to help, and we were soon being served an excellent local brew by our hostess. Gormley and I figured that our unit would realize they left us behind—and would eventually show up to collect us. But the two of us wound up sitting there drinking, and then eating, for hours, with no sign of our buddies.

Eventually the local farmers grew tired of my buddy and I chatting up our hostess, and one of them challenged me to arm wrestle. The farmer was both angry and lit after having a few beers, and I got the feeling that I needed to win this challenge—or face the group's wrath.

Motivated primarily by fear, I slammed the stunned farmer's wrist flat on the table. I had been told that twisting the wrist inward was the secret. It is. I then offered to buy everyone a beer (with my buddy's money, of course). All went well, and a short while later we all shook hands as the bar closed. But we had a problem—the sleeping gear was on the APC, and we had no means of communication with the unit and not much cash. Our newfound female friend agreed to let us sleep on the wood benches in the restaurant. The next morning, we awoke and were allowed to shower and shave in her personal bathroom. She refused to accept any money from us.

With no one showing up to rescue us, we decided to walk in the general direction that the APCs had headed in the previous night. We walked for hours down dirt roads through the forest. Then we saw a convoy of American vehicles heading toward us.

I flagged down a jeep with a captain in the passenger seat, staring down at some topographic map, and asked him where our unit was located. He said that they were at least 10 miles ahead of us. But when I asked him to make contact or otherwise assist us, he announced that he'd just received new orders and had to leave immediately. He and the rest of the convoy roared down the dirt road, abandoning Gormley and I once again.

What had started off as an amusing little adventure was slowly turning into a nightmare. We couldn't understand why our unit wasn't trying to track us down, and why the captain couldn't have at least put in a call to headquarters about us. We walked for hours more, hoping to find a train or bus stop.

Eventually, we stumbled upon a German air force base, where we were promptly taken to the base commander, a squared-away-looking colonel and jet fighter pilot. After I explained our situation, including the brush-off from the American convoy, he became very agitated. He grabbed the phone and lit into every American military official he could find until he was able to take care of the problem. We were taken to a railhead and placed on a train to Cooke Barracks, where we hung out until the unit returned from maneuvers.

In a bizarre twist, the army actually accused Gormley and me of "desertion" and attempted to bring us up on formal charges. They refused to listen to what Gormley and I had to say about being left in the woods and our efforts to get reunited with our unit. I had no choice but to retain a criminal defense attorney, who successfully tracked down the German air force colonel, who was now in San Diego. The colonel was apoplectic and vowed to fly back to Germany to speak in our defense at any proceedings called by the army. My superiors said nothing to me but subsequently withdrew the charges. It was all as if nothing had happened.

A few weeks later, word came down that Brown would soon be returning to the company, and my solo time would be up. Because of a great deal of grumbling, the roommate structure was going to be rearranged across the board. In Brown's absence, I made a strong case for rooming with another African-American soldier, with whom I got along well. That worked out, for me. But it was bad news for the new roommate Brown was paired with—and would sexually assault.

When that happened, the company was put on lockdown and an investigation was done. But witnesses said little and the investigation didn't get very far. Both men were transferred out to different companies. The incident triggered animosity within the company, and a cold chill permeated the barracks. Though some saw this as a purely racial matter, it was far different to me. I had African-American friends, white friends and Latino friends. Hell, Brown and I were friends—though he probably wouldn't have acknowledged that in public. This was about predators and prey, and the game continued 24/7.

As time slid by, Kane and I shared an uneasy but nonconfrontational existence. He was growing more vocally militant and aggressive, clearly unnerving a lot of white soldiers. One late morning in May, when I was walking alone in the huge motor pool in Hohenfels, he called me over and asked for a favor. He told me he wanted to have a private conversation with a white sergeant. He'd just been promoted to E-4, which was one rank below sergeant. Was he crazy enough to actually assault an

NCO while we were on the base—and in the middle of the day? Kane's face held a sly smile, and he asked if I could close the loading ramp on the APC he was working out of. I did so, and walked away thinking that there was no way he'd dare go that far.

But Kane did, indeed, assault the sergeant, leaving him with two black eyes. Not surprisingly, he was immediately charged with a court-martial offense. I was, of course, the last person to see the two of them before the incident—and the only witness other than Kane and the sergeant. When Kane's case came to court, I was called upon to testify—and did so honestly. Kane was furious with me for testifying. He was found guilty as charged and taken away in handcuffs by military police—only to be given a second chance by superiors and allowed to return to the unit.

While Kane was locked up in a military stockade, I became acquainted with a white soldier from Cook County, Illinois, known simply as "Doc." My new friend proudly carried around in his wallet the newspaper clippings describing his deeds of derring-do as a criminal prior to enlisting. Some three or four months later, the two of us wound up getting arrested by MPs on the base after a fight; both of us were charged with assault. I was found guilty and knocked down a pay grade, which I later recovered. Doc, who had a long rap sheet, was sentenced to do time in the army's correctional facility in Mannheim, Germany.

After the verdict was handed down, Doc was sent back to the barracks with a police escort, to collect his belongings. He asked me to help him pack. Doc's prison escort was the heavyset Sergeant Chesty, who had signed out a .45-caliber pistol and nine rounds of ammunition just in case things got out of hand with Doc. Chesty seemed bored watching Doc pack his few belongings and so was amusing himself by playing quick-draw with his loaded .45. What he had somehow failed to remember was that at some point before getting to the barracks, he had racked the gun—pulling back and releasing the slide mechanism on the pistol to load a round into the chamber. The .45 was ready to fire.

Me outside Cook Barracks in Göppingen, Germany.
The second-floor window (over my left shoulder) is where the incident
with the stray .45-caliber bullet took place.

Chesty had apparently missed the firearms safety course that every new recruit is required to take.

Time and again, the sergeant acted like a modern-day Wyatt Earp, pulling the pistol from his holster and spinning it back into place. Then he pointed the pistol at me, loosely forming a grip and said, "Hey, Brad." He pulled the trigger with the pistol pointed at my chest. The gun went off with a deafening explosion, and I felt a burn on my wrist. My eyes darted to both Doc and Chesty. All three of us were covered in white dust, but otherwise we were okay. The bullet had grazed my wrist, ricocheted off the rock-hard plaster wall, flown out an open window and disappeared. The company was away on a training exercise at the time, and we were the lone witnesses to the gun's firing.

The unintended discharge of a .45-caliber pistol on the base was a serious offense, and we all knew that Sergeant Chesty could soon be joining Doc in jail if the incident was reported—or if he couldn't return all nine .45-caliber rounds that he'd been given. I glanced at Doc, telegraphing my amazement at the sergeant's stupidity. Neither one of us held any animosity toward Chesty, nor did we see any point in getting the guy in trouble. No one said anything, but we all went to work cleaning up the mess from the wall and moving a locker to cover the large hole left by the bullet. We then "found" a .45-caliber round to replace the spent one that was lost. Chesty babbled his undying thanks to Doc and me and proceeded to escort the prisoner to jail. It was the last time I ever saw or heard from Doc.

Life on the base increasingly fell into a rhythm for me—grueling days of training on our base or some other army facility in the German countryside, visits to assorted bars and nightclubs during weekend leave (and dealing with the inevitable hangover afterwards) and the occasional trip to a whorehouse like the House of Three Colors in Stuttgart.

There were also some memorable longer trips, including one that several of us made to Paris via bus. We took in some of the tourist sites—the Eiffel Tower, the Louvre, and the Palace of Versailles—and enjoyed some very nice (and relatively inexpensive) French wines. And we amused ourselves with a side-trip to Pigalle, where we found some women of the night at 1 p.m. But all of the activity seemed to take place against a never-ending stream of violence. At least, those are my most vivid memories, the ones that made the biggest impression on me during my tour of duty.

During one unforgettable training mission to Hohenfels, I caught the flu. It was the only time during my three-year tour of duty that I ever got that sick. Excused from the normal routine, I was allowed the privilege of just lying in my sleeping bag on a cot. My temperature was between 103 and 104 degrees, and the mess hall and bathrooms were a long walk down a dark pathway from my company's sleeping area. At no time did

I ever receive so much as a gesture of kindness from anyone in my squad. A couple of guys filled up my canteen, using a nearby faucet, but that was it.

Weak and with no appetite, I just lay in my cot, sweating profusely into my sleeping bag hour after hour. I tried to keep hydrated using the water in my canteen and periodically stumbled to the latrine to relieve myself.

I asked my squad leader if I could get sent back to the rear, as I was feeling very weak, but he said "Top"—the top sergeant—wouldn't send anyone to the medical unit unless their temperature hit 105 degrees. That was apparently the way they did it in Vietnam, at least according to Top. My sergeant's experience had apparently been different. During his two tours in 'Nam, soldiers were sent to the rear if their temperatures hit 102. One way or the other, there wasn't anything he was willing to do about my plight.

Late during my second night in the cot, some of the African-American men in my unit were viciously fucking around with some of the white guys, deliberately choking out people who were sleeping—or feigning sleep—in their cots. We were in a darkened, open dormitory-style area housing some 70 men. I could hear what sounded like five or six men in the distance, clearly drunk and up to no good. It sounded like Big T, Brown, Kane and a couple of their buddies. As they moved around the space, I heard muffled screams and commotions as items went flying. I knew PFC Woodson had already taken a beating from the group, and it sounded like they were moving on to their next intended victim.

Months earlier, I'd decided to carry a switchblade with me when I was on base, and I had it with me that night in my sleeping bag. I held the weapon in my left hand, with the blade pointed down. I could feel the cool steel against the inside of my wrist. I was weak, but I had all the strength and determination I needed to stab someone in the face. I wasn't scared to act. In fact, I wanted blood on my knife that night.

Deep down, I was angry. Maybe I was angry with the U.S. Army for turning a blind eye to the violence in its ranks. Maybe I was done with watching some of my buddies getting beaten up. Maybe I was just done with all the shit in Cooke Barracks.

I remember that I was determined to brutally punish my attacker— even though I assumed that would be the end of my army "career." I didn't care. Fuck them. If I was on my own, so be it. I heard the guys move closer and slightly shifted the grip on my knife.

For reasons that I will never know, the group passed me by that night, and my carefully sharpened steel blade wasn't dirtied. Maybe it was better that way. Sometime later, the barracks quieted down and I fell asleep. The next morning, I awoke in my sleeping bag, which was drenched with my sweat. My switchblade was still laced in my fingers. The choked and beaten soldiers sported only minor battle scars and were seemingly possessed of a collective amnesia. It was the same sort of amnesia that was suffered by the NCOs who had heard, or perhaps even witnessed, the violence that night and done nothing to stop it. I had a feeling that I would soon see still more violence in my unit.

CHAPTER TEN

A VIEW FROM THE ABYSS

One evening during the winter of 1974, before turning in to my bunk in Cooke Barracks, I noticed that Sergeant Bill Collins was assigned as CQ, or Charge of Quarters, tasked with guarding the entryway to our three-story barracks, which held about a hundred men. The CQ sat in a chair in the entryway, next to the stairs that led up to the second and third floors. There was no back door, so everyone had to pass by him.

I'd always been impressed with Collins because he had a large row of service ribbons, as well as a torso severely scarred by shrapnel. Collins was a battle-hardened tough guy, and we'd often gone drinking together when we were off duty. With Collins on duty as CQ tonight, I was pretty confident that I'd get a good night's sleep. It was midweek, and we all had to be up at 5:30 a.m. for our daily physical training and four-mile run. Collins had the balls to deal with anyone daring to come in drunk and loud.

Two identical buildings held the men of B Company. There were another two that held C Company. All four fronted on an open field used for training, and they were about 30 yards apart from each other. Inside, all of the rooms in the barracks had the same layout, with over-sized casement windows on the wall directly opposite the door and bunk beds placed on either the left or right side of the room. The bunks were all covered in the same white sheets and thick green wool blankets.

Shouting from a bunch of very drunk men awoke me from a sound sleep around 1:30 a.m. I recognized Kane's voice and some of the other guys', too. The group was crashing around and literally shaking the walls. It was as if a battle was taking place in the hallway. So much for my faith in Collins. I wondered where the fuck he was.

Kane, Big T and a couple of other guys were trying to kick in the door to a room occupied by two black guys—my friend Bo Peters from South Carolina, and Sean Smith, a soft-spoken guy from Dallas. Their room was on the first floor, just a few doors down from mine. Peters was a ferocious dude, and at one point the two of us had roomed together. We got along well. Smith generally kept to himself and rarely if ever made trouble. He had befriended a German woman in her 20s who lived near the base, and there were rumors that he'd sometimes smuggle her onto the base late at night, though I'd never seen her.

"Come on, man. You gotta share with a brother, don't you think," Kane shouted amid kicks and punches to the steel door. "A brother gotta share. You gotta share that pussy."

Kane and the others wanted to share Smith's girl—no matter whether he and his girlfriend were willing or not. Gang rape was what they had in mind, and the only thing between them and their "prize" was the heavy metal door to Smith's room. The girl had taken a big risk even coming onto the base, but there was probably no way that she could have anticipated this kind of trouble.

As the shouting and the pounding on the door continued, I put on my fatigue pants and boots and went out into the corridor. I was terrified of being attacked by the men but even more troubled by the idea of ignoring what was going on. I figured I could find Sergeant Collins, who had to be close. Maybe he'd just wandered away from the barracks to break the monotony of sitting all night. Still, it was the middle of the night, and noise like this carried—though probably not as far as the officers' quarters. What the fuck was going on, and why wasn't someone stopping it?

Kane had managed to break through the door to Smith's room, and he and the others were headed inside. Big T brought up the rear, holding a .45 pistol in his right hand. All eyes were on the girl, and I quietly walked past the door, hoping they wouldn't spot me. There was no way that I dared intervene, especially with Big T carrying a gun.

The girl was sitting on the bed, with one of the green blankets wrapped around her like a shawl. She was white, with long dark-brown hair. Smith and Peters were sitting on each side of her, looking glum. For a split second, the girl stared at me, silently screaming for help. Her look telegraphed both panic and fear. Peters saw me, too, and subtly shook his head no. His message was clear: move along, and don't intervene.

I kept walking, going through the foyer and past the CQ's empty chair. Kane and the others hadn't seen me walk by. Where the hell was Sergeant Collins? I went outside and ran down to the adjacent barracks looking for him. But he was nowhere to be found.

I stood alone in front of my barracks, the cold German air filling my lungs. It was pitch black, and no one was around. The noise and shouting inside the barracks had stopped.

Intervening in any way, be it by a phone call to the MPs, or by busting in there myself, seemed out of the question because of the risk to my own life. It didn't take a Ph.D. to imagine what was going on inside that room, or what the aftermath would be for the victim.

I went back to my bunk and fell asleep. There was nothing I could do that night—or at least that's what I thought at the time. Little did I know that the image of that woman would stay with me forever.

The next morning, I wondered what my next steps should be, if any. The safest thing for me to do, by far, was to shut up. That much was clear. I wondered if Collins had deliberately deserted his post at the barracks, or if—perhaps—there was some good explanation for why he wasn't there. That was unlikely, for sure. Should I report the incident and expose Collins's desertion from his post, knowing full well that that would be the end of my "career" in the army, and perhaps of my life?

Where did my sense of morality begin or end?

Reporting the incident would certainly have destroyed Sergeant Collins's career, and it would have sent the most dangerous men on the post, including one with a handgun, looking for vengeance or determined to neutralize the threat—me. I was also fairly certain that the case (if any) was certain to come down to a "he said/she said" scenario, with the men who assaulted the woman insisting that the sex was consensual. I very much doubted that she would have the nerve to stand up to the men and tell the truth about what happened that night. There was no way that Smith would be able to protect her, and I was positive that he wasn't going to be reporting the rape to anyone, no matter if it was his girlfriend or not. Ultimately, he valued his life more than hers. If it went down as consensual sex, that would still be a serious violation, because soldiers aren't allowed to bring any outsiders onto the base. But I doubted that the charge would result in any of the assailants going to jail. There was also the possibility that someone could catch Big T with a loaded weapon in his possession. But it seemed highly unlikely that someone would be able to do that and live to tell about it.

I was way too inured to the oxymoron of military justice at this point; there was no justice in the U.S. Army. Doing the right thing held only one certainty: I would be a pariah, a rat with no real hope that so much as one single person would support me.

The next day was business as usual in the barracks, with no indication that anything criminal had occurred the prior evening. All was forgotten, at least for most of the men in the barracks. If I hadn't seen her eyes, maybe I, too, could have pretended it never happened. There were probably about 100 men in the barracks that night, virtually all of whom pretended to sleep through screaming, banging, crashing and ultimately gang rape. I saw not one single person even so much as put the lights on in their room, and I wondered why.

As a 19-year-old hanging out in my bunk in Cooke Barracks in Göppingen, Germany, I didn't really spend much time thinking about the violence or the racism that I encountered. It was simply part of my experience. No doubt, it wasn't the environment that I had dreamt of before I decided to enlist. But truthfully, who can imagine from the outside what the army is *really* like?

Later, I wondered if what I experienced was commonplace in the army or not. Were all the U.S. Armed Forces around the world as violent, and sometimes evil, as they were in the late 1970s in Germany, right after the Vietnam War?

For the most part, Cooke Barracks was closed off from the prying eyes of the press. We were thousands of miles from home, in a base that was largely removed from German society and its norms. In some sense, it was a microcosm of American society, with blacks, whites and Hispanics living together. But unlike back home, we lived together in close quarters 24 hours a day, seven days a week, with access to virtually unlimited quantities of booze and drugs. We had no choice but to deal with each other all the time.

The U.S. Army, the great green machine, had forced all of us together, no matter what we had been accustomed to back home. Some of us wondered what the army was even doing in Germany and whether it would even be possible for our relatively small number of soldiers to ward off a full-scale, Soviet/Eastern Bloc offensive through the plains of central Germany, the Fulda Gap. We were training for a war that most of us figured we'd probably wind up losing—though we rarely talked about it. Many black soldiers quietly wondered why they should be the ones in harm's way when the nation didn't seem all that grateful or willing to provide the sort of opportunities that were commonplace for people with white skin.

The officer corps was almost completely comprised of white, college-educated men, while the majority of the rank-and-file soldiers were black and Hispanic. In the combat arms branches, such as infantry, the blacks and Hispanics usually outnumbered, or were at least on par with, the number of white soldiers. They also tended to be considerably more street-smart; they enlisted at a slightly older age, too.

Many of the black men whom I knew were fine soldiers. But there was a small percentage who were militant, violent and truly intimidating to those around them.

No doubt, the level of violence that I experienced in the army hardened me and perhaps set the stage for my decision to enter a motorcycle gang, where the violence was even greater. For years, I wondered why I seemed to be surrounded by violence in the army, and why my experience was so different from others who followed similar paths. I suspect that there was something about my size and level of fitness that made me the perfect target. Someone who stood over six feet and weighed a muscular 195 pounds was a more impressive target than someone who stood five foot six and weighed 150. No one would be impressed if you took out one of the wimpy Southern kids in the barracks. But they may well be impressed, and feel intimidated, if you took out someone who was big and fairly muscular, like I was. I was large enough to merit a "pat on the back" for the guy who took me on, but not so large as to be a serious threat to someone. Bullies don't like to lose fights.

To be certain, any honest soldier who served could likely tell people stories of racial intimidation and violence. Going into the army, I had no idea that sort of thing even existed. I doubt I would have enlisted had I known what was happening inside Cooke Barracks.

The weird thing is that I can't really complain about the violence I experienced in the army. Ultimately, it made me stronger, both physically and mentally. Maybe I should send my recruiter a fruit basket.

CHAPTER ELEVEN

THE DEEPEST RING OF HELL

At approximately 0630 hours one spring morning, the men of Bravo Company were headed back to our barracks, nearing the end of a required four-mile run. Wearing white T-shirts, fatigue pants and combat boots, we ran in step with an NCO calling cadence. Charlie Company was running in the opposite direction—and in tight quarters with us.

A black soldier from Charlie Company, one I'd never even talked to, grabbed and pulled my arm.

"I don't play that shit," I said, before nailing him with a very clean right cross. The move sent him flailing at speed through his formation. Before he even had time to stand, both companies stopped dead in their tracks and started glaring at each other.

Seconds later, a black sergeant from Charlie Company began walking in my direction, clearly hoping to retaliate. My platoon's Sergeant First Class Tre Mallard, a tough white Cajun, stepped in front of him and took a stance telegraphing his willingness to fight. Mallard ordered the other sergeant to stand down, which he did—but only after giving me an angry stare. This wasn't over by a long shot.

Striking me would certainly have meant a court-martial and serious trouble for the sergeant from Charlie Company. Or at least it should have, under the Uniform Code of Military Justice. Under those rules, he was obligated to protect his men and to see to "the good order of the situation." But there was no threat to the sergeant's men when he came toward me. The soldier I'd hit was being helped to his feet, and I'd simply stood my ground. In my mind, I'd reacted as I had to. But clearly the soldier would have had to even the score or face serious ridicule (or worse) for letting himself get battered by a white soldier. There was no way that I wanted to provoke a full-fledged fight between the two units. I knew full well that I would have been in deep trouble had I done so.

The soldier who yanked my arm did not know me; the two of us had never had any beef. My guess is that he attacked me simply because he saw me as a soft target. No doubt, my counterattack surprised him—though one can only speculate what he expected me to do.

I suppose most black soldiers believed that their white counterparts were simply inferior as street fighters. Whatever success I enjoyed in this altercation probably had a lot to do with his shock at being counterattacked. I certainly didn't have any special fighting skills at that point in my life, and I never possessed that natural knockout punch that some men seem to be born with.

I was frightened by the violent and militant black men who were often trying to stare me down; I was frightened a great deal of the time there, and for good reason. But for me, there was a greater fear than that of a physical beating. It was the fear of looking in the mirror and seeing a coward, a pussy. I wanted to view myself in the way Sergeant Jackson from Fort Polk likely viewed himself: with a grim, fire-eyed defiance of any weakness related to battle, either armed or unarmed. So it would seem my greater fear won out.

For days I heard rumors of my impending death at the hands of some of the black soldiers from C Company. But for reasons that were never clear, no one came after me. In the end, the original attack was just another act of random violence, the sort that I saw repeatedly during my tour of duty. The violence hardened me in a way that I didn't fully understand at the time. As time went on, I would slowly become numb to the danger. My sense of fear lessened a bit each time, and so, too, did my sense of caring for the men around me. I suppose I would expect that to happen in men who've seen combat and risked their lives in the field. But we were all on the same side—and still on friendly soil.

One Saturday afternoon, I watched as a fight broke out at the mess hall between a white private and a black sergeant assigned to my squad. Most of the men were off the base, enjoying weekend leave. The two men had apparently gotten into some debate inside the mess hall. The white soldier was in civilian clothes, and the sergeant, who was on duty, was in his fatigue uniform.

I watched from a hilltop some distance away as the sergeant left the mess hall and ran across the commons into our barracks, where he changed into civilian clothes and then came back outside—where he stood and waited for the white soldier to come out. The sergeant then laid a solid beating on the soldier, who looked scared to death and never even attempted to fight back. Eventually, he fell to the ground, where he was kicked in the face. A handful of the victim's buddies had no choice but to stand by and watch the incident transpire; they were surrounded by a large group of blacks who were making it clear that they, too, wanted a slice of the pie. The fight soon ended, with the victim lying bloodied on the ground. The sergeant walked back into the barracks, changed into his uniform and continued with his duties.

No one ever reported the incident, and there was no indication that it was ever investigated by anyone. Sadly, I was among those who saw the fight and did nothing. I never even considered reporting the matter, because I knew that doing so would put me in grave danger. My personal survival took precedence over my sense of honor and morality that day, a fact that still sickens me. The immortal Dante tells us that the deepest ring of Hell is reserved for those who protect their neutrality in times of danger. I suppose I knew at the time that, no matter what I did, no single individual would be capable of affecting any change in the violent environment in which I lived.

The U.S. Army would have to make sweeping changes in policy impacting all levels of the force, ranging from the rank-and-file troops up to the officers, who needed to be more hands-on and confront what was really happening in the ranks. Alcoholic ncos had to be treated and dealt with. Violent and verbally abusive soldiers had to pay a real and harsh yet fair punishment for their transgressions. And everyone needed to accept that the only color that could be recognized for any reason was green—the color of our uniforms. Personally, I believe that the army made dramatic changes, and that a soldier's world today is far different than the dysfunctional environment I experienced. One thing is clear: U.S. forces have been very effective in the battlefield since 9/11.

I had no idea how the army would treat me if I stabbed someone with a switchblade knife. Yet I rarely went anywhere without one. I certainly had never stabbed anyone before and was quite certain a very long jail sentence would await me if I did. The real reason I carried it was simple: I was frequently scared, and I hoped that the nasty presence of the blade would preempt its use. I should have realized that carrying it for a long enough period of time almost guaranteed I'd end up in a perilous no-win situation. Still, fear often trumps sound reasoning, and the fear I felt was real.

Some weeks later, I was walking alone on the base on a Saturday afternoon, off duty, and was about to enter my dorm. I had been assigned a new roommate, a black guy who had some time in and seemed like a decent roommate. A group of black soldiers in civilian clothes was hanging around the entrance to Cooke Barracks, mostly members of my company. Big T was among them, holding court and passing around a couple of bottles of Thunderbird. I foolishly had hopes of making it inside unnoticed.

"Hey, Bradshaw, how the fuck are you," Kane shouted as I walked past him and headed into the barracks. "Lookin' forward to catchin' up with you later, bro!"

After being court-martialed for beating up the sergeant in the motor pool at Hohenfels, Kane was back—and in my face. I was the sole witness who'd testified against him, and he'd spent some hard time in a military prison before returning to base and hooking up with his old buddies, including Big T. I'd spoken up and done the right thing, and now I was in serious danger once again. I really had only myself to blame.

My new roommate was still putting his locker in order, and we chatted briefly before I dug out my well-worn copy of Frederick Forsyth's *The Dogs of War* and dropped onto my bunk to read. Minutes later, I heard a group of loud and drunk men outside my door. I put the book down on the green blanket and waited for the inevitable.

The door burst open, with Big T and Kane leading the way. The other wine-drinking members of the group followed close behind. Kane was holding the heavy end of a broken pool cue.

"Bro, ya know that 90 percent of all black men go to jail," Big T said, looking in Kane's direction. "Jail is part of the black experience, and you need to be part of that. This is the white fucker who should be dealt with. So be black and do what you know has to be done."

My roommate stood still, not certain of what he should do—if anything. The men behind Kane were shouting encouragement, urging him to take me on. For a split second, I sat paralyzed on my bunk. Then I grabbed the switchblade from under the pillow, stood and flipped the blade out, ready to finish whatever Kane started.

Kane stared at me, looking euphoric. He glanced down at the blade, lunged at me with the pool cue and missed. I lunged, too, but struck air.

A sergeant who was part of the group tackled Kane and urged him to give it up. Kane looked determined to continue even as some of the men grabbed him and dragged him out of the room. Big T looked at me with a smirk before turning and exiting the room with the others.

Someone closed the door as they exited, and I stood there, still firmly holding the switchblade in my right hand. My roommate and I looked at each other but said nothing.

It was almost as if Kane and I had become gladiators, forced to play roles that neither of us wanted, in a very real game that we couldn't stop. Kane had no choice but to demonstrate that he wasn't going to let me get away with testifying against him in court-martial proceedings. And I had no choice but to defend myself by whatever means were necessary, even if that meant using a weapon that I should never have had. Kane and I had both entered the army to be soldiers, pure and simple. Yet we were fighting against each other, and not some enemy, real or perceived, of the United States. We were both in our own personal hell.

I was fortunate that the sergeant had broken up the fight when he did. Had I stabbed Kane, everyone in the room that night would have testified against me, and I would have gone to prison, disgraced and dishonorably discharged. No one would have dared to speak in my defense, especially since the switchblade that probably saved my life was illegal to possess.

Curiously, no one said anything to me afterwards—not my roommate or any of the other witnesses. It didn't seem to make any difference in how I was treated by the men, either. In the end, it was just another day in the army. No blood had been shed, and so it was hardly worth the bother of conversation.

★ ★ ★

One night during the late fall of 1975, I was hanging out in the barracks, pleasantly intoxicated and drifting off to sleep, when my friend Steve Comer got into a heated exchange with another soldier from C Company about some small thing. The two of them began to grapple, but the other soldier was able to break free and take off, with Comer in hot pursuit. Wondering what was going on, and thinking that my buddy may need some help, I took off after him.

Chasing across the grassy commons after Steve, I ran headlong into an off-duty NCO from C Company who was walking with a bunch of soldiers, all of whom happened to be African-American. The NCO fired a slick left jab to my eye, the opening salvo in a serious beat-down. I never left my feet, but went to a knee a couple of times, only to recover and get hit with another brutal onslaught.

I fought back, but it was immediately clear to all of us on the field that night who the victor was. Still, the fight continued long after the NCO had demonstrated to everyone present that he was a stronger, tougher, more able fighter than I was at the time. There was no reason for the NCO to continue, and yet he did, inflicting blow after blow against someone who had made the unforgivable mistake of crashing into him in the dark.

Afterwards, Comer and some of the guys took me to the emergency medical facility on the base, where I learned that my orbital socket was fractured. The next day, I learned that the NCO in question was a member in good standing at Smokin' Joe Frazier's gym in Philadelphia. Perhaps not surprisingly, I learned, he had studied with savage diligence.

MPs were dispatched to investigate, and I told them that I'd taken a bad fall down the stairs in the barracks. Not believing the story for a second, they chuckled and left, shaking their heads.

I lost an important part of myself that day. When the fight was over, my sense of compassion for others was gone, replaced by an emptiness and a steel resolve to protect myself no matter what the cost, and no matter who might get hurt. I had become so inured to the perpetual violence surrounding me that I simply accepted it. There was no point for me to hope for justice or dream of some kinder, gentler world. Life was a brutal struggle, interspersed with a few brief periods of fun to keep you ready to get back into the fray. Weakness in any form is the enemy, and fear is a weapon that can be used against you. In my Brave New World, the rules were simple: prepare for battle, and never show weakness. Author Joseph Conrad was right—most men went to their graves ignorant to the last of what the world held in perfidy and violence.

The NCO felt the need to demonstrate his boxing prowess on the unskilled and vulnerable. Even if he had justification to strike me, and perhaps he did, he went way too far. Filled with his own bloodlust and adrenaline, my attacker was perhaps the most important teacher I could have had. Through all the blood and pain, I had learned to break through and see life in a radically different way, to live each day as a warrior, to be the proverbial tough guy.

It seemed an eternity since I'd lain in bed with the flu in my parents' house, reading Norman Mailer's *The Naked and the Dead*. I'd revered Sam Croft at the time as the cold-blooded killer who looked death and hardship straight in the eye. Now I embodied some of the same elements as the character I had once revered; I had learned to put my feelings and conscience aside, to file them away for a while and forget about them. It wouldn't be until another great teacher, Renzo Gracie, entered my life that I would once again find my soul.

CHAPTER TWELVE
QUIET DAYS IN KEY WEST

I was psyched to be 90 days to ETS, or End Term of Service, when I would be discharged from the army and head back to the States. The closer I got to my discharge, the more careful I became about my behavior—and avoiding any sort of altercation that could delay ETS.

I'd saved up about a month of leave time, which would allow me to get out earlier than normal. As I counted down the days, I circled the base with clipboard and papers in hand, going through the army's elaborate and time-consuming process of making sure that everything was in order before I was discharged. That meant paying off my tab at the base commissary, returning gear and making sure that all my service medical records and administrative/personnel files were in order—performance evaluations, certificates, and DD Form 2586, "Verification of Military Experience and Training."

Finally, my time was up and I grabbed a train from Göppingen back to Frankfurt and hopped on a plane for the eight-hour flight back to Newark. I needed to go back to Fort Dix to complete the final step of the discharge process. In one of life's little ironies, someone failed to call my name from the long list of men and women being discharged, and I sat in a waiting room for six hours. It was only after I stood up and started asking what was going on that the clerk realized I'd been forgotten and got things straightened out.

I headed back to my parents' house and moved back into my old bedroom, which looked just the way it did when I'd left three years earlier. But I was different, and it felt weird to be back. My parents probably felt the same way. None of us were at ease.

One morning, my mother quietly walked into my room—probably to drop off some laundry that she'd done—and woke me from a deep sleep. I snapped awake and jumped up, ready to attack her. She was stunned and promptly left the room. The moment affirmed what both of us already knew: I was different from the teenage boy she'd said goodbye to after I enlisted.

My always-reserved dad looked at me differently, too. Bud had something to celebrate now with his buddies at his weekly poker games: his son was a veteran, just back from Germany. I knew I'd fallen short of his expectations by quitting the high school football team. He'd wanted—no, *expected*—me to become a county or state football champ. But at least I'd served our great nation and was a veteran. That was something. Otherwise, Dad was the same as he'd always been.

I'd been home for about three weeks when a friend of mine, Henry Rathmaker, suggested that we take his Camaro, drive down to Key West, Florida, and have some fun. I had no idea at the time what the Florida Keys were. Still, with no job and nothing holding me in New Jersey, I gladly accepted, and we headed south together. It didn't take long to pack, because I had next to nothing.

Rathmaker and I rented a cheap two-bedroom apartment on the second floor of the Marine Hotel, with a balcony overlooking the turquoise waters of the Straits of Florida, for just $175 a month, including utilities. The hotel, with its Spartan accommodations and peeling paint, was far from a four-star resort. Still, it had its own swimming pool, and the receptionist promised that if you showed your key across the street at the Sands, you could get access to the small private beach there. I wound up spending countless hours on that gem of a beach and the adjacent wooden pier, hanging out, drinking beer and enjoying some of the passing sights—including the attractive female tourists. Palm-tree-studded beaches, bikini-wearing American girls; I felt like I had died and gone to Heaven.

My buddy and I shared the apartment for about two months until he got a job offer up north and hit the road. I kept the place even though it was bigger than I needed. But I realized that I had to stick to a budget if I intended to keep living the good life without a job. My skills, limited to soldiering and fighting, were not in high demand in sleepy Key West.

I bought a used 10-speed bike for transportation and calculated that if I limited myself to just one meal a day, I could hold out pretty much indefinitely. I knew I could grab cheap takeout food from a Cuban place in town. I allowed myself a generous $6 a day for booze. The Blue Parrot sold cheap beer and even provided a container to go for my bike ride home. After all, it wasn't like I could get into much trouble pedaling my rusty 10-speed. While the tourists were watching the sunset at Mallory Square, I was visiting the low-end bars, where you could buy six shots of tequila for a dollar.

With Rathmaker gone, my apartment felt more humble and emptier than before. I had a black-and-white TV with a wire antenna on top, and a sleeping bag on the bed. Most of my clothing was army surplus—two pairs of fatigue pants cut into shorts, some green T-shirts, a couple of sleeveless undershirts and a pair of sneakers. No underwear. The women who shared my bachelor lair didn't find it all that quaint and cozy, which helped to ensure that they weren't overly interested in returning.

I went to the unemployment office to collect what I felt was my just due. I hadn't yet acquired my current belief that it's abhorrent to collect unemployment insurance when able and healthy.

The office clerk reasonably explained that, in order to stay eligible, I needed to show proof that I'd attempted to find work at a minimum of five locations a week. The skills of bayoneting, shooting, drunken brawling and topographical land navigation were nowhere to be found in the want ads. I had no comment for the clerk but likely looked perturbed, as I had no idea how to find work in Key West—or any of the Florida Keys for that matter.

The clerk cocked his head to one side, frowned and asked me what was bothering me. I told him what I had been doing for the last three years.

Could I prove it? he asked.

I showed him my Department of Defense DD214 separation papers.

The clerk acquiesced and agreed to give me the benefits, job search or no job search. Come in every other Friday with the papers filled out, he instructed, promising not to look too closely. It was worth about $75 a week to me, which wasn't bad given my $175-a-month rent.

Key West had an amusing Conch Train that gave tourists a pleasant, low-speed ride around the island. It ran on rubber tires, not steel wheels, and was powered by a V8 gasoline engine, not steam. But tourists seemed to like it, in part because it was cheap and ran right by all the island's places of note, including Hemingway's former home. The train typically carried a mix of elderly retirees, milk-white tourists who'd just arrived from the mainland, a handful of lonely and bored single women and the occasional stoned freak laughing like a hyena. I watched it for a while and devised a battle plan to identify and then meet women who might find a well-tanned young stud interesting—well, at least for an afternoon or evening.

I'd noticed that the train picked up speed in front of Smathers Beach. I learned to get on my bike in advance and then race the train as it went past the beach, passing it at full speed, shirtless and sweating from exertion in the hot sun. If I saw anyone of interest, I'd just happen to stop for a cold beverage at the very point where the train stopped to let off its passengers. Admittedly, my act was extremely shallow. But it was also great fun, and an excellent way to pick up women in this era before AIDS. Of course, if I couldn't find anyone of interest on the Conch Train, there were plenty of other places to look, including the beach, swimming pool and bars.

I affected a sort of sad yet heroic pose. Deeply scarred by life's injustices and moving on from a tragic love affair, I was in need of the right tourist woman to fuck me into being a whole man. It's a role that's been done a thousand times, but as with good cop/bad cop, simple playacting often works. The target just needed to have the seed of wanting to believe. I suffered my fair share of rejections. But rejection never bothered me for long since there were plenty of other transient women in Key West. It wouldn't take long before another sexy woman would come along, and I'd move on to my next target.

My time in Key West was certainly pleasant enough. I'd recharged my batteries and found out what it was like to sleep deeply in the clean salt air without worrying that some armed man was going to bust into my room and try to murder me. But in time, chasing the Conch Train grew lame. If I didn't live there, I would have found it difficult to believe a small city could be so tolerant, laid-back and peaceful. I didn't even make it a year. Relaxing in paradise didn't fit, kind of like a dinner jacket with one sleeve too long. I missed the adrenaline rush that I'd gotten on almost a daily basis in the army. I missed the action, and maybe I even missed the danger. Whatever the issue, staying in Key West was not in the cards for me.

It was Helen Keller who told us, "Life is either a great adventure, or it is nothing." I had no real idea what was to come, but I didn't want it to be boring.

I headed back to Middletown with no plan, no job skills and no prospects for work. I moved back into my parents' place, got a job doing construction work and played third base on a local softball team. I went out most nights and often wound up spending the night at a friend's house.

My brother, Mike, had opened up a karate school across the street from the train station in nearby Red Bank: Bradshaw's Karate. He worked at a bank during the day and was at the school, running classes, most nights and weekends. Like many karate schools, it was a basic storefront operation with a small counter up front, wood paneling on the walls and a large carpeted area that we used for training and grappling. I trained there regularly, studying Korean Karate under my brother and his buddies and doing some heavy-duty weight lifting. Mike had a sense of business acumen that I clearly didn't have, and some superb fighting skills. He had trained under a local legend. He also was being instructed by a very tough group of Jamaicans from a brutal and prestigious school in New York City. I was reveling in the training and couldn't have cared less about any sort of career advancement.

The Jamaicans were the elite students of famed karate star Tadashi Nakamura. On weekends they would come down to the Jersey Shore in a group, their girlfriends in tow. The women were terrific fighters as well, smiling like jungle cats while they taped up their wrists for ju-kumite, or free fighting. The Jamaicans spoke of the warrior code and Bushido. They were traditionally educated and well schooled in oriental martial discipline and philosophy. But more importantly, in my mind, they walked the walk. They considered themselves classical warriors in a modern world. There wasn't a phony bone in any of their bodies. Training and fighting with them was a test of your mettle every time, and the standards they set for my brother and I were the very same ones they set for themselves.

These were the hardest and toughest men and women I had ever had the great good fortune to associate with. Humility and self-deprecating humor were the order of the day. Showing off or acting disrespectfully was not tolerated.

One sweat-soaked Saturday afternoon, Venezuelan Santiago Vasquez came into the school. He was in incredible physical condition and warmed up doing full splits. He told us he wanted a "friendly" sparring session and asked if we would be amenable taking turns fighting him—five of us, in all—with short breaks between each bout. Assured of his prowess, he made it clear with his body language and facial smirk that this was a splendid idea. As the kumite began, Vasquez's smirk evaporated, replaced by despair as he went toe to toe with fighters who wouldn't back down no matter what the circumstances. After the fight, Vasquez's body was bruised, but his self-esteem was devastated.

Vasquez broke down in tears in front of the group. In many gyms, his tears would have been perceived as pathetic or unmanly. Not so on that night. Ultimately, the way in which he handled himself earned him real respect from the group.

"A tiger can't help being a tiger," one of the Jamaican fighters explained. "His nature compels him to seek combat. The Chinese say that when two tigers fight, one dies and the other is seriously injured."

He continued: "Our warrior nature also compelled us to end this combat, since in this world a superior person seeks justice. And an act of kindness is the highest form of action, and is the mark of the superior man. Understand, my friend: you are not fighting normal people here."

Vasquez became a member and quickly a real leader in the school. Later he became a renowned undercover narcotics police officer in Kansas City, Kansas.

The sun was starting to dip lower in the sky one hot day in August as I got onto the Garden State Parkway on my new deep blue 1975 Harley-Davidson Sportster, twisted the throttle and ran it up through all four gears. The 900-cc bike always sounded great on the open road. I'd used some of the money I'd made in construction as a down payment on the Harley. I had already started to customize it by adding an extended chrome front fork.

I was headed northwest to my brother's apartment in Matawan, off exit 120. Mike and I both played on a softball team sponsored by the United Counties Trust Company, where Mike worked during the day.

*The gang of five—me on the left, my grandfather Bill,
my father Bud, and my brother Mike in the foreground.
Mike's son, Michael, is on my grandfather's lap.*

I played third base, and Mike played center field. We were scheduled
to play the River Plaza Fire House softball team, and my brother had
decided to invite both teams to his place for a beer party the night
before the game.

Mike lived in one of the many nondescript apartment complexes
that were sprouting up in the Central and North Jersey areas—perhaps
not the best place to have a beer party for a bunch of young guys. The
walls were paper-thin, and your neighbors were literally just a few feet
away in each direction. Mike was the corporate type and not at all the
sort of person who would draw undue negative attention from the rest
of the yuppies-in-training that he worked with.

The team that Mike and I played on was pretty chilled out. But the
other team was captained by my cousin, Bill Hendricks, who was known
to be a mediocre player with a competitive edge and a volatile temper.

Bill had spent three years as an MP in Germany, most of it prior to my arrival. I had visited him at his posting and seen the healthy respect he received from his fellow soldiers. He had also endured some brutal and violent encounters, and survived using much the same methods as I had.

As the party progressed, we continued drinking heavily. It was as if Budweiser was going to stop making the stuff the next day—which definitely wasn't the case. We'd already purchased the keg that we'd be drinking at the game the following day. The voices got louder, prompting us to crank up the music time and again so that it could be heard over the din.

One of the guys came up with the brilliant suggestion of having a friendly boxing match on the second-floor landing. It was too long a walk to head down to one of the grassy areas adjacent to the apartment building, and too far from the booze. I peered down over the rusty three-foot metal railing surrounding the landing. It was about a 20-foot fall to the concrete sidewalk below.

Mike dug around in his closet, came out with two pairs of 16-ounce boxing gloves and offered to referee the matches. I was fortunate enough to be called for the first match; I'd be representing my team, and my six-foot-three, 215-pound cousin Bill would be representing the other team. I briefly wondered what my brother's neighbors were thinking about this crowd and why they didn't call the police. No matter to me. The fight was on, and I was fully confident that Bill would not hold back just because we'd grown up together and were relatives. No doubt he loved me. But he was also intent on knocking me out. If my front teeth were collateral damage in the action, so be it. We didn't have any mouthpieces anyway.

My corner man shouted words of encouragement—to stick and move. Perhaps more sage advice would have been "Don't do it," or "Try to avoid getting knocked over the railing." No matter. The Heavyweight Championship of Who Gives a Shit was poised to begin.

Bill and I both attempted the "stick and move" strategy for about two seconds. Then we moved to the center of the landing and punched each other as hard as we could. My brother briefly attempted to break a clinch but was promptly launched backward through his open apartment door, landing ass-first on the floor. One of the neighbors also tried to intervene, at least until Bill and I gave him an angry look and he silently retreated into his apartment. We continued beating each other until we couldn't breathe or punch, thus ending round one.

The second round ended the same as the first, and neither of us wanted a third round. So we ponied up to the beer supply and tried to drink, though we both had serious pain when opening our jaws from the trauma of the temporal lobe area being smashed; the only cure for this pain was drinking more beer.

The game the next day is a bit of a blur, a blend of angry hangovers and a hot and humid summer day. Bill participated in only three or four fistfights—not bad, given that his team got shellacked and someone certainly needed to pay. Bill and I almost had a much-anticipated rematch several times, but each time one of us cooled down just enough to save face and not have to relive the fun-filled festivities of the prior evening. We ended the day with an empty vow that we were done with each other as comrades. Later, Bill came to be a trustworthy and reliable ally who stood with me without question when serious threats came my way.

Sometime after my discharge from the army, I began to evaluate my friends and relatives using what I called "the foxhole test." In a foxhole, confronted by a powerful enemy, would I trust this person with my life? I believed I could judge people on my own, using just my intuition. I resolved that I couldn't be close to those who failed the test. Ironically, there were few people that I was able to judge one way or the other; I was brooding, unsmiling and compassionless. Few people wanted anything to do with me.

I landed the perfect job, working for a person who looked and acted menacing and didn't care about upward mobility—contractor Tom Rondell, a shrewd, divorced ladies' man who was building a small development of upscale houses. His method of obtaining maximum profit was to find the cheapest contractors possible—and then browbeat them to give him the best possible prices. His goal was simple: build a new house cheaply and quickly, and sell it for the highest amount the market would allow. My responsibility was simple as well: ensure that Tom didn't get shorted by his grossly underpaid workers and make sure they didn't beat the shit out of him.

CHAPTER THIRTEEN
BEYOND GOOD & EVIL

The phone rang one fall morning. It was my longtime friend Bob Grant, a well-educated guy who was tough as nails and could be a serious problem for his opponents in a bar fight. Though capable of significant violence, this guy was affable, gregarious and fun when drunk. He was also a married homeowner and businessman in Middletown with assets to lose and a reputation to uphold. "Have I got a story for you," he said, inviting me to have a beer with him later in the day.

Grant and I were in the army during roughly the same time period, though he was discharged about six months before me. He was an MP with a ferocious reputation for violence—and for not getting caught when dispensing his own form of justice. Once, after I got out of the army, I was picked up by local police after I got into a fistfight and foolishly left an ID bracelet with my name on it next to the dude I had knocked out. Grant's subsequent advice for me was pretty simple: avoid carrying any kind of ID during that sort of mission: no patches, no dog tags, nothing.

Over a couple of beers, Grant described to me how he'd been hanging out one evening in Fair Haven at a bar called the Lock, Stock & Barrel, drinking Scotch and talking with another guy. Grant said that one of his more colorful stories included the word *fuck*. But one well-dressed young woman at the bar was appalled at his use of the word—and opted to confront him.

"Excuse me, but would you mind refraining from using that sort of language?" she asked.

"I don't know, honey, exactly which language would you prefer—French?" Grant replied. "Well, shit; don't speak a word of it."

"You did it again. You have a really foul mouth."

"Hey, let's start over again," Grant said.

"I don't think so!" she angrily replied.

Before Grant could reply, the bartender pointed at him and shouted, "You are flagged. Pay up and get out! Now!"

Almost immediately, the bartender started to move toward Grant. Pissed, Grant picked up a drink glass off the bar and hurled it at the man's head. He missed.

The glass struck and shattered the huge mirror that hung behind the bar. Shards of glass rained down behind the very large, well-built and now startled bartender. Grant took his cue and headed for the door, crossing the street and going down to the cold, swiftly moving river, which was nearly a mile wide. Hearing police sirens in the distance, he ran down the embankment, "borrowed" a rowboat he found tied up along the shore and quickly rowed across the river.

Soon he had disappeared into the dark, moonless night. Grant felt certain that no one in the bar knew his name and that it would be difficult, if not impossible, to identify him. He'd driven a friend's car to the bar that night and so couldn't be identified that way, either.

Grant ditched the boat on the other side of the river and walked the seven miles to his house without seeing anyone. Once home, he grabbed a beer and hung out with his wife, who was still awake.

The doorbell rang around 3 a.m., and his wife hopped up to see who was there. She instantly recognized their visitor and opened the door. In walked Middletown Police Officer James Pressfield, a trusted lifelong friend of Grant's who'd noticed that the lights were on and was hoping for a cup of coffee.

Half-drunk and still high on adrenaline, Grant made a bad mistake: he opened up and described to the officer what had just happened at the bar. Pressfield seemed to love the story and reveled in the details, laughing uproariously at Grant's description of his escape across the river and long, long walk home. Pressfield assured Grant and his wife that the police would never catch him.

"You are home free, my man. Nothing to fear," Pressfield said. "Relax and go to bed, and don't worry about those bozos across the river. They can't catch anything bigger than cold."

Grant thanked his buddy and retired to bed soon after the officer returned to patrol.

But, Grant continued, things went very differently.

At 8:30 the following morning, the doorbell rang again. Two detectives from the Middletown Police Department stood at the door, explaining to Grant and his wife that they wanted to take custody of him immediately in connection with the incident in the bar. Grant sleepily feigned ignorance of any wrongdoing, but the lead detective cautioned him to stop talking.

The detective then described, in great detail, what Grant had done the previous evening. The description matched nearly word for word what Grant had said to Officer Pressfield.

"We aren't looking for bail here, just formally charging you," the detective said. "We'll give you a lift back here, if you promise to play nice."

"I will cooperate completely, but can I ask one question?"

The detective wryly grinned. "Let me guess. You're gonna ask how did we figure all this out? Did someone tell us?"

"You must be reading my mail."

"Listen, you look like an intelligent person. My partner and I start work at eight. Need I connect the dots?" The implication was that Pressfield had left Grant's house, completed his patrol and then reported what had transpired to his superiors. As soon as the shift change had taken place, the detectives were sent out to make the arrest.

Grant was furious at Pressfield—and pissed at himself for trusting his friend of many years. After his processing in the Middletown Police Department's headquarters, he spoke with the arresting detective.

"Honestly sir, I have only one confession to make," Grant said to the detective. "I don't trust anyone with dangerous information, but I would trust my closest friend. James's betrayal hurts worse than this arrest."

The detective didn't hesitate in his reply: "If James is your friend, you don't need enemies. If this was involving a serious injury or a major theft, that's one thing. But no one was hurt at the bar—luckily, I might add. And the rowboat was recovered from the dock where it was tied up. It really makes a good story. But I don't like rats, even when they help me clear cases."

The detective paused for a second, and then continued: "But in a way I'm almost glad it happened. Want to know why?"

"Tell me," Grant replied.

"Because, without anyone getting hurt, I know I can never trust your pal James," the detective said. "He does this to you, I'm nothing to him. Stand-up he most certainly is not."

When Grant had finished telling me the story, he seemed energized. He wanted payback against Pressfield but knew it was going to be a serious problem. It's one thing to have a bar fight, but quite another to put a beat-down on a sworn police officer. It also didn't take a genius to figure out that the cops would come looking for Grant if something suddenly happened to Pressfield.

We ordered another round of beers, and I gave the matter some thought.

Turning to face my buddy, I said, "You can have no knowledge of any act of revenge whatsoever. If these fucking cops even suspect you, and they will, James being the pussy that he is, you are fucked. They will bust your balls for all eternity. Trust me; James does not get a pass on this because he's hooked up with the blue mafia. I'm flying a black flag on this and we will not discuss it again."

"You ain't flying anything on this without me," Grant said.

"You'll just have to shut the fuck up," I said. "Not to worry, though, no doubt I'll need a favor from you someday. Anyway, this one will be fun."

"What do you guess you're gonna do?" Grant asked.

"I have no idea what you are talking about."

My assessment of James Pressfield completely changed after hearing from Grant about the bar incident. Though Pressfield was big and carried himself like a tough guy, I believed that deep down he was a pussy. The cop used his size, badge and gun to bully and control people—and there were plenty of people in Middletown who agreed with that assessment. At that point, Pressfield and I had known each other for years through our mutual friendship with Grant, and we'd gotten along pretty well. But behind my back, I knew that he quietly boasted of having taken me down. That was pure fiction. If Pressfield was as tough as his reputation, he was going to get an opportunity to prove it—in the dark, with no witnesses but me, his attacker.

I happened to know that the cop lived in a rented farmhouse on a large, run-down estate in southern Middletown; I'd been there for Grant's bachelor party, years earlier. You had to drive down a long road—some parts gravel, and others just dirt—and go past the empty former manor house to get to Pressfield's place. There was a sharp right-hand turn in the road, and then a quick left, which forced drivers to slow almost to a crawl. Large trees and thick brambles bordered the road on both sides. Past the sharp turn, there was a good 300 yards of gravel road before you reached Pressfield's house. The entire property, and the road itself, were unlit.

The south side of town was largely a cow pasture at the time; the north was far more populated (and well lit). I knew this part of town quite well because my parents' home was only a mile away from Pressfield's. It was common knowledge that most of the Middletown Police Department's marked units were assigned to the northern half of town because that's where most of the action was.

Despite its remote location, Pressfield never worried about trouble anywhere near his house because he was six foot three, weighed 220 pounds and was a cop. By regulation, he was armed with at least a handgun 24 hours a day, seven days a week.

My "plan" was simple: I intended to ambush Pressfield on the dark road to his house after the end of one of his four-to-midnight shifts. I was familiar with the Camaro he drove. There were two variables—timing and whether or not he'd be alone. I wondered if he would drive straight home or stop to suck down some free drinks at Mulrain's Tavern on Route 35, right across the highway from the Middletown Police Department. If he picked up some chick in the bar on the way home, then I was going to abort. Otherwise, it was game on.

Late one cloudy summer night, I walked the five miles to Pressfield's house from my place in Belford and began planning my makeshift assault. There was no Comanche moon, and the place was both dark and silent. I found a couple of fallen tree limbs and placed them across the road to force the cop to stop his car and remove the obstruction. My years in the army had taught me a few things about tactics in the field. The obstruction didn't seem that unnatural; it looked like the limbs had been knocked down by the wind. When he got out, I'd have an opportunity to see if there was anyone with him or not. From my vantage point behind a tree about 30 feet away, where I waited in the shadows, it would also be easy enough to see if he was being followed by a friend in another vehicle.

As I sat in the darkness, I thought about a book I had read only a few weeks earlier, *Beyond Good and Evil*, by Friedrich Nietzsche: "One has to test oneself to see that one is destined for independence and command—and do it at the right time. One should not dodge one's tests, though they may be the most dangerous game one could play and are tests that are taken in the end before no witness or judge but ourselves."

There was a part of me that was looking for an excuse not to assault Pressfield. The whole event was out of character for me, and I wondered time and again if I should just call the whole thing off and walk back home. But Nietzsche's words kept echoing in my head. It was as if Nietzsche was telling me that this was one of life's tests.

By 12:30, there was no sign of Pressfield, and I settled in—it was going to be a while. Then, at about 2:20 a.m., the Camaro's round headlights appeared in the distance. There was no indication of anyone following. I was sweating bullets. It was highly likely that Pressfield had spent the last couple of hours drinking, which meant that he'd be half in the bag and likely quite tired, too. Alcohol is not your friend when speed and split-second thinking are needed.

I was wearing a long-sleeved dark sweatshirt and blue jeans. I wore a rubber mask—the face of a wizened and deformed bald old man—and black leather driving gloves. I carried two other things with me: a small flashlight and a roll of quarters. I had no real "weapons" with me that night—no knife and no gun. I wanted this to be a good old-fashioned beating and something he'd remember. For me, it was all about personal honor and justice.

Pressfield slowed the car as soon as the headlights picked up the branches blocking the road. I could see the reflection of the car's red brake lights coming on. He flicked on the high beams and slowed to a stop about six or eight feet from the obstruction. I heard the door pop open and watched as the overhead light inside the vehicle came on. There was only one person in the car: my intended target.

He got out slowly, wearing a white T-shirt and his uniform pants—the outfit that cops generally wore when drinking publicly after a shift. The uniform shirt cannot be worn off duty. He sighed loudly and muttered a few curses as he walked toward the tree limbs.

I immediately left my hiding spot and took several quick strides toward him. I grabbed the roll of quarters out of my pants pocket and held it tightly in the palm of my right hand. The weight of the coins would make my punch even more powerful. Next, I pulled the flashlight from my sweatshirt, flicked it on and held it so that it would illuminate the mask from below and make me appear even more threatening. Even the topography worked in my favor: the field by the edge of the rutted road was six or eight inches higher than the dirt tracks, forcing Pressfield to look up at me.

The cop saw me the instant I turned the flashlight on, but he seemed unable to move or otherwise react, at least for a second or two. I could hear his breathing become labored. He inhaled and exhaled in fits and starts. Slowly his eyes rose to meet mine, and he began to shout—not for help but out of fear. James the rat realized that he was alone and would have no choice but to fend for himself. His house, his refuge, was barely a thousand feet away. But it didn't make any difference how far it was, because there was no way he could make it there. Oddly, he made no effort to reach for his gun.

With one more stride, I closed the distance and punched Pressfield in the nose. I could feel the soft cartilage break from the blow, made heavier by the roll of quarters, and watched as he fell back and landed on his ass.

I immediately straddled him and struck him time and again in the area around his left eye. I wanted him to be flying his "look, world, I got the shit kicked out of me" flag for an extended period.

Pressfield started blubbering like some preschool child who'd just been bitten by a pit viper. His pathetic demeanor only fueled my adrenaline and made the blows come harder and faster.

He was broken, both mentally and physically.

With my boot across his throat, I pulled Pressfield's off-duty .38-caliber revolver from his waistband and threw it into the darkened, overgrown field. I made sure he could see the area where I'd tossed his gun so that he wouldn't be able to claim it was stolen. Then I reached inside the Camaro to shut the engine off, removed the keys and tossed them into the field.

I gave Pressfield a kick in the balls with my black engineer boot, picked up the flashlight that I'd dropped a few feet away, and walked into the dark night. I stopped by the creek at Poricy Park to toss the flashlight into the black water. I held on to my $10 worth of quarters, intent on using them over the next few days. Money was money.

I have little doubt that Pressfield claimed to his fellow officers and anyone else who would listen to him that he'd been sucker punched and beaten by a gang of 10 or more men. Being such a tough cop, he likely claimed that some of his former arrestees were possible suspects.

I learned from Grant that he was briefly questioned about the assault, but he literally knew nothing about it and the cops had no evidence of any sort. All they had to go by was the partial description from Pressfield and maybe some boot prints left in the soil—but there was nothing else, and no apparent motive.

I have long believed that you cannot reveal what you don't know, and so I never told Grant what I did.

Big tough James Pressfield quit his job with the Middletown Police Department shortly after the beating. Years later, after I joined the very same police department, I heard from some of the guys that Pressfield had never seemed to recover from the savage beating he'd taken that night from a cowardly mob of young thugs. It seems Pressfield couldn't find the light at the end of the tunnel. Too bad. If he does find it some-day, I hope it's a train.

CHAPTER FOURTEEN

WHISKEY JOE & THE BREED

A few months later, I started renting a bungalow with a former army buddy, Steve Comer, in the blue-collar community of Keansburg. The 'Burg offered great water views north toward Manhattan, a cheap little amusement park that was popular with summer tourists, and not much else. Many houses there were not much more than summer bungalows that had been converted into year-round homes, and more than a few were in dire need of maintenance. Old cars and the occasional motorcycle sat outside them. Our place was down by the water, in a neighborhood with tiny yards.

Comer and I were hanging at a local bar one night in the late fall of 1976 when we saw "Whiskey Joe," a member of the Breed Motorcycle Club, sitting at the bar, drinking—no surprise—straight whiskey. Steve had been "rehabilitated" of his once-violent nature during a brief stint in military prison following a fight. After we shared a few drinks, he suggested that we ask Whiskey Joe about riding with his outlaw club, which had been formed in Asbury Park in 1965 and was at one time among the strongest and most feared biker gangs in the Northeast.

Whiskey, who had long, thick black hair combed straight back and a thick black beard that covered much of his face, was easy to talk to. He was wearing typical biker clothes—blue jeans, a T-shirt and engineer boots. After some casual banter, I asked him if he and the Breed were looking for more riders. He chuckled and said yes. Over a few more drinks, Steve and I agreed to pick up Whiskey in our car, or "cage," and make the half-hour drive up to a bar in Perth Amboy to meet some of the guys.

The Breed had a well-deserved reputation as a nasty bunch, aligned with the Hells Angels. The club colors—the jackets bearing the club's emblems—displayed a red-and-white American flag with a circle of stars in the area where the blue field and 50 stars would normally be. The Breed was about as patriotic as Sherman's burning down of Atlanta and Columbia was a demonstration of zealous patriotic duty. They were a bona fide one-percent outlaw gang, and they made no effort to conceal that fact in any manner.

Motorcycle clubs in the U.S. are considered "outlaw" clubs when they aren't sanctioned by the American Motorcyclist Association, or AMA, and don't adhere to the association's rules. Rather, outlaw clubs have their own set of bylaws that provides the foundation of the outlaw biker culture. Story has it that at some point the AMA said that 99 percent of all motorcyclists are law-abiding citizens. That gave rise to the notion of "one-percenters," the outlaws who didn't follow the rules.

The one-percent patch, typically sewn onto the sleeveless jacket worn by members of outlaw clubs, is one to be taken seriously. Only a bona fide outlaw biker would dare display it. It is earned, not bought. One-percenters play the game for keeps.

I cringe these days when I see movies and TV shows depicting outlaw bikers as buffoons, latent queens, cretins or swollen-bellied drunks who can't get out of their own way. Bikers may lack book smarts, but they are street-savvy and fearless. Day in and day out, they wear their Breed or Pagan colors, billboards displaying their membership to all they come into contact with. Making that bold statement, and walking the line on it, makes for a cunning and oftentimes vicious category of being. To dismiss any bona fide outlaw biker as pathetic loser or mental lightweight is a dangerous underestimation.

Flying the colors is a gigantic "fuck you" to all citizens and every cop. The outlaw may individually like some citizens and even certain cops. But for the rest of the non-outlaw world and most non-aligned clubs, the insignia, be it a winged death's head (Hells Angels), a Fire God (Pagans), a skull with crossed pistons (Outlaws) or a sombrero-wearing gunslinger (Bandidos) is a massive and heartfelt "go fuck yourself."

Most outlaw bikers see themselves as modern versions of the 19th-century mountain man—dangerous, tougher-than-life anachronisms, forced to put up with modern laws that need not apply to them. They live life on their own terms. They have no need for government, police or other societal norms. They need only their bikes, brothers, women and the open road. As to women, the ditty "My bike's number one, you're number two. Don't call me, I'll call you" is roundly applauded.

Anyone foolish enough to take on a member of any outlaw club will find the club's wrath coming down on them. Club members stand for each other unconditionally. A club member is a member for life, and never forgotten or unfairly dismissed. They'll tell you that they would rot in jail before ratting to the Man about any club business or other club member. Why, then, would a young guy from Middletown be interested in joining the Breed? For me, joining an outlaw club was the ultimate act of defiance. Like Thomas Carlyle. Grim Fire-Eyed Defiance.

I had neither grievance with nor hatred for any specific entity or person. The circumstances of my life had left me with an overwhelming emotion: defiance. And the bikers were its true outward essence. The average American male who pays his taxes and plays the game, follows the rules and plays it safe at all times, seeking security at every turn, knows this in his heart: *What I wouldn't give*, he thinks, *for one day telling everyone that I feel like telling it to: "FUCK YOU. What I wouldn't give to have one day when I can grab that woman who is batting her eyelashes at me, throw her down on the floor and have a wild pile-driver fuck. What I wouldn't give for one day with the wind in my face, surrounded by my comrades in arms, taking what we want and doing what we want, as our just due.*

That was how the Pagans lived life. Fuck the cops, tell your woman—your "bitch," as they would say—to shut the fuck up, and drink, drug and fight as you see fit. No guilt, no remorse, just outright defiance. Well, like the Jamaicans say: everyone want go Heaven, nobody want die.

All outlaw clubs have a system allowing "hang-arounds," guys who tag along with gang members with an eye toward eventually getting into the club. They are generally treated respectfully if they act properly. Each hang-around has to be sponsored by a bona fide club member, who is responsible for him. If the hang-around doesn't piss people off, he's allowed to become a "prospect," the next step toward becoming an actual member. Prospects are like recruits in the military: they go through a training period before being accepted. Military recruits and biker gang prospects are both treated like shit—ordered around and humiliated on a regular basis. But that's where the similarity ends. One is training to be a member of the legions defending the U.S. Constitution. The other is training to be a cutthroat member of the legions of the damned.

If you are a prospect for a bona fide outlaw motorcycle club, you're obligated to follow any order given to you by a superior—no matter what. I knew how to take orders from my time in the army. I had tough-guy killers like Sergeants Koncha, Mallard, Jackson and others who gave me orders. Those men earned the right to issue orders in the crucible of battle. I was honored to do what I was told by those men, who had survived combat and come back whole to show others how to do the same. But I had a problem being pushed around by someone whose greatest accomplishment in life was knowing how to use a socket wrench—at best. That seemed dishonorable to me, and I wasn't willing to do it. If I was going to get into a motorcycle club, it would be on my terms.

Steve, Whiskey and I drove in my cage to Perth Amboy, a blue-collar city with a feeling of rot. It was bitterly cold outside when we arrived at a workingman's bar, the type where there's a hearty crowd even at 6 a.m., enjoying that liquid breakfast of champions, a shot of Fleischmann's rye whiskey with a beer back.

With Whiskey leading the way, Steve and I met a couple of guys from the Breed and heard of another who was on the way. All three of them went by their nicknames—"Grip," "Crimes" and "Cisco."

I would come to find out that Grip earned his nickname because, after he drank enough wine, there was absolutely no crime he would not commit; he would lose his "grip." The guy had a pinched face and a swarthy complexion and seemed perpetually dyspeptic. If I had a daughter, I would chain her up rather than let her spend time in this guy's company. Crimes had one leg missing and was quite adept at moving with a prosthetic. The story was that he'd lost the leg in some kind of motorcycle accident. But the perpetual angry look on his face, coupled with his demeanor, made me wonder if he'd eaten the missing append-age. Cisco would have cast perfectly for a prison drama in need of Aryan Brotherhood stand-ins. Whiskey was the life of the party. His speed-and-whiskey-induced charm kept the action rolling.

A loud crashing sound came from the bar's front door. Enter "Wild Billy," who chose to smash the door open with a kick rather than use the knob. Billy was a snazzy dresser—bare-chested, his black leather jacket open so all could admire his triple-canopy chest hair. The guy seemed pissed off about something. But Whiskey assured me that Billy was always pissed off because he worked on a garbage truck—and hated it.

The six of us grabbed a table and started doing some drinking together. Since Steve and I could not be trusted with any information about club business, the banter was light. Whiskey even got some laughs from the group. This was not the kind of discussion where you gave your opinion on the latest popular books or offered insightful commentary on political issues. Steve and I kept a low profile, nodded when appropriate and answered the few questions posed to us truthfully. Getting caught in a lie with any once-percenter was not a smart thing to do.

I was trying to get the guys to drink to the point where things would get interesting. They, in turn, were looking for signs of whether we had the "chops" to be part of the Breed. They were also suspicious that we might be Pagans trying to infiltrate their group. If that had been the case, we would have been risking serious bloodshed—or death. There was reason to believe that we could be Pagans, because Keansburg, where Steve and I lived, was considered Pagan turf.

"Zorro," a smaller and slightly darker-complexioned version of Father Christmas, showed up sometime later. He immediately referred to Steve and me as Pagans—even though we'd never even met a Pagan—and never let up with shitty comments about it. Whiskey thought he was awesome. I wanted to punch him in the throat.

The evening ended without incident, and Whiskey Joe assured Steve and me that it was okay for us to hang around with the other guys in the club. He told us to catch up with him the following Friday at the same place. Because of the constant turf warfare between the Breed and the Pagans, members of both clubs were very careful about where and when they got together.

That following Friday, Whiskey told us that we'd be going on a long ride upstate to Troy, New York, which was frigidly cold. I had the misfortune of drawing Crimes as my cage partner for the trip. He did little more than grunt at any comment or attempt at conversation, and I spent hours asking myself what I was doing with a member of the Breed. Still, some strange force seemed to be pulling me deeper into the outlaw lifestyle. It was as if I needed to work some kind of risky high-wire act.

Our first stop in Troy was a motorcycle show, where we hooked up with some of our new buddies, including Whiskey, Grip and Cisco. Though no one was wearing colors or otherwise identifying themselves, it seemed clear that there were a bunch of other members of the Breed at the event. It was easy to identify who the heavies were—and it was also obvious that there was a great deal of sizing up and glaring taking place between certain subgroups. The tension was thick. Still, the cops seemed not at all intimidated. We were only at the show briefly before being commanded to head to a local nightclub by one of the Breed's leaders—a soft-spoken, muscular guy who stood six foot 10.

The nightclub was upscale and vast, with several bars, loud live music, a serious crowd, including lots of well-dressed women, and plenty of dancing. It also had some king-sized bouncers working at the entrance who said nothing and allowed all the Breed members to go inside without objection. The Breed leader, "the Giant," had donned his colors, as had all the other members. Steve and I were the only hangers-on there.

The Giant towered next to me at the bar. I found him to be an interesting drinking companion. There was probably not enough whiskey in Texas to get him drunk, but he gave it his all anyway. The cost for all this booze didn't seem to be an issue for the Breed leader or any of the other guys. Somehow the bartenders got very forgetful about collecting what we owed.

None of the guys from the Breed were willing to do any dancing—despite the sexy chicks on the dance floor. Bikers don't dance. Pussies dance, jerk-offs dance, but not real bikers.

After more than a few drinks, the Giant explained that he had to start his "dime" soon—a 10-year jail sentence—and so drinking good booze, and lots of it, was a good way to spend some of the free time he had left. As he drank his whiskey, the Giant explained that the sentence stemmed from a guilty verdict in a rape case, and that doing the dime was actually not so bad an outcome. It was all part of doing business, and if you couldn't handle it, you shouldn't play at that level.

While I was busy chatting with the Giant, I couldn't help but notice Crimes playing a bizarre game: calling himself "the Kissing Bandit," he kissed and groped only those women at the bar who had dates with them—with impunity. He had strategically placed himself near the Giant and another member of the Breed, "Ape." Weighing well in excess of 350 pounds, Ape was perhaps the most revolting person that I've ever seen—grossly fat, with long, unkempt hair and beard and clothing to match. He was a mammoth stinking asshole. But with the Giant and Ape nearby, none of the men at the bar dared to protect their dates from Crimes. Under Ape's amused countenance, a lot of women fell victim to the kissing bandit, their dates sheepishly looking away.

Hoping to curb some of Crimes's moves, I asked the Giant what he thought about his buddy's antics. The Giant just sadly shook his head and said, "It ain't my way of doing business, but Crimes has had my back more than once. I would kill a motherfucker if they put their hands on my old lady like he's doing. But as you can see, they don't seem too concerned, now, do they?"

In the wee hours of the morning, the Giant decided he was done and headed out. Crimes decided that the rest of us should head over to Ape's house to continue the evening's festivities. On the way there, Crimes got so excited about his kissing bandit exploits that he rolled the car window down and began firing his pistol wildly. It didn't make a damned bit of difference to him where the bullets landed, so long as he didn't hit anyone from the Breed. With his drunken demeanor, it was highly unlikely that he was actually going to hit anyone or anything.

Ape's sprawling old house was spacious enough for about 14 of us in all, including 10 Breed members, a couple of women the guys had picked up at the bar, and Steve and me. Crank (crystalized methamphetamine) and beer were plentiful, and the conversation was mostly about the savage beatings that Breed members, including Ape, claimed to have laid on Pagans. Thankfully, Zorro wasn't there, so Steve and I didn't have to defend ourselves against claims of being undercover Pagans.

It wasn't long before Ape brought out a film projector and showed the most disgusting bestiality films that I've ever seen. He howled with laughter, even seeing to it that the women there watched as well. His film "collection" seemed to be his pride and joy.

If there was a way to do it, I would have volunteered for electroshock treatments to rid my mind of the images I saw at Ape's place.

After returning from the frozen north, Steve and I continued to spend occasional evenings with Whiskey Joe, whom we both truly liked, and some of the others, most notably Grip and Cisco. The winter was the time for Northeastern bikers to dismantle, repaint and repair their choppers.

CHAPTER FIFTEEN

ENTERING THE LITTLE BIGHORN

Most guys with Harleys tend to put them away for the winter under a cover in their garage. For Steve and me, things were different. Our Harleys were the most valuable and important possessions we owned—and we kept them in the living room of our bungalow year-round. That was where we cleaned them and did basic maintenance. Motorcycle parts were strewn all over the living room floor. It wasn't like we were inviting the guys over to have a Super Bowl party anyway.

That winter, Steve needed to have some serious work done on the front end of his dark-blue Shovelhead Harley, something that the two of us couldn't pull off in our living room. Steve told Cisco that he'd put a longer front fork on the bike and that he needed someone to adjust the rake on the front end to keep the bike properly balanced, and Cisco agreed to take care of it.

What we hadn't expected was Cisco's decision to break into our place to retrieve the part for repair. He smashed a window by the front door, reached in and opened the door. From what we could tell, he left only with the bike's front end, but it was kind of hard to tell if anything else was missing. Steve and I were pissed, and we knew that Cisco was making a statement—that he was dominant, the alpha dog.

Neither of us was intimidated by this guy, and we wanted to make sure he got that message, no matter whether we were hang-arounds or not. I am sure that Cisco was rarely challenged by the people who crossed his path. He was tall, muscular, never smiled and looked like a hard-core outlaw. But Steve and I had seen this act before, and we weren't going to stand still for someone breaking into our place.

Two days later, Steve and I were sitting in my cage with Cisco and Whiskey Joe, and Steve decided the time was right to bring up the break-in.

"This is fucking bullshit," Steve said. "I asked for help with my front end, but this is my house."

"I would kill the motherfucker who breaks into my house," I said. "I got no problem with Cisco coming in anytime, but fuck breaking in. What the fuck?"

Both Steve and I spoke with more bravado than we felt. But we had no choice. We knew that Cisco would keep coming back for more if we didn't put an end to this now.

"I couldn't give a fuck to what some fucking hang-around thinks," Cisco said. "These fucks ain't wearing a patch. Whiskey, I am seriously losing patience with this shit."

Steve and I looked at each other but said nothing.

"Everybody calm the fuck down," Whiskey Joe said, laughing. "Cisco, you got to understand these cats are going from a triple-A club to the big leagues overnight. You guys better learn how to deal with patch holders right quick. This shit is real. It's not a fucking game. Figure it the fuck out."

Before we broke up that day, we agreed to meet at Whiskey's place and get together with "Crazy Horse" and the guys on Staten Island—very solid Breed territory that Crazy Horse ran with an iron fist. Afterwards, Steve and I headed back to our bungalow, where we had cardboard covering the broken window and a nice chill breeze blowing through the place.

I had a vague idea of what Crazy Horse was like, and it wasn't pleasant. Even the Giant and Ape shook their heads in serious respect for his violent and tormented state. "That Crazy Horse is a sick fuck, but he takes care of business," the Giant said that night in Troy. "You don't have to ever clean up after him."

The original Crazy Horse was a brilliant military leader of the Sioux Indian Nation. Given to trances and prophetic omens, he was both a shaman and a gifted killer feared for his excellence in combat. He was a believer in the spirit Wovoka, who gave the Sioux Nation the ghost dance. He was a serious problem for General George Armstrong Custer and the Seventh Cavalry at the Little Big Horn. The Crazy Horse I met on Staten Island was a brutal and psychotic megalomaniac—and far worse in real life than I had imagined in my pre-meeting nightmares. He shared only a name with the leader of the Sioux Nation.

We drove to Staten Island in two separate cages. Steve drove my car, with me riding shotgun and Whiskey stretched out in the back seat. We followed a car with Crimes, Cisco and Grip inside. When we were close to the Staten Island nightclub, Crimes pulled over to the curb and Steve pulled in right behind him. Steve and I wondered why we were stopping, but Whiskey told us to just sit tight.

Steve and I watched as Crimes and Cisco got out of the car, walked across the street and confronted a group of about six men and women who'd been hanging out chatting. Crimes and Cisco pulled out hand-guns, and we could see them collecting belongings from each member of the group. Then they slowly sauntered back to our cars as the group watched them in stunned silence.

Cisco headed over to us and popped his head in through the open back window, looking at Whiskey. "We just took them off for their drugs and money," he said calmly, handing Whiskey a wad of cash and a small plastic bag of marijuana.

Whiskey stuffed the cash in his pocket and reached forward to jam the weed into the pocket of my black leather jacket. "Hold on to this shit," he said.

Cisco and Crimes headed back to their cage and we drove to the nightclub. There were several places on the same block, so we had our choice of where to party. A group of men and women, all wearing Breed colors, were standing outside one of them.

Crazy Horse stood about six feet tall, with a wiry build and wavy black hair that hung to the middle of his back, and the colors he wore were extremely faded—an obvious sign of being with the Breed for many years. His flowing, long hair reminded me of some historic image of an American Indian on horseback—only this guy was not the sort of person you want to smoke a peace pipe with. He looked at Steve and me as if we were pieces of shit, but said nothing to us. His "bitch" just sneered at us.

Steve and I shared a look as we asked ourselves what we were doing here in the company of these people, and wondered if any of the six people who'd just been ripped off by Cisco and Crimes had called the police. Steve whispered that he didn't think anyone in the group had taken down my license plate number. Both of us had visions of a lengthy stay at Rikers Island. Now if we could just leave and celebrate away from this plague of locusts that we had stupidly decided to party with.

Crazy Horse turned around and headed toward the workingman's club nearest to us, his woman in tow. The bouncers stood aside and made no attempt to collect the cover charge from anyone in our group. All the upstanding citizens behind us had no choice but to pay. We followed Crazy to the bar, where he pushed people aside and swept their glasses and bottles to the floor with a sweep of his arm. This was our territory now.

"Me and my fucking crew need beers," Crazy announced. "Give them Bud, in bottles, not glasses. Give me that whiskey and a bunch of shot glasses, too."

The bartender did exactly as he was told and didn't ask for a dime.

"Get me a fucking tire iron, hang-arounds," he said. "And make it fucking quick."

Crazy fired one of the shot glasses at the lights over the pool table to emphasize that he wanted the tire iron immediately. Broken shards dropped onto the table as stunned patrons backed away but said nothing. The bouncers, too, were silent.

"What kind of tire iron do you want?" I asked sarcastically. My comment was not well received, and I decided that I would be wise to find a tire iron promptly. Steve and I made our way quickly toward the door. Behind us, we could hear Crazy Horse shouting something about "fucking hang-arounds."

"Fuck, Steve, maybe we should just drive away," I said to my buddy once we were outside. "That motherfucker is stone crazy, and he is going to bring all manner of trouble down on our asses."

"Yeah, but these fucks will kill us for sure if we run off," Steve said. "We got to show some balls here."

I knew Steve was right. The Breed would have come after us in force if we had fled.

"I am not gonna show them nothing like fear," I replied. "If we have to go down, let's go looking that motherfucker in the eyes."

"If we make the night, you want out of this shit?" Steve asked.

"Fucking right. Best get out early before we get one goddamn inch deeper."

The two of us shook hands and popped open the trunk to my car to look for a tire iron. I thank my Lord and Savior Jesus Christ that I left a tire iron in the trunk. If Jesus knew what that tire iron was for, he would no doubt take it up with me later, assuming that I got to Heaven one day. I was pretty sure I wasn't in any danger of bumping into Crazy Horse there.

Steve snuck the tire iron past the bouncer and presented it to His Majesty, who was screaming at people, telling them not to leave the bar, because the party had just started. Whiskey Joe and the other members of the Breed seemed not to care about his shouts. They'd evidently seen this show more than once before. But dozens of bar patrons seemed unsure what to do; they stood quietly and tried to avoid body or eye contact with anyone wearing colors.

Crazy took the tire iron and smashed out what was left of the lights above the pool table. Then he used it to smash open the change reservoir from the inside of the pool table. Bits and pieces of the table went flying as the guy continued to hammer at it with the tire iron while screaming some nonsense at the crowd. His woman and a couple of the other chicks that were hanging with us pocketed the coins. No one seemed to see anything, and the formidable-looking bouncers were nowhere to be found.

"Let's get the fuck out of this dump," Crazy Horse suddenly announced. "We gotta take this party to the usual spot."

I guess even Crazy Horse felt a little awkward about sticking around in the place he'd just ripped off—not to mention destroying both the expensive pool table and the light fixture that once hung above it. All of us headed out to our cages. Just as the three of us were about to get back into my car, I saw a bunch of New York Police Department officers approaching us. Two of them headed straight for Crazy Horse—one holding a pair of handcuffs.

One cop grabbed Crazy Horse by the arm and shoved him face-first onto the trunk of a nearby police vehicle. Other cops came in close and took multiple shots at his body. His woman was tossed to the ground as another officer put a knee on her back and reached for an arm. Crazy Horse laughed hysterically, shouting to Whiskey that the cops were arresting him on a warrant for some prior scuffle with the law.

The cop closest to me slammed the car door on my leg as I was trying to get in. My leg hurt like hell, and I bent down to rub it. At the same time, I reached into my jacket pocket, pulled out the bag of marijuana and tossed it under the car. I had almost forgotten about the drugs, with the Wild West show going on around me.

The cops demanded ID from all of us, which we provided. All of us, even Whiskey, addressed them as "Officer" and were firmly polite.

"I guess you didn't see my leg, no problem," I said to the cop who'd slammed the door on me. "I just got out of the army. Shit happens in jobs like this. We're clean, if you want to check."

The officer took a good, long look at my military ID card. It seemed just enough to keep him from getting real shitty with me and seeing what would shake out. I had no idea that I'd be the one playing tough cop in just a few short years.

No one had spotted the bag of grass I'd tossed under the car, and I figured I was good.

The cops told Steve, Whiskey and me to get the fuck out of Staten Island right fucking now.

Whiskey insisted on taking the wheel this time. He was determined to find the precinct that the cops would take Crazy Horse to. Fortunately, he had plenty of cash to bail out our fearless leader, thanks to the armed robbery the guys had pulled off just a few hours earlier. Foot to the floor, Whiskey blasted through five red lights in a row. We actually beat the cops back to the precinct. I suspect that the cops spent a little extra time with Crazy Horse outside the bar, adjusting their captive's attitude.

Much to our relief, Whiskey told Steve and me to head back to New Jersey, and he would handle springing the boss. "We'll catch up this week and get you guys straightened out, one way or the other," he said.

As we headed west over the Outerbridge Crossing, Steve and I contemplated how much more time we could stand hanging with the guys from the Breed.

"We've got to get my front end back and then tell Whiskey this shit ain't working for us," Steve said. "I am not reliving this shit again. No fucking way. We'll be doing time before the summer is out."

"Whiskey ain't going to take this well," I replied. "Cisco will go off the wall—and Grip, Zorro, Wild Billy. Shit. We will make some serious enemies, man, if we walk."

"If?" Steve asked.

"When," I replied.

The two of us sat silently for a while, contemplating our immediate future.

"You know what, man? We did not survive that shit overseas to get pushed around in the world," I said. "We did not expect this shit, and fuck all these motherfuckers. If Whiskey don't see it, fuck him, too. I don't remember him explaining shit about being slaves to these fucks. I would be much happier dead than prospecting for Crazy Horse."

"Looking at it that way, yeah, man, there is no way. None," Steve said.

CHAPTER SIXTEEN

GOOD EVENING, MR. MOLOTOV

"Whiskey," I said, "this shit is over for Steve and me. Over, and no chance of it turning around. He needs the front end of his bike, and we part ways. No bad blood, but this ain't for me and him."

"I need my parts back, man," Steve echoed. "I got the money, but I'm with Chuck. No way I'm staying with this. No fucking way at all."

Steve and I had set up a meet with Whiskey Joe at the Globe Bar on East Front Street in Red Bank, with the goal of making a graceful—and healthy—exit from the Breed. At the time, the Globe Bar was a classic gin mill where the most popular order was a shot with a beer back. The meeting took place early one evening in March, right before the start of the riding season, and the three of us were sitting at the big rectangular bar, with a pool table behind us. Steve and I were both drinking beer, and Whiskey was drinking his usual—whiskey, straight.

Whiskey had no immediate response for us but instead just sat there and slowly had a couple of shots.

"Can't handle it, huh," he finally said, leaning forward and resting his elbows on the bar.

"Yeah, can't handle it. Right, Whiskey. We just can't hack it," I said, with a slight edge. I thought that if I showed weakness at any point with any members of the Breed, they would seize on it like a squad of jackals.

"What's the problem, nobody served you coffee yet?" Whiskey said.

Steve and I knew we were taking a risk by even raising the idea of leaving the motorcycle club. We'd observed some pretty serious criminal acts, and knew many members of the Breed—and where they lived and got together for meetings. It was no secret that various police agencies, including the Federal Bureau of Investigation, wanted to know more about the club's members.

Guys in the Breed wore colors at sporadic times, usually when they were together and rolling as a pack. They took security very seriously and took pains to make sure they weren't followed when going to someone's house or apartment. We routinely entered and exited buildings through alleyways and basements to throw off any undercovers who might be trying to follow us. At first, I thought that members of the Breed were just playing some kind of game on Steve and me. But after a while I realized that this was cold, hard reality and absolutely not a game.

Leaving the Breed wasn't going to be a game, either. We knew that Whiskey Joe would take some real heat for bringing in two hang-arounds who quit under suspicious circumstances. But leaving wasn't up for discussion. Steve and I were determined to get out, no matter what the consequences.

Whiskey and I glared at each other but said nothing.

"We got no problem with anyone in your club," Steve said. "It's all the way cool there. We don't feel like we fit in. We don't know jack shit about anything anyway. And we sure as shit ain't giving the fucking Man anything. We just want to cut it clean."

Whiskey had another shot and brooded for a while. I sensed what I always did about him: he was a hard man, smarter than he appeared. A real no-bullshit tough guy. And we'd put him on the spot. He'd vouched for us, and now were we betraying that trust by wanting to leave. He was pissed off and planning out his next move.

I don't think he thought we'd "pussied out." But he would be stung by the club for bringing us in. Finally, he made his play.

"Then one of you guys got to meet Front End John up north. You can't just kiss us goodbye. Negotiate with him. Tell him you can't handle it, or whatever the fuck you want to say. But somebody got to show, somebody's gotta explain. I ain't doing it for you," Whiskey said. "I got my own shit to explain 'bout this fucking bullshit."

Steve caught my eye and asked me to go for a quick walk with him. We headed back toward the men's room.

"I know you, you fuck," Steve said, standing inches from me, his finger in my face. "You're gonna go up there and take care of this shit with Front End John, right? You're thinkin' that, right?"

"You're reading my mind," I said. "I ain't afraid of these cocksuckers, and only one person needs to go. You got this girlfriend you're all in love with, and I really don't give a fuck about anything. Yeah, let me put this shit to rest."

"Did you ever stop and think how fucking stupid you are?" Steve asked.

"No, tell me how the fuck stupid I am."

"Front End John is the front end of a car," Steve said emphatically. "You go meet these fucks and you are going to have an accident with all the right witnesses. You will meet a Front End. Just not a human one."

Steve and I said nothing further and walked back to our bar stools. I had learned the hard way how to deal with danger in life. There is but one way: attack danger like a good infielder plays a ground ball. You go after it. You don't back up and let it play you. Whiskey had no problem with my defiant attitude. He was a tough infielder as well.

"No fucking meeting, no fucking negotiations," I told him. "You owe Steve his front end. Give it back. We forget this ever even started."

Whiskey leaned forward and stared at me. I could smell the booze on his breath.

"You bought yourself a real problem," Whiskey said. "No walking away from this one, no fucking way. Give me a call. You know, so you can pay for your front end. Season's starting. You can't ride without half the bike."

Whiskey threw down some money on the bar and stood to leave.

"I got the bar bill," I said. "Don't look so sad. We're going to be getting together real soon."

A few days later, Steve called and told me that he'd tried and failed to get his front end back. He described how he'd called Whiskey's house and first gotten the guy's wife on the phone. She verbally abused him for a while before handing the phone to Whiskey, who cranked up the volume and made it clear that there was no chance of Steve ever getting the part back, no matter what he did.

Steve was furious, in part because we were getting close to riding season and he really wanted to get his Shovelhead out of our living room and back on the road. The plan that the two of us hatched over the phone wouldn't have won any awards from army tacticians. Basically, it was a frontal assault that would be mounted by Steve and me and our buddy "Lesh," who owned an auto repair shop in town. We were going to drive up in front of Whiskey's modest two-story house on West Street in Red Bank, hit the car horn until someone came out and demand that we be given the front end back. If that didn't work, we were going to toss a Molotov cocktail onto Whiskey's front porch. What better way to get some action?

There were some challenges with the plan. We had no idea if Whiskey would be home. Would other people be there? Would anyone be armed? How were we going to get away, given that the house was in the middle of town and just a couple of blocks from the busy commercial areas around Riverside Avenue and West Front Street? Was Steve's front end even in the house? And there was one other issue: the Red Bank Police Department was two blocks away, on Monmouth Street. You could walk from police headquarters to Whiskey's house in four minutes.

Shortly after nightfall, Steve, Lesh and I hit the road, heading into

Red Bank in Lesh's car to do some reconnaissance. We'd fortified our-selves before the trip with a liberal dose of alcohol. The lights were on in Whiskey's house, and there were a couple of cars parked out front. Otherwise, things looked quiet, so we decided to go ahead with our plan. We went back to Lesh's place and swapped cars, using Steve's for this trip. Lesh, who was psyched to be part of some real action in town and didn't worry about consequences, hopped in the back seat, holding a Molotov cocktail and a lighter.

I pulled the car right up in front of Whiskey's house and hit the horn. Steve yelled for Whiskey to come out. Instead, Whiskey's wife came out.

"Go fuck yourselves," she yelled from the porch of the wood-frame house, which was set back about 20 feet from the road. She gave Steve the finger to punctuate her statement.

Lesh took her response as a firm no and immediately lobbed the firebomb onto the porch, where it exploded in flames and set the porch on fire. Whiskey's wife beat a hasty retreat inside.

The flames started to spread, and the roof over the porch also caught fire. I hit the gas and we sped off into the night.

Back at Lesh's place, we switched cars again. Steve, Lesh and I re-turned to Whiskey's place in my cage to see what was going on. I was behind the wheel, and Steve was riding shotgun—literally carrying a loaded shotgun that was pointed out the passenger-side window of the car as we drove back into town at around 8:30.

We found Whiskey and a bunch of his buddies standing outside the house, working to put out the fire. Some other members of the Breed were there, too.

Small-arms fire rang out as I drove past. We ducked and sped away—but not before the car was struck by several bullets.

Some perverse voice told me to pull a K-turn on Wall Street and make one last pass in front of Whiskey's place. I was stunned to see my nemesis walking across the street alone—and wondered if he'd been using the pay phone at the Brothers Tavern. I'd seen him do that before as a way of ensuring that the authorities couldn't trace his calls.

My mind flashed back to the shitty conversation we'd had when I told him I wasn't going to run with his wolf pack. I flashed to the kissing bandit, the armed robbery of those people in Staten Island and Crazy Horse's intimidation of countless others. I snapped, put the pedal to the metal and aimed the car straight at Whiskey. He was going to meet my Front End John.

A split second before impact, Whiskey jumped up. He rolled across the hood and slammed into the windshield before rolling off and crashing onto the pavement. I left him there and continued driving. But Red Bank Police cars were blocking the street ahead, and five cops immediately took the three of us into custody.

The cops seemed unsure what to do with us. They knew Steve and me, knew that we were ex-military and had stood with them in bar fights. We had nothing but respect for the police. But they also knew that this insane scene demanded action. Whiskey and his wife had already identified us as the ones responsible for the Molotov cocktail. Then there was the issue of possessing a loaded shotgun in a vehicle, and my attempt to run over Whiskey, which had been witnessed by three police officers. In the face of overwhelming evidence, we took full responsibility for what we'd done.

We were taken to a large, open room in the police headquarters. A couple of officers were sitting at their desks, looking at us. Two other officers and a detective lieutenant confronted us and demanded to know what was going on. "You guys are usually good eggs but this is way out of line," he said. "Loaded shotguns, gunshots in my town . . . This shit is fucking getting sorted out."

Suddenly the door smashed open, and in walked a limping and apoplectic Whiskey Joe. Pointing at me, he screamed, "You missed me, you motherfucker!" He turned his attention to the cops and continued his tirade. "Just where the fuck were you, you goddamn motherfuckers, when these pussies were trying to burn down my house? I pay your fucking salaries, you lazy mother—" Whiskey never got a chance to finish his sentence: three police officers grabbed him by the arms and removed him.

"Get the fuck outta here, don't look back. Just disappear. And make sure you stay away for a while," one of the cops told us. "Your ass just got yanked from the fire. Get moving."

The three of us walked out of police headquarters without a word to anyone. We worried that someone in charge would change his mind and call us back inside.

I walked back to my car, which was still parked by Whiskey's house. When I got there, Milo Esteves, president of the North Jersey Breed at the time, was leaning on my car. The two of us were alone.

"Did you ever have a problem with the Breed Motorcycle Club before?" he asked.

"No."

"Well, you sure fucking do now," he said.

Completely drained by the evening's events, I met his stare and said, "Okay."

I hopped in my bullet-ridden car and drove away, wondering about my life expectancy.

CHAPTER SEVENTEEN
SHAKING THE TIGER'S TAIL

Things were quiet for two or three weeks, with no visits from members of the Breed. It was hard to believe that Whiskey and his buddies would let Steve and me get away with the firebombing, but maybe they were just hanging low for a while.

I continued to hang out at the Globe Bar in Red Bank with my friends. One rainy night in late March, I was having a beer there when the phone rang. The bartender picked it up.

"It's for you," he said, handing the phone across the bar to me. I'd never received any phone calls at the Globe before; this was truly a first, and I wondered if the caller would be friend or foe.

"You haven't been coming around," Jake Slater said casually. "We never see you." A legendary figure on the Jersey Shore, Slater was the very persona of a tough biker, a man feared by all who crossed his path, and respected by some.

"I've been busy," I said. "But when are you getting something together?"

"Tonight, as in now," Slater said. "I'll give you directions, you gotta come by. Some of the guys want to meet you."

"Okay, give it to me. I'm in."

I'd met Jake on a couple of occasions. He lived in Atlantic High-lands, where he pretty much ruled the community. Jake stood about six foot three and weighed a muscular 260 pounds. His black hair was moderate length and wavy, and he always had a beard—sometimes a full one, sometimes a Fu Manchu. He was missing one of his front teeth, which gave him a gap-toothed smile. Jake always wore a black leather glove on his right hand, with silver metal studs on it, and a matching chap on his right forearm.

Slater reminded me a bit of Big T from my army days. Both men were naturally massive in size, loved violent domination and were charismatic and intelligent. Both could also be disarmingly charming one moment and sadistic and deadly the next. I genuinely liked Slater and enjoyed the brief time I'd spent with him. I knew he was being seriously courted by the Pagans Motorcycle Club, and I was still a little gun-shy from my time with the Breed, so I never attempted to locate him or frequent the places where he could often be found drinking truly prodigious amounts of rye whiskey.

I paid my tab at the Globe, headed out and hopped into my old Ford Galaxie for the short ride to Slater's designated meeting place, his buddy Steve Stone's house in the Port Monmouth section of Middletown. About 12 people were there when I arrived late that evening; I only knew two from high school and around town. A few others I recognized as members of the Asbury Park chapter of the Pagans Motorcycle Club. No one at the house was wearing colors, and the mood was light and friendly. What was perhaps most remarkable about the gathering was the setting: the interior of the house had been gutted, and we were looking at wall studs, outlets and plumbing. There was no Sheetrock in the place, at least not the parts that I saw.

This felt like a different crowd than the Breed, and I didn't get the sense that these guys would be watching bestiality films or looking to stick people up at gunpoint. The conversation was all about bikes, bars, bitches and not taking shit from anyone. This was a tough group, and the Pagan reputation for ferocity didn't seem in question. But there were no kissing bandits here.

I also got the sense that I was being observed by some of the guys, and wondered if I was being vetted as a potential member of the Pagans. I knew that the club was looking to expand its territory, and the North Jersey coast was in play.

After spending a couple of hours at the house, the group decided to hit a bar in Keansburg, where I lived. Keansburg was an interesting choice as a place to party for the likes of us—a square mile of bungalows and bars, split evenly between Italians and Irish at the time, with a distinctly lower-end blue-collar feel. It was a very close-knit community, with outsiders only nominally welcome. The place was legendary for notorious bar fighters, and the police had a reputation for helping to ensure that outsiders who caused problems didn't want to return anytime soon. Going to Keansburg guaranteed that this was going to be an interesting evening.

We rode to Keansburg in several different vehicles, with Slater and another guy in one car, Stone driving a van and me alone in my car. Jake picked a bar called Memories, which had a reputation as a bucket of blood—a place where fights between patrons were as commonplace as shot glasses and beer mugs.

Memories was doing a brisk business for a weekday evening. It seemed as if the patrons weren't sure what to do with us and so opted to leave us alone. Jake was acting quite differently from when he had left the house. Later, I learned that he was hitting the "green" heavily on the way over. The Pagan drug of choice was parsley-laced PCP, which we referred to simply as "green" because of its color. I'd tried the stuff only once and sworn to never use it again. Green is smoked like marijuana, but the PCP it contains leaves a man so high that pain means nothing. Satan laughs and spreads his wings every time someone consumes green.

Slater shelled out for multiple rounds of shots for the group, and we were soon in an alcoholic glow, some burning brighter than others. As I swallowed another shot, I noticed that Slater was getting into a game of pool with one of the locals. A couple of guys were standing at the far end of the table as Slater crouched low to break with the cue ball. One of the men leaned down as well so that he could follow Slater's break. Jake struck the cue ball low and hard, driving it up off the table and straight into the man's face.

The injured man bellowed loudly with a mix of anger and pain. Slater immediately flipped his cue stick around so that he was holding it by the thin end, and began smashing the untouched balls in the rack, sending them flying everywhere.

A wild brawl broke out as Slater and the rest of our guys took on the locals with everything that was at hand, including smashed beer bottles, pool cues, beer mugs, bar stools, feet and fists.

Bodies flew and tables broke as the brawl continued. Everyone seemed to be moving in slow motion around me as I focused on taking out the men directly in front of me. My army days came back to me as I picked my shots and avoided the flying limbs and projectiles.

Countless police vehicles screeched to a halt outside the bar. The Keansburg Police had issued a mutual aid call, asking all the surrounding towns to send as many available units as possible. There were squad cars from Middletown, Union Beach and Hazlet—and all the cops were ready to mix it up with us. They were determined to bring a quick end to this brawl, and it didn't seem to make much difference to them how it all ended.

That night at Memories was like a western film fight. When we got outside, there was a wild light show from the flashing red lights on all the police vehicles. The police weren't the only ones who had shown up in force. Drinkers had descended on Memories from other nearby bars, and they, too, wanted a shot at us. Some of the bar patrons threw empty beer bottles in our direction. If the cops hadn't been there, we would likely have faced a very different, and brutal, kind of street fight that evening.

As police flooded into the bar and brought things under control, Slater went to speak to a member of the Middletown Police Department whom he seemed to know. Later, I learned that the cop was the brother of the guy Stone who had been in the bar with us and who hadn't fared so well in the free-for-all.

While Slater was talking to the Middletown cop, I got into it with one of the officers from Keansburg, telling him to go fuck himself after he seemed to be showing off to the large and angry crowd. I instantly regretted my remark, because I'd long vowed not to piss off the cops. But I was stoned on adrenaline that night, and the two of us shared some very angry looks. I wondered if I'd just put a bull's-eye on my back. Years later, the two of us would become good buddies, both working undercover drug operations.

No one was anxious to point the finger at anyone else, and it seemed impossible for police to start identifying and cuffing those responsible for starting the brawl. Soon enough, we were allowed to get into our cars and drive out of Keansburg.

Stone and Slater were among the first to leave in the van. But Stone didn't get far before crashing into a utility pole. He wound up with a compound fracture to his leg. Slater was pretty banged up but otherwise okay. While the police were focusing their attention on the one-car crash, I headed off in the opposite direction—happy to make it away from the bar after that raucous hell ride of an evening.

The next day, I got a call from Slater, who wanted to take me to lunch. Apparently I'd passed my vetting at Memories. The two of us hung out at a luncheonette in Middletown before heading over to Riverview Hospital in Red Bank to visit Stone. We listened to him harass the nurses about not getting enough pain meds until Slater tired of his act and we left. Later, as we drove back to Middletown in Slater's cage, he told me about the possibility of establishing a new chapter of the Pagans Motorcycle Club to provide muscle for the area of Monmouth County near Sandy Hook. The president of that new chapter, the Sandy Hook Pagans, was going to be one Jake Slater.

★   ★   ★

The Pagans Motorcycle Club was not a large group, with a membership estimated to be between three hundred and four hundred at any given time. Membership constantly fluctuated depending on the number of members who were in jail. Several other clubs were larger, including the Hells Angels, the Outlaws and the Bandidos, but the Pagans made up in ferocity what they lacked in numbers.

Although the Pagans would state emphatically that the East Coast, from Maine to Florida and west as far as Ohio, was solid ground belonging to their club, the territory was interspersed, with areas held by other outlaw clubs, some defiant, some working to get along. The Warlocks were in Pennsylvania and Delaware, which was very strong Pagan turf. And the Warlocks were very hard-core. They operated in a manner just short of war, and any meeting of members by coincidence was a powder keg of tension.

The Hells Angels had a large and tough chapter in NYC, but if they strayed into Long Island, the Pagans felt justified in retaliating. The Breed also teamed up with the Hells Angels, and so the Pagans were always at war with both the Breed and the Hells Angels. But the Breed were the ones most hated by the Pagans. At the time, the Feds had what they called the "Big Four" on their radar: the Hells Angels, Bandidos, Outlaws and Pagans.

I knew very little about either the Breed or the Pagans when I was to starting to get involved with them. I didn't care about the history of any of the outlaw motorcycle clubs at the time—or what others thought of them. If I liked the guys, I would ride in an outlaw club.

One thing was certain, and I learned it very quickly: I was surrounding myself with some very bad hombres. These were not idle threat makers or phonies. Jail and violent death were a daily part of life. It would be a very unwise practice indeed for any life insurance company to provide a policy for any outlaw bikers.

Like most chapters, the Sandy Hook Pagans Motorcycle Club would be small in number—comprised of Jake Slater, me and six others. Out of the eight men, only three appeared physically intimidating and cause for concern in a street fight—Jake, me and a guy named Ray Wolfe.

None of the clubs would ever disclose the actual number of members they had, but only big-city chapters had large numbers of soldiers. And in Pagan gatherings, chapters would mingle so that a small chapter could appear more formidable than it really was. Each chapter was run a bit like a Lions or Kiwanis Club: meetings were held at scheduled times, and each chapter had a president, a vice president, a sergeant-at-arms, a secretary and a treasurer.

It was very unclear at first whether the Sandy Hook Pagans would become a reality. What was clear was that the Pagans Motorcycle Club wanted to expand its influence, and the Jersey Shore was its target. Slater seemed perfectly suited to become the president of the new club, a tough-guy biker with a solid reputation for violence.

But none of us were willing to do any prospecting. So it was up to Slater to convince the national president of the Pagans, Paul Ferry, aka "Oouch," along with the 13 board members and most of the other club presidents, that the Sandy Hook Pagans should be granted instant club colors. That had never been done before, and the decision would be made by a group of men who had all prospected. Oouch had taken over for John "Satan" Marron, who was doing life in a maximum security prison in Virginia for a double murder. If Slater was successful but then something went wrong later, his ass would be on the line.

CHAPTER EIGHTEEN

THE SANDY HOOK PAGANS

About two weeks later, word came down from Slater that the eight of us needed to meet at Stone's house late one afternoon. We were told that we should bring our Harleys and that we would be meeting with Pagan leaders about setting up the new Sandy Hook chapter.

When we got to the house, two U-Haul trucks were parked out front, and Slater told us to load our custom choppers onboard—and to then get in the back of the panel trucks with our bikes. Suddenly we realized that this was going to be a clandestine meeting and we weren't supposed to know where it would take place. Slater was going to drive one of the trucks, and "Vinny," the president of the Asbury Park chapter, would be driving the other. Vinny had spiderweb tattoos on both of his elbows. I was told at the time that they indicated membership in the Aryan Brotherhood, but I never asked and so had no idea if that was true. Others say the tattoos are worn by men who have done, or are doing, jail time.

Inside the U-Hauls, the Harleys leaned heavily on their kickstands, and we used some blocks of wood as wheel chocks to prevent them from shifting. We also loaded some bottled beer on board, figuring that we'd want something to drink during the ride. We had a hunch that we were going to visit with Pagan leaders in their secret headquarters on Long Island.

The vans were loud, but the ride was okay—better than we'd expected. The overhead light in the cargo area was left on, and we were able to move around the area, standing or sitting on the bikes, drinking beer and talking. The ride continued for about two hours, most of it on highways, judging from the road noise.

When the rear doors were finally opened, we found ourselves in an industrial area off the Long Island Expressway, in a compound surrounded by an eight-foot-tall chain-link fence topped with concertina wire. It was close to dusk, with long shadows across the property and distant noise from the highway. In the center of the compound was an unpainted concrete-block structure with a flat roof, a steel entry door, a larger garage door and no signage of any kind. The fencing was reminiscent of the stuff used around county jails, and I wondered if the security was designed to keep people in or out, or perhaps both. A couple of Harleys and trucks were parked near the structure. But otherwise there was no clue as to what the building might have been used for. As Slater commanded, we pulled our bikes off the U-Haul trucks and parked them behind the building.

A member of the Asbury Park Pagans wearing colors motioned to us to follow him, and we entered the Pagan equivalent of the White House; our group would indeed be meeting with the national president of the Pagans. We were in a large meeting-hall-type space, with doors in the rear that apparently led to other rooms deeper inside the building. The room had a large bar along one wall, with plenty of tables and chairs. The walls were covered with lavish woodwork, and numerous elaborate plaques on the walls honored fallen members. The space itself was quite comfortable. But the occupants made me wonder if I was going to live through the night.

About 30 or so Pagans, most of them wearing colors, gathered around us—furious that non-members were being given access to this very special place, where we had no right to be. Some of them held "war clubs"—thick, heavy wooden walking sticks with the Pagan war god carved into the top as a handle. The war clubs were quite artistic and highly valued by members. They also looked stout and able to inflict serious danger on anyone daring to challenge a Pagan.

"Who the fuck are you?" demanded an angry, bearded Pagan with a large beer belly and very wide girth. He stood just inches from my face and casually swung a war club in his right hand. "Who the fuck are you to walk into my house?"

The others shouted at us from all angles and made equally threatening gestures. Nobody in our group had any sense of what was going to happen at this meeting, but I certainly hadn't expected a bunch of angry men to be staring us down and threatening our lives. My senses were telling me that I was in serious danger, but I was determined to stand my ground. I did not react in fear or anger but tried to point out that I'd come with Jake Slater, and that I'd been invited. My remarks prompted more screaming and acrimony, but no one hit me with a war club.

None of the Pagans bothered Slater, who walked right through the crowd and headed for the back of the room, where he just stood around for a few minutes, fiddling with something in his hands.

We waited. Though the potential for a shit storm was clear, I wasn't all that worried about getting smashed up by one or more Pagans, and the guys I was with seemed equally nonchalant about the danger. Somehow, we'd felt comfortable coming to the Pagan headquarters because we were with Slater. But now the guy had physically distanced himself from us and we were left to fend for ourselves.

I wanted to partner up with the Pagans and had no problem if they wanted to see if I was a pussy or not. I had pumped iron for years and started learning Korean Karate from my brother Mike and his Jamaican friends, and felt very confident in a street fight. This would be my first chance to show I had steel. I wanted to show that I was as hard and tough as the hardest, toughest man in the Pagans. This club was seeded with some very dangerous men. It also was home to some members who didn't appear as intimidating but were in fact assassins.

Looking back, I now realize that we were probably in far more danger than I thought. No one knew where we'd gone that day, and we'd spent hours traveling in the back of two U-Hauls. What if this meeting didn't go down as planned, and they decided we weren't worthy of being Pagans? Would anyone have been able to track down the seven of us if we'd gone missing? It would have been real easy for those guys to get rid of us and our bikes.

Things simmered down a bit when a door at the rear of the building opened and Oouch, the national president, came into the room and embraced Slater. He walked in with a posse that treated him with deference. Oouch acknowledged our presence with a nod, grabbed Slater and several of the other men nearby and retreated into the back room for a private meeting.

Oouch, pronounced "Ooch," was well built and stood about six feet tall, with long, fairly thick black hair that reached his back, full sleeve tattoos and a genuine air of command. Over time, I learned that he was respected as the natural leader that he was. He never seemed loud or abrasive and held a calm intelligence.

There seemed nothing for the rest of us to do until Oouch finished his meeting with Slater.

I turned to look at the heavy-set Pagan who'd been threatening me with the war club and asked if I could buy both of us a beer. Beer cost the same at all Pagan venues at the time—just 35 cents for a bottle. He agreed, and the two of us walked over toward the bar.

The private meeting between Oouch and Slater continued for hours, and our guys just quietly hung at the bar, sipping beer and undergoing periodic rounds of questioning from the members. With no windows in the building, no clocks on the walls and no one with a watch, we had no idea how much time had passed. We just sat, bought beers for everyone, and waited. The fact that we were buying all the beer seemed to reduce the tension a bit.

Still, there was an air of suspicion of the seven of us from New Jersey, and it was clear that people who were not prospects or patch holders did not normally gain entrance to this building. The issue of prospecting never came up, at least not in a way that reflected on us. Had these guys been aware of my negative personal attitude on prospecting, I am certain that our meeting would have had a decidedly different flavor.

Slater eventually emerged from the private room in the back and told us it was time to leave. We walked outside as a group and were shocked to realize that the sun was coming up; we'd been in the building all night. Slater said we'd be riding back to New Jersey on our bikes, and that he and Vinny would lead the way in the U-Hauls. Some members of the Asbury Park Pagans who'd been in the headquarters would be joining us for the ride home; they all donned their colors before getting on their Harleys.

We left the compound and turned onto a secondary road. Within two blocks, three marked Nassau County Police Department vehicles pulled up behind us, switched on their emergency lights and pulled us over. They asked for the usual documents—license, registration and insurance cards—and asked where we were coming from and where we were going. Though we'd been drinking, I guess we weren't drunk enough to warrant any roadside sobriety tests. They checked out our IDs and sent us on our way.

Traffic was moving quickly on the Long Island Expressway (LIE) westbound, and we quickly settled into formation, staggered on the left and right sides of the lanes and riding behind the U-Hauls.

Most drivers gave outlaw bikers a wide berth, and that was true for most of the people who were on the LIE this morning—there were not many chopped bikes on the road, and damned few outlaws. But a group of wasted college kids decided to hassle us, driving very close to the bikes at a speed close to 80 miles per hour. They flipped us the bird and inched closer to the bikes, a risky maneuver no matter what the circumstances.

One of the Asbury Park Pagans was riding in front of me in the left lane when the car sped up and came between some of the bikers. He turned back to look at the vehicle for a second, then reached into his vest pocket, pulled something out and hurled it at the vehicle. I couldn't see what he threw, but I knew it had to be pretty small.

The sedan's windshield suddenly imploded, showering the car's four occupants with glass. I watched as the stunned driver lost control and the vehicle started to fishtail across the highway. We continued cruising west and I never got a chance to look back and see what happened.

Later, we stopped for gas and I asked the Asbury Park Pagan what had happened. I told him that I never saw anything leave his hand.

"I whipped a spark plug at the shitheads," he said casually. "I think it's the ceramic part that causes the glass to explode. I never ride anywhere without them in a handy pocket."

"Yeah, man," I replied. "Shit, one second there was a windshield there, and the next second there was nothing. Holy fuck."

"You're not worried about those fucks, are you?" he asked.

"Nah, fuck no. I just never seen anything like that shit before."

"Stick around and you will see shit you won't believe, all the fucking time," he said.

Several days later, Slater called us together for the first official meeting of the Sandy Hook Pagans in our new Atlantic Highlands clubhouse. He had secured a nondescript one-story cement-block building off Avenue A. It was just a few blocks from the town's business district, which included several bars and the Atlantic Highlands Police Department. We were literally within walking distance of police headquarters. But no one saw that as any kind of a problem.

The flat-roofed building had four commercial-grade garage doors along the front, along with one steel entry door. It was adjacent to another building that also had a row of garage doors along the front. The space, which looked like it was intended for storage for a plumbing or

Me standing in front of the former Pagan clubhouse, just a few blocks from the police headquarters in Atlantic Highlands. We used the building for weekly meetings and met there before rides to Asbury Park and other locations. (Photo by Douglas P. Love)

landscaping company, was big enough to hold our prized Harleys. There was also room for tables, chairs and a couple of slightly used couches for the eight of us. That was about it; there was a bathroom, but no shower.

Slater walked to the back of our new clubhouse and announced to the group that the Pagans Motorcycle Club had green-lighted the creation of the new Sandy Hook chapter. Now was the time for us to decide if we wanted in or not, he said. Once we had our colors, it would be too late for us to back out; we would be "patched" members of the outlaw motorcycle club. You could be granted a "retirement" after 10 years.

What he didn't say was that in 10 years the odds were overwhelming that you would be either dead or enduring a nice, long stint in prison.

No one voiced any objection, so Slater went ahead and named the officers of the club (there was no election) and handed out the patches, which were to be sewn onto a sleeveless, collarless denim jacket. Over time, the jacket would fade and naturally show its age; it was never supposed to be washed. We were to wear the colors proudly and treat them as something even more valuable than our custom choppers.

The colors for the Pagans Motorcycle Club included a series of four patches grouped together on the back of the vest. At the top was a patch that said simply "Pagans," with either blue or red letters on a white background. Below it was an image of the Pagan Fire God, a sort of angry Norse icon. And below that were two square patches, one with the letter M and another with the letter C, signifying Motorcycle Club. We were also given a diamond-shaped image that was imprinted with "1%," meaning that we were now members of an outlaw one-percent motorcycle club. Only a true, no-shit outlaw biker would dare to wear this on a patch or even on a T-shirt. It was a statement in itself.

The patches were new and shiny in a motorcycle club in which old and faded was revered. Indeed, some members had colors so faded and worn that they could only be read by someone standing just a few feet away. Normally, a biker would carry his colors with him for life; they were his most important possession, and there were dire consequences to anyone who lost them. Even cops knew enough not to screw with a biker's colors—or to be prepared for a serious reprisal. Wearing Pagan colors gave a man instant respect on the street; Leo DiCaprio might be able to travel anywhere in the world and buy yachts and mansions with his millions, but no one commanded more respect, no one was more feared, than a one-percenter.

As expected, Slater said he would be president and Stone would be vice president. Two other guys were named secretary and treasurer, and I was named sergeant-at-arms—responsible for enforcing club rules and adjusting a member's attitude as needed. There were only three members of the Sandy Hook Pagans who didn't serve as one of the group's officers.

The chapter would have mandatory club runs on Memorial Day, the Fourth of July and Labor Day. All members would be required to participate in those rides unless they were in jail or hospitalized. All the club's members would also have to pay the agreed-upon dues, and everyone's Harley had to be up and running by April. It was also understood that members had to obey orders from their superiors in the club's chain of command. Anyone who violated club rules would be subject to being made a prospect—essentially removing any status they may have earned within the club.

Slater also made it clear that we were never allowed to get into a car, or cage, with our colors on; they were only to be worn when we were on our Harleys. Violators would be beaten.

And so I began my new life as a Pagan. As a veteran club member explained to me, I was never supposed to work, ever; I was too good to work. I would have a "bitch" who would be working and providing for me. We were warriors of the Fire God. And God help those who dared fuck with a Pagan. Nevertheless, many Pagans held down jobs— everything from working a garbage truck to owning an auto body shop. The choice belonged to individual club members, and some worked and some didn't. There was no stigma attached to having a woman put bread on the table. Wives and girlfriends were untouchable. They were with the Pagan they were with. Women who were just hanging with the club were available. There was a clear delineation between a wife or a girlfriend and just a "bitch" hanging with the club.

CHAPTER NINETEEN

LIFE WAS EASIER
WHEN I WAS CRUEL

One Saturday morning near the end of March 1977, we met up at the garage clubhouse for the first official ride of the Sandy Hook Pagans. We were headed to Philadelphia to see a motorcycle show inside the Spectrum, an indoor arena that had opened a decade earlier and was the first arena that Bruce Springsteen ever played, in 1976. The arena was packed with row upon row of motorcycles, including dozens of chopped Harleys loaded with brilliantly shining chrome; most of the bikes were for sale.

The Philadelphia Police Department had a very large presence and was strictly enforcing a "no gang colors" policy. In a way, the policy was a very good idea, because it showed that the cops were ready to make war no matter how fucking tough you and your club thought you were. The police were more heavily armed than the gangs, and they successfully kept a very volatile situation under control.

Not wearing gang colors hardly prevented one-percenters from displaying other articles, such as leather forearm gauntlets with club insignia. And since this was a very large gathering of warring tribes, most members of any given gang stayed close to one another. You would need to be blind not to discern the gang members in the crowd. Every outlaw club was represented by a sizeable group, and there were innumerable men who could only be described as ferocious in both appearance and attitude.

The Pagans were strongly represented, but other powerful clubs were represented, too. The Wheels of Soul were there in significant numbers; this was a very rare breed of outlaw motorcycle club because it had both white and African-American members. Traditionally, outlaw clubs were more akin to the Aryan Brotherhood and about as minority-friendly as the Ku Klux Klan.

The Wheels of Soul looked very heavy indeed. Their leader was large enough to be an object of morbid curiosity. I briefly wondered how he wound up as an outlaw biker rather than a mauler of running backs and quarterbacks before some national stadium audience. He was white, stood nearly seven feet tall and weighed at least 350 pounds. Although he wasn't overly muscular, he looked hard and thick—like a cement truck. And I thought he'd be equally difficult to stop in a street fight.

We didn't take on the Wheels of Soul, but we did beat the shit out of six or seven guys who happened to be standing on the steps outside the arena. We'd spent a couple of hours looking at the bikes and decided to head out to a local watering hole. As a group of about 10 of us were leaving, we saw some guys on the steps and beat them up. I have no idea what the rationale was behind the slugfest, but I simply did as I was told.

The men fought back, but not aggressively. Because there were more Pagans nearby, I suspect they didn't dare try to win a skirmish against us, only to find themselves losing a bigger and more dangerous battle against our buddies. They took their beatings like good dogs, and clearly had no intention of going to the police or otherwise filing any complaint about our behavior. What was clear was that they weren't patch holders from another club; they were just a group of wannabe outlaws who somehow offended a patch-wearing Pagan and paid for it.

About 50 of us descended on a tavern that catered to a blue-collar crowd and sold mostly shots and beers. I didn't see anyone in the place who wasn't a Pagan, and all of us were drinking heavily. Many in the crowd wore faded colors—longtime members. I tried to avoid getting involved in any serious conversations, worried that I would end up hearing something that I wasn't supposed to.

The bar owner, a man in his fifties, and his wife were serving beer to the crowd with astonishing speed—and collecting money at the same speed. Though clearly stressed about the quality of the clientele, the husband-and-wife team also seemed pleased to be raking in wads of cash. It wasn't unusual for bar owners to make a substantial amount of money off one of our parties, but it always came with the risk that we'd get pissed off about something and opt to destroy the place. It was a risk they took, whether they knew it or not. Sometimes even bar owners, employees and patrons can find themselves part of the demolition project. In this case, all was going well—at least for a while.

I was standing by the jukebox when the bar's front door opened. In sauntered a slender white male who was about 30 years old and fashionably dressed, with a neck scarf tied demurely around his neck. The man bumped into a veteran Pagan, who promptly landed a series of hard punches on him and threw him out the door. Few of the Pagans in the bar even noticed what was going on. The bar owner appeared mildly concerned, but there were no broken bones, and it didn't look like this was going to result in a police response. What made the incident seem odd to me was that the guy seemed okay with the idea of taking a few hits to his face.

Minutes later, the same man walked back in the door with the same beatific smile on his face, and not looking all that bad given the hits he'd sustained. Again he bumped into the same veteran Pagan, who most people would have been inclined to avoid at all costs. This time, two very adept Pagans laid a quick and nasty beating on the man, who crashed to the floor—but kept on smiling as if Farrah Fawcett was playing his trombone. He was pushed through a gauntlet of uninterested outlaws and hurled through the door; he crashed onto the pavement head-first. I caught another worried look on the owner's face. But he seemed unsure what to do, if anything. With 50 Pagans in the bar, he may well have thought it dangerous to start hassling one of them.

Then, for a third time, the same man walked back into the bar. Personally, I made it a point to affect a sniper's calm whenever I was within the bowels of the Fire God Nation. But I will confess that seeing this grinning pain-junkie mince back in a third time was a remarkable and bizarre sight that got my full attention. This time, a gigantic and truly furious Pagan slammed his way through the group and grabbed the offending character as if he was an oversized Raggedy Ann.

"No!" the burly, sweat-soaked bar owner screamed at the top of his lungs, drawing the full attention of everyone in the place—including the one oversized Pagan he was hoping to reach.

The scream had its desired effect, and my fellow Pagan walked the victim to the door, sternly pushed him to the street and ordered a couple of prospects to make sure that he not re-enter.

The bar owner truly saved the guy's life, and he was not given any grief whatsoever for screaming an order at a member of the Pagan Nation. Somehow, the man had earned the quiet respect of the Pagans he'd been serving, and the group was willing to dial back its level of violence. I later learned that there really was no code of conduct for such situations. Under slightly different circumstances, the bar owner may have found himself under attack, too. If the right combination of alcohol and green were consumed, even respectful conduct by a citizen could lead to violence.

Because we hadn't prospected, we were being watched closely by the leaders of the Pagans, and they expected us to make our presence known in New Jersey. Slater knew that there'd be all manner of hell to pay for him personally if he didn't make sure the club was active. We had to show the Pagan colors while riding together with other club members, support other clubs and get into at least some trouble on a regular basis.

The trouble often revolved around a night of drinking at a bar.

Since Thursday nights were our club meeting nights, we would meet for a while at our headquarters off Avenue A, where we invariably wound up complaining about someone who owed back dues, talking about any rumored police activity that might impact us and occasionally getting serious about war party plans involving the Hells Angels and my former buddies with the Breed.

One Thursday evening soon after our Philadelphia trip, Slater told us we'd be riding up to a bar farther north to help support the North Jersey chapter, whose membership had been decimated by members serving extended jail terms. We parked our bikes in front of a dingy bar and went inside for a few beers.

"Pagans! I was a Pagan once," one guy said, laughing, as we walked in the door.

If he had been a Pagan, he would have known better than to joke about it. As the sergeant-at-arms, I knew I needed to have a talk with him immediately. As I got closer to him, he started reciting scripture to me.

"Zip it on the Pagan stuff or I am going to visit you with a little of the old shit fuck, and you ain't gonna like it," I said.

The guy immediately changed the subject, and I thought, *Another soul saved—at least for the evening.*

Most of the women at the bar looked like they'd been through one or more wars. There were only two of note, and both were riding with Pagans. One of them was white, the other Hispanic. The white chick was stunning, in a white, sleeveless undershirt that showed off her physique. She had long, sharp fingernails and wore a hat that would look perfect on an Irish cabbie; it hung on the side of her long, wavy blonde hair. Both women stood toe-to-toe with the guys and struck an attitude of "let's just get wasted and fuck with somebody."

Just when I thought the evening would prove to be a quiet one, the two women began to beat the shit out of each other for reasons unknown to anyone else in the bar. They threw wild punches, gouged skin with their fingernails and eventually dropped to the floor, grappling and rolling as each sought the upper hand. Both had stamina and a palpable hatred spurring them on.

The Pagans who were with these two were enjoying the spectacle too much to consider stopping it. Indeed, no one wanted it to end, and certainly the two women weren't ready to quit. But as the fighting continued, even the Pagans decided that this battle had to stop. Two men waded in and pulled the snarling adversaries apart.

At that point, I headed outdoors for some fresh air. I've never smoked, and most of the bars I visited during my years as a Pagan were invariably smoke-filled. Outside, one of the North Jersey prospects was guarding our bikes against the very real possibility of a Breed attack. A similar attack had recently taken place at a nearby watering hole, so the prospect was attentive and ready for action.

As I was looking at something on my bike, an African-American man, about 30 years old, approached and asked if there was anything he could do for me. I said no and hoped he'd just leave.

"I can boost a stereo, or steal anything you want, real quick-like," he said.

"Yeah, thanks, but I don't want anything."

"You wanna fuck me in the ass?" he inquired.

"No, I don't want to fuck you in the ass, in the mouth or any fucking where."

"You sure 'bout that? Dragon fucked my ass in Rahway [state prison] for years. He sure liked it," the guy said.

"Good for Dragon. Now get the fuck lost."

Before we got on the highway, we stopped to top off the gas tanks in our Harleys. Custom bikes have small gas tanks, so running out of gas is a real concern. We all filled up on premium. I was riding the last bike in line, and the station attendant asked me to pay for all of the gas he'd pumped.

"I ain't fucking paying," I told him.

He didn't repeat the question, and simply let us all ride off into the night. It was better to lose a few gallons of gas than risk a beating from a bunch of Pagans.

The reality was that you had to be ruthless and not care too much about the fate of others if you rode with the Pagans. This was a club that had ordered a member to execute a highly ranked Mob soldier in front of several Philadelphia police officers. He knew the cops would witness the murder, but he shot the guy anyway. Being a member of the Pagans was all or nothing. Mere citizens were expendable. It wasn't that citizens were hated—just that they weren't considered any more important than a pawn in a chess game. They could be sacrificed for a greater good—at least as "good" was defined by the Pagans MC.

A few days later, I was awakened by my girlfriend, Jane, who would later become my wife. She said she'd been attacked at Marine Park in Red Bank.

Jane tearfully explained that she'd been hanging in the park with friends smoking weed when some young guys came by and demanded that she hand it over. When she refused, one of the guys slapped her in the face and took the joint. I was pissed that anyone would treat my girlfriend like that, so I grabbed my Pagan colors and car keys and headed to the park with Jane in tow.

It didn't take long before I found a guy who not only confirmed my girlfriend's story but offered to give me the thief's home address. He even offered to show me the way there if he could just hang out and watch the action, which I agreed to.

With turn-by-turn directions shouted out by my new buddy, it took only a few minutes to reach the place on the busy Route 520 in Red Bank. I banged loudly on the front door using a clenched fist—what's known in karate as a hammer fist.

As soon as the guy started to open the door, I hit it hard with a front thrust kick that sent the door flying inward and propelled the thief backward into the middle of his living room. He landed on his ass and immediately curled up into the fetal position, afraid to even start something with me.

Jane and my new buddy from the park followed me in and closed the front door behind us. A black Labrador retriever crouched under a coffee table, barking loudly but staying put. I threatened to kick the dog, though I never would have followed through on that threat. Dogs and other animals have nothing to fear from me; it's men that can get me pissed off.

I swore at the thief, who remained curled up on the floor, and landed some kicks and punches on him. The truth was, I had no intention of seriously beating the guy or leaving any lasting injuries. My plan was to inflict some damage on his belongings and send a strong message that violence against my girlfriend amounted to violence against the Pagans MC, which would not be tolerated.

One punch bloodied the guy's lip. I ordered him to kiss Jane's feet, but quickly abandoned that plan as blood dripped onto her boots. My next stop was his kitchen, where I tossed dishes onto the floor and pulled some stuff out of the refrigerator, creating an instant feast for the dog, who'd decided that we weren't so bad after all.

I was about to use a front snap kick and take out what appeared to be a new and expensive console TV when the offender crawled with remarkable agility to the front of the screen and begged me on his knees to leave the TV untouched. He got his wish and received a kick to his solar plexus instead. I am certain he thought this was a good trade-off.

I promised he would be spared any further contact with the Pagan Nation if he refrained from slapping my girlfriend and didn't contact the police, two requests that he vowed to comply with.

We left a couple of minutes later, and I dropped my enthusiastic new friend off back at the park. He was thrilled to have been able to be an observer and seemed to admire me for teaching the thief a lesson.

"You guys do this shit all the time, man?" he asked.

I sagely nodded my head. "Yeah, but it's only taking care of business, man."

Several weeks later, Slater invited me along on another trip to Long Island to visit Oouch, the Pagan president. This time, the plan was to meet him at his home. Slater borrowed a customer's blue Volkswagen Bug. Jake always had a stable of vehicles available to him, thanks to his auto body shop business in Atlantic Highlands. He routinely "borrowed" his customer's vehicles, and the car we were in was one of them.

What I didn't know was that Slater had made a deal to buy two ounces of methamphetamine from the club, which he would then re-sell in New Jersey. I was simply along for the ride as he made the pickup. Selling drugs was one way that some club members were able to afford their lives of leisure and custom bikes. I just wasn't into that kind of work, though I, too, was looking for a new way to generate some cash. I had grown tired of working for the home builder, even though keeping his men in line wasn't all that difficult or time-consuming.

The directions to Oouch's home were probably straightforward. But Slater "got lost" along the way, and we spent more than an hour and a half driving around Long Island as he searched for Oouch's house. Eventually we got there. Looking back, I'd guess that Slater simply wanted to ensure that I didn't know the precise location of Oouch's house; the trick worked, and I had no idea where we were.

The ranch house was on a wooded lot. Slater and I were greeted by Oouch at the front door and invited inside the comfortable home. Several other Pagans were in the place, and Slater disappeared into the back of the house for hours. I sat and chatted with Oouch for part of the time, making casual conversation about the Pagan Nation. We talked about the club's history and recent expansion, and some of the other outlaw clubs, too. He smiled kindly at my naiveté and was an adroit speaker. I made sure to never ask penetrating questions in any regard; the more you knew, the more you put yourself in danger.

As the sun rose the next morning, Slater and I were headed back to New Jersey, two big guys in one very little car. Later that day, I circled back to Slater's house and visited him and his very attractive, dark-haired girlfriend, Jean. It was only then that I learned that the leader of the Sandy Hook Pagans had received on consignment a couple of ounces of methamphetamine made and produced by the club during our visit to Oouch's place.

Unfortunately for Jake, he knew relatively little about drugs other than the green that he used from time to time and the powders that he snorted, and he had inadvertently left the meth in direct sunlight. When he awoke later in the day, he found that he had two bags of useless fluid. I never spoke to Slater again about the matter, but I'm sure he had to make good on the deal and pay his fellow Pagans for the destroyed meth.

CHAPTER TWENTY

THE WOMAN IN THE WHITE DRESS

Looking for a way to make some quick money, I started thinking about doing collections work as the muscle for a loan shark in Bayshore, New Jersey. Donning club colors and asking people to pay what they owed plus the vigorish, or "vig" (interest), was a very easy way to make money, as I'd learned from the Philadelphia Pagans.

In Philly, there was a very large and nasty group of Pagans who were already working with some elements of the Mob, doing collections. Pagans were almost overqualified for collecting money from deadbeats who were stupid enough, or desperate enough, to borrow money from illegitimate enterprises. Intimidating people who borrowed from the Mob was child's play for the Philadelphia Pagans. More broadly, Pagans were known as nomadic killers; they were hard to locate, with club-houses that were not openly visible and locations that changed in an instant. Pagan colors, unlike those for some of the other outlaw clubs, also didn't show area affiliations; there was nothing on the vest to indicate whether the individual was from New York or Philadelphia, for example.

Through acquaintances, I'd heard of a guy in Bayshore who needed muscle, Carl Redler. The guy dressed like a bum and lived with his elderly mother on the second floor of a cheap motel. But he was remarkably intelligent and worth tens of millions of dollars. Heavyset and standing about five foot 10, he sported cheap jackets that resembled leather but were made from polyester. He kept his dark-colored hair slicked back, like the Fonz. During the day, you could find him in a bar in Bayshore—one of the many properties he owned—where he'd happily cash anyone's paycheck, no questions asked. He was also willing to loan money to anyone who asked.

But Redler's easygoing demeanor was severely challenged by anyone who dared to fall behind on his payments. Screwing this guy on the money you'd borrowed—even the vig on the amount—was foolhardy at best.

My work for him was perhaps even easier than my construction job. It usually didn't take any more than a very nasty slap, shove or verbal threat of mayhem to collect on past-due payments. So I made enough money to keep my bike in good repair and pay for a round or two of drinks when needed. I was always bewildered by the guys who were behind on their payments to Redler—including the gamblers, who had this never-ending belief that they were going to hit the jackpot any day.

Just as the summer of 1977 began, a nightclub called the Playground opened in the busy little city of Long Branch. Attached to a motel, the bar was across the street from the beach and boardwalk, and booked the hottest nightclub shows on the shore. It offered everything a Pagan could want—gorgeous girls, complete with free motel rooms right next door; unlimited inexpensive drinks for anyone wearing colors; and needed visibility for the club.

The manager somehow thought he'd end up dead if he didn't immediately agree to all of our requests. It wasn't true (I would have known of any threat against him, as sergeant-at-arms for the club) but it kept the drinks flowing and the motel rooms available when needed.

We were ecstatic at the find, and we quickly realized that we needed to take steps to ensure that we remained on good terms with everyone,

Getting ready to head out to Long Branch during the summer of 1977.

which meant that there would be no brawls or activities that had the potential to destroy the club's interior. Over time, the Playground became our place, and Pagans from other more distant clubs would often travel to Long Branch just to hang out with us.

The Sandy Hook Pagans became part of the scene at the club, and we got along with the management, bouncers, patrons and even the band members who played there. Our many visits to the club helped solidify the perception of our chapter as "the Hollywood Pagans," cruising the Jersey Shore, hooking up with hot women and hanging at upscale clubs. I don't recall a single act of violence by the Pagans at the Playground. When the itch for a street fight came on strong, we simply moved to a different venue.

The woman in the white dress stands out among all the chicks that we hung with at the Playground. Led by Jake Slater as usual, we happened to get to the club early that Thursday evening and were having a round of brews before the band went to the stage. A woman walked in who was so staggeringly hot that she had the attention of every Pagan in attendance plus all the other guys in the nightclub. She wore a white dress with light-reflecting trim that showed off her fabulous shape, and a pair of sexy shoes with stiletto heels.

I looked away from her briefly and sipped at my bottled beer, trying not to get caught staring in her direction. Then I felt a light hand on my shoulder and turned to see her standing next to me and looking into my eyes.

"Chuck, is that you?" she asked.

Stunned, I quickly realized that I'd graduated from high school with this girl. It was Bridgette, who had once been my best friend's girlfriend. Back then, I'd felt that I had about as much of a chance scoring with her as being asked by the Russians to become their next cosmonaut. Now, wearing outlaw colors, I was in a different position.

Bridgette kissed me on the lips, and we chatted about our pasts for a few minutes. I caught Slater glancing in my direction; his look telegraphed shock that I knew this chick well enough to get a kiss.

"Chuck, I like to make it with more than one guy," Bridgette said, clearly no longer the girl I knew in high school. "I just know you have some friends."

It took me a second or two to react to her bombshell proposal. "Would this cat and that guy be alright?" I asked, pointing to a couple of other Pagans at the bar.

"Oh yeah, your place or mine?" she said.

"Well, it just so happens I have a standing arrangement for a room in the back, in the motel," I replied. "Grab a drink and I'll set it up. This is Jake. He can entertain you for a minute."

I beelined it to the motel lobby, where I found both the nightclub manager and a female front desk manager. I asked for my usual room upstairs.

"No can do," came his sheepish reply.

"What the fuck. Why not?"

"Convention weekend. Booked solid. I am really, really sorry," he replied with a fearful stutter.

"Who the fuck's in my room?"

"I checked them in," the female front desk manager offered.

I walked behind the front desk and grabbed the spare key to my room off the rack. It was time for me to handle this personally. "They are going to have to find another place to park their asses, whoever the fuck they are," I said before heading toward the stairs.

"I don't think you'll have a problem," the front desk manager said with a sheepish grin.

"I saw what you lined up, and believe me, I understand. But what are you going to do? They paid cash for the night," the club manager shouted at my back.

"I'll deal with this. Not to worry."

Upstairs, I banged on the door to my room and announced, "It's the police. Open up."

I heard some hushed voices in the room and someone scurrying around. Seconds later, the door opened. A man with a towel wrapped around his waist stood there looking blankly at me. He took a few steps back as he realized that I wasn't a police officer after all, but a Pagan wearing colors.

I handed the man $50, told him there'd been a mix-up about the room and said that he would have to leave. In those days, $50 was plenty to find a good room, and he seemed willing to accept both the money and my order to leave. Then I noticed a man pretending to be asleep in the bed, the covers pulled up to his chin. What the fuck was going on here?

I pushed aside the guy in the towel, strode into the room and yanked the covers off the bed—revealing a guy dressed in lingerie.

Now I better understood the front desk manager's comment about me likely not having a problem getting the room's occupants to vacate.

I repeated my order to get out of the room, now. Both men scrambled to comply, tossing on street clothes and stuffing their things into overnight bags. Seconds later, they were on their way toward the door.

I grabbed the $50 back from towel man as he headed through the door. They would be on their own for motel accommodations.

I stopped at the front desk to tell the manager that the room was now mine, and that I'd appreciate it if someone could change the sheets and give us some new towels. Next, I walked back into the Playground, collected Bridgette and my two buddies, and went back upstairs.

AIDS didn't exist at the time, and many sexual mores had been kicked to the curb during the '70s. Women had easy access to effective contraception, and the mood on the street was "just do it, baby." Being a Pagan truly enhanced my ability to be with certain types of women; it also shut the door to other types. The vibe between me and a woman was established very quickly. Plenty of women were turned off by the biker image. But there were plenty for whom the bad-boy biker held serious appeal. It made little difference to me at the time which way things went. The Jersey Shore was, and perhaps still is, a target-rich environment.

No doubt, there were Pagans for whom group sex was common. But that wasn't the case for the Sandy Hook chapter; we simply didn't roll that way. I also carried as baggage the image of that German girl being raped, and anything that vaguely reminded me of that scene was a nightmare.

But any deep-seated repulsion I had for pulling out my junk in close proximity to other males melted in Bridgette's presence. She looked even better unclothed than she had downstairs. The four of us fucked and sucked for what seemed like an eternity. Then there was a knock on the hotel room door.

I pulled my pants on and walked out onto the second-floor landing. It was the manager.

"Does your, uh, girlfriend have a boyfriend, about six foot three, with a black beard?" he asked.

"Hold on," I said, returning to the room to ask Bridgette.

"Yeah, so?" she replied.

"Yeah, that's him," I told the manager. "Why?"

"Well, he is on his way up. He seems pissed off."

I walked back into the room and shut the door. "A good time has been had by all, but why don't we let these two lovebirds work it out?"

"Fine with me," Bridgette replied as the door crashed open and her mad boyfriend walked in. He seemed ready for a fight—until he got a look at the three outlaw bikers standing around. Then his attitude seemed to change.

"It's cool, guys. Go have a beer," Bridgette said. "I'll deal with it. Really, he's no problem."

She kissed us all and we said our farewells as her boyfriend stood quietly in a corner of the room, hands on his hips, looking down.

CHAPTER TWENTY-ONE

SYMPATHY FOR THE DEVIL

I never did learn all the details of the story about "Boo," the member of the Asbury Park Pagans who had his colors stolen by the Breed on Staten Island. But I knew the basics: Boo had been riding his Harley across Staten Island when some members of the Breed spotted him and gave chase. Boo pulled off the highway and ducked into a bar, hoping to slip out the back and escape—but got caught in the process. They beat the shit out of him. When they were done, they left him for dead and rode off with his colors.

The Breed must have done some ferocious job on the guy, because he was a scary motherfucker without compassion for anyone or anything— with the possible exception of the satanic dog he often rode with.

Jake was furious and immediately hatched a plan to get Boo's colors back by abducting a member of the Breed and holding him for ransom. The actual kidnapping took place a few days later, outside a motorcycle show in Asbury Park—nominally Pagan territory, and a dangerous place for the Breed to be hanging out. But a Breed member called "Thunderstorm" was there. A bunch of the guys confronted him and forced him at shotgun-point into a van, where he was trussed up like a deer for a ride into the New Jersey countryside.

As sergeant-at-arms, I was summoned to the isolated cottage in Colts Neck where Thunderstorm was being held by Jake and five other

Pagans. When I got there, the guy was trussed up, blindfolded and beaten, lying on his side in the cottage's bathroom tub. Two of the guys were standing guard over him with the aforementioned shotgun and a bowie knife, and several of them were talking about various ways to torture our prisoner including skinning him alive and burning him to death.

I didn't know or care about Thunderstorm, and I knew that at least a couple of the guys in the room were ready to do whatever Jake wanted—even if it meant being involved in a murder. But there were two other issues that seemed relevant. If we killed Thunderstorm, we wouldn't have anything to trade for Boo's colors. And if we tortured or killed a member of the Breed, the fighting between the clubs would become lethal, and any one of us could wind up dead.

As sergeant-at-arms, I was expected to participate in whatever plan was decided on. Unlike the Uniform Code of Military Justice, Pagan law has no provision for refusal to follow illegal orders. I had no intention of getting myself killed for this asshole, but I was going to try to finesse the situation if I could.

Two of the guys got fed up with all the talk about torture. They grabbed Thunderstorm from the tub and dragged him out to the living room. They put a thin blanket over his head and torso and drenched it with gasoline. Thunderstorm started to shake violently and pleaded for his life.

Suddenly, the large plastic sheet on the floor beneath the man seemed irrelevant. If this plan went ahead, the whole cottage would be burned to the ground. I grabbed Slater and told him that we needed to talk, privately. We went into the kitchen.

"Bro, fuck that motherfucker, but we should play it cool and not fuck this guy up. We got to stop the shit," I pleaded.

Slater gave me a look that was uniquely his, one that blended a threat with a condescending cocking of the eyebrow and a sardonic smile. "Yeah, and what the fuck are you suggesting about dealing with this piece a shit?"

"Listen, I am talking low so fuckhead can't hear. We keep this guy tied up, but let's at least give him some water," I said. "Bro, when I was in the army, capture and torture was a heavy topic. But the best reason not to torture this fuck is because if you or any one of us gets taken, they won't feel obligated to skin us alive—not if we treat this guy okay. I am not complaining about harming some motherfucking member of the Breed. But I am talking straight strategy. The kind of shit a president does looking out for his bros."

Slater nodded, smiled and said, "Sometimes you surprise me." He halted the abuse and even ordered one of the guys to get Thunderstorm some water.

Thunderstorm pleaded with Slater to let him go and swore that he would quit the Breed the second he was released. Eventually, it was decided that we would go ahead with the plan to swap our prisoner for Boo's stolen colors. There was only one condition: Thunderstorm would have to remove the Breed tattoo, a rectangular red-and-blue flag that covered the outside portion of his left upper arm. Because there was no way for us to surgically remove it without severe physical harm, it was agreed that we would scrape black ink over the area to cover it. Thunderstorm readily agreed.

Slater contacted one of the Breed's leaders, and they agreed to meet for the swap in downtown Red Bank, not far from where Whiskey Joe and I had had our showdown—and literally a few blocks from the Red Bank Police headquarters. Jake handled all the negotiations after conferring with some of the very hard-core guys in our group.

With bikers on both sides carrying loaded shotguns and driving heavily armed war wagons, Thunderstorm was swapped for Boo's colors without incident. We didn't see one Red Bank squad car, a lucky break for all involved—especially Thunderstorm.

★　　★　　★

In the late 1970s, the Orchid Lounge in the heart of gritty Asbury Park had a clientele that was overwhelmingly African-American. Most whites knew better than to walk through the door, which was popular with members of the Kingsmen Motorcycle Club, an all-black, non-one-percenter club whose members proudly rode Japanese motorcycles. Though we weren't exactly friends, the Sandy Hook Pagans did have an open invitation from the Kingsmen to hang out with them at the Orchid Lounge. The only white males I ever saw at the Orchid were fellow members of the Pagans. Even as guests of the Kingsmen, we were always on the very cusp of a bloodbath. Still, they were good company and we genuinely enjoyed hanging with them.

One day before an Orchid Lounge drink-fest, I ran into a couple of guys in Asbury Park who thought it would be "really cool" to have some colors-wearing Pagans come to a party that their girlfriends were throwing at a nearby home on the following Thursday evening—which also happened to be meeting night for the Sandy Hook Pagans. The party was going to be in someone's backyard, and there would be a live band playing. Frankly, I thought the guys were crazy for inviting Pagans to a house party, but it was their call, and I cheerfully agreed.

At the Orchid later that evening, I extended the invitation to the members of the Kingsmen MC. I painted a picture of sexually liberated chicks and lots of booze, and they immediately made plans to join us.

That Thursday evening, I briefly met up with some of my Pagan brothers at our clubhouse in Atlantic Highlands before getting on our Harleys for the half-hour trip south to Asbury Park. Along the way, one of the guys had trouble with his bike, so we all sat and waited while he sorted out the problem and got it roadworthy again. It was after midnight when we finally rolled into the city by the sea.

As we got closer to the address that I'd been given, members of the Kingsmen MC raced past us in the opposite direction, headed away from the house party. We saw red lights from marked police cars in the distance, and heard more police responding at high speed with sirens blaring. It was clear that some serious shit had gone down, but we had no idea what.

Dozens of partyers were rioting and fighting with the cops in the home's front yard and in the street when we arrived. The cops had their nightsticks out and were making it quite clear that they would restore law and order, no matter how many citizens had to be taken down. Before we could dismount, a group of police from nearby Long Branch descended on us. It looked like the Asbury Park cops had called for mutual aid from other departments. One of the cops grabbed my handlebars with his left hand while holding a nightstick at the ready in his right.

"If you don't take this bike and get the fuck out of here, I'm gonna hook it and you fuckers are going down hard," he said.

None of us wanted to see our bikes taken away on the back of a tow truck for the trip to a police impound. We all looked at each other, shrugged our shoulders and rode to a nearby nightclub, where we drank without incident.

I had no remorse for the problem my invitation seemed to have caused. The Kingsmen were stand-up and knew very well how the game was played. A week or so later, I had a beer with some of the Kingsmen members and we talked about the party. They said the sexy and seemingly willing white women were less than sexually liberated when it meant crossing racial lines, and the white guys seemed intimidated and defensive. As a result, the scene got real ugly, real fast.

When the cops came, the white guys at the party got shitty with them for failing to protect residents against the intruding bikers. The complaints from the crowd prompted the cops to focus their attention on the invited partygoers—and ignore the bikers, who didn't seem to be doing anything wrong. While the partygoers and the cops fought it out, the Kingsmen jumped on their bikes and headed out of town. They thought the night was a blast and were not in the least put out by the cops or circumstances; it was just another night on the other side of life.

★　　★　　★

The Jersey Shore area where the Sandy Hook Pagans rode was mostly rural until after World War II, when it blossomed and became a major rail hub to New York City. Economically, the area was unusually diverse, spotted with wealthy enclaves including Highlands, Rumson, Deal and Wanamassa, and impoverished areas including Keansburg and much of Asbury Park. In the half hour it took us to ride our chopped Harleys from Atlantic Highlands to the bars and nightclubs in Asbury Park, we would cruise by weathered summer bungalows; dark, rat-infested apartments; and stunning high-end homes surrounded by manicured lawns and privet hedges.

Most nights that we rode together as a club were spent at dive bars. But on some evenings we'd check out more upscale places—like Tradewinds, a sprawling oceanfront club with a beautiful pool and the very best entertainment on the Jersey Shore. It was just a short ride from Atlantic Highlands.

One hot Saturday night in 1977, a bunch of us headed for Tradewinds. Members of other Pagan clubs had heard about our plan and decided to join us. As usual, Jake Slater was in the lead. When we got there, Jake palmed a wad of money to one of the preppy young bouncers out front, and a dozen of us headed inside the packed club. The bouncers seemed uncertain how to handle our presence, and they paced nervously. Somehow, the hours spent in climate-controlled gyms, building those biceps and pecs that drove the teen girls giggly, were not so formidable in the presence of outlaw bikers wearing colors. The girls for the most part seemed to be doing their best to look cool and check us out when they thought we weren't looking. The males at the bar seemed to be drinking faster.

The tension in the air was the sort we enjoyed the most, as the girls seemed drawn to the bad-boy bikers in their midst and the males grew increasingly jealous. We knew that it was only a matter of time before a brawl started, that some jock three sheets to the wind would say or do something tragicomic, thus opening the doors to what the thugs in

Me and my custom Harley-Davidson
Sportster during the summer of '77
outside my parents' Middletown home.

A Clockwork Orange called "a bit of the old ultra-violence." I was pacing my drinking because I felt, given the numbers, that we would be fighting for a while. You can't fight at your best if you're half in the bag. Most of our guys seemed similarly inclined. Still, the mood among us was loose and jovial.

The way we gauged the climate for battle was simple: when a high enough percentage of the people in the nightclub started giving us glares of outright hostility, or began mocking us, the time for confrontation was growing near. Our policy was the same as that of the Prussian general and military theorist Carl Philipp Gottfried von Clausewitz—a brutal frontal attack, followed by more of the same. We also shared the Prussian's penchant for total war. This did not mean we shot and sliced the enemy (at least not under the circumstances presented by the Tradewinds crowd) but that we were completely and ruthlessly committed to the task at hand. We knew our opponents were woefully unprepared for the battle that was sure to come.

Around 2 a.m., a chant rose from the crowd to "kick the Pagans' asses." Ironically, we hadn't done anything to provoke the anger. We had been hanging out at the bar, drinking and talking among ourselves. Though there were plenty of young chicks in the place, we hadn't bothered any of them. It was as if we presented an alien aura, and our unsmiling and sardonic attitude toward the patrons seemed to fuel their passions. Many of them were also drinking heavily.

Some muscular 21-year-old guy shoulder-checked one of our men, Snake, near the bathroom. Snake was considerably shorter than the guy who bumped him. But what the 21-year-old didn't know was that this particular Pagan would strike if given the slightest provocation—which is why he had that nickname. Snake head-butted his antagonist and beat him with his fists and elbows into a limp, bloody pile on the floor. A bunch of the other jocks jumped into the fray and were quickly dispatched with the aid of wooden bar stools and fists.

Someone in the back flicked on all the emergency lights in the club, and many of the patrons headed for the doors rather than get involved.

We, too, thought that the fight was pretty much over. Jake told our guys to saddle up and get out of town before the cops arrived. He and I hung around near the bar for another few minutes, talking to one of the bouncers who'd actually stood with us against the crowd.

The two of us looked out the exit doors and saw a mob standing there, demanding revenge. We glanced at each other for a split second before moving to take care of business. Jake threw the doors open and walked outside, with me a half step behind.

Slater dropped two guys with one punch to each of them from his massive right hand. He then swung his helmet like some Roman gladiator, shattering the faces of several more attackers. That seemed to be the end, or at least that's what we thought. Exhausted and exhilarated, we walked toward our motorcycles.

As I turned my head to say something to Jake, I saw some big guy racing toward him, ready to attack. I threw my helmet like a Nolan Ryan fastball and caught the guy in the center of his face. The impact knocked the attacker off his feet, and he crumpled onto his back in the street. I grabbed him by his arm and pulled him onto the sidewalk so he didn't get run over. His face was a mess, blood pouring from his nose and mouth.

Me and my faithful companion,
Big Foot.

Jake and I turned and continued walking toward our Harleys. We'd find another bar to finish out the night.

More than a decade later, at a Tai-Chi seminar in Red Bank, I ran across the guy I'd dragged off the street. By then, I was heavily into the martial arts and working as a cop in Middletown. When I walked into the event, several old friends were standing off to the side with amused looks on their faces. They said nothing to me but seemed intent on observing what I was doing. After a few minutes, I introduced myself to the guy standing next to me. He told me his name—Chris Stevens—and said that we'd met before, in Sea Bright.

Suddenly, I realized that Stevens was the man I'd hit with the helmet. His father and my dad were actually good friends. Chris and I later trained in Brazilian Jiu Jitsu against each other, quite aggressively. Neither of us ever spoke of that night in Sea Bright, and he never made any effort to get even with me for the injuries that he still wore.

CHAPTER TWENTY-TWO
ALL THINGS MUST PASS

The orders came down from Jake Slater, as they usually did: it was time to ride to Long Island for a war party. There would be no questions, and attendance was mandatory. When we arrived on the island late that night, we gathered in a pitch-black industrial park near the Long Island Expressway. The guys from the Pagan national headquarters had heard rumors that a group of Hells Angels was coming onto the island as part of an effort to flex their club's muscle and expand into our territory. Though most of us had ridden there on our Harleys, we had a couple of war wagons with us, loaded with clubs and at least a few shotguns. The cars varied; there were some sedans, and one of the guys had a Chevy El Camino.

The Sandy Hook Pagans rarely ran drugs, but some clubs used drug sales as a way to generate cash. The bigger your club's territory, the more cash you could generate. The Pagans had long owned all of Long Island, but the Hells Angels had control over New York City and wanted to expand their territory to the east.

I don't know who handled the battlefield logistics for the Pagans that night, but whoever it was seemed to have at least some military experience. A bunch of us were directed to take up positions in an L-shape that would have allowed us to ambush the Hells Angels if they started anything. I was carrying a 12-gauge pump shotgun with a sleeve of extra shells.

Surprisingly, the night ended quietly. Some members of the Hells Angels did ride into town, but they kept their distance and there was no confrontation. I put the shotgun back into the trunk of our war wagon, and we all rode back to Atlantic Highlands in the still of the night.

I had seen my share of Hells Angels, and it seemed to me they were very much like us in appearance. Our colors were different: the Hells Angels used leather jackets while we used denim, and their jackets carried a patch on the lower portion of the back—more accurately, a "bottom rocker panel"—that announced what chapter of the outlaw gang they rode with. We were at war for territory with both the Hells Angels and the Breed. That was the way it had been for years, and likely would remain well into the future.

There were a couple of other times when we believed we'd clash with the Hells Angels. I remember one day when there was a motorcycle rally on Long Island that drew mostly non-one-percent motorcycle enthusiasts. We'd heard that the Hells Angels were going to attend the rally in a show of strength. The move was unacceptable, and we had no choice but to respond. So we gassed up our bikes, loaded our war wagons and headed across the Verrazano-Narrows Bridge to the island.

After a tense period, we learned that the Hells Angels were elsewhere, and there would be no chance of conflict. Some of the guys were so anxious for a fight that they got into a brawl with enthusiasts attending the rally. The enthusiasts had done nothing wrong but had been in the wrong place at the wrong time. Several of them got punched out because they were around pissed off Pagans who had no one to fight. The enthusiasts meekly accepted their beatings and dared not fight back. No one was in a good mood. The beer didn't even taste good.

In time, I could feel myself beginning to burn out. As a club, we'd all been running too fast and too long in the hopes of proving to the national leadership that we were worthy of wearing colors. The tension was evident, and I was certain that it would only get worse. One of the chapter's members had already been demoted to a prospect, and our vice president was in deep shit because he couldn't find his colors. We were all feeling something of a sensory overload, and it was taking a toll.

Slater was on a wild ride of pure, unadulterated megalomania. He fed off the dark landscape that we patrolled on our choppers. His capacity for long party nights riddled with ultra-violence fueled his ego. He led from the front, to be sure, was generous with his money and could be downright charming. But he was hypoglycemic, and alcohol turned him into an utterly fearless and less than tactical general. Jake consumed whiskey and soda in large beer mugs that seemed to unleash a fury within. Add green to the mix and, as William Shakespeare said, "Cry 'Havoc!' and let slip the dogs of war."

Jake was capable of acts of wanton cruelty. And then, in seconds, he could shift gears and talk kindly to a person in a wheelchair. If sufficiently sober, he would also spend time with a child stricken with cancer and conduct himself with remarkable compassion. He seemed to follow some sort of inner guide that none of us could understand or predict. But he was mostly dark and violent. He certainly possessed a high IQ and could be amazingly perceptive. Being his sergeant-at-arms meant keeping my head on a swivel and never showing weakness. When you rode with Jake, you were always watching your every move—and ready for the unexpected.

We knew that some of the more hard-core patch holders in the Pagans condescendingly referred to us as the Hollywood Pagans—banging uptown pussy and riding the Jersey Shore like we were living the lyrics from some Bruce Springsteen song. To prove we were more than that, we were committed to performing random acts of brutality. Slater was more than willing to make a bold statement, and I was 100 percent in support of this position at the time—provided that those random acts were showered down on other outlaw bikers. But Jake didn't see a difference between the outlaws and normal citizens. That disagreement created a divide between us that I could see, feel and taste.

Jake also had a personal demon that compelled him to dominate all those around him. No matter how close to him you were, unless you were a higher-ranking member of the Pagans, he would at one time or another brutalize you. I saw full beer cans thrown with velocity into a member's face and watched other members get slammed in the face with the metal-studded leather forearm guard that Slater habitually wore. Usually it happened only once. I knew my day would come.

At one point, Slater was charged with the brutal knife slaying of an African-American. The charges seemed ironclad until witnesses became ghosts and some very well-paid lawyers laid waste to the remainder of the evidence.

He was once the victim of an unprovoked attack in which he was seen beaten to the ground by a lone baseball-bat-wielding attacker. Witnesses later told me that Jake seemed all but dead, but suddenly he got off the ground and shook the beating off—a feat few of us could manage.

One of Slater's rare but memorable losses was to "Black-Tar" Larry. A laconic roofer who liked to drink alone and wasn't considered a tough guy, Larry was trying to enjoy a beer at Vacation Bar in Highlands when Slater and some of his friends made their drunken entrance. Larry put up with Jake's boisterous intimidation for a while. Then he snapped and did the unthinkable, furiously attacking Jake with his fists. Jake was stunned and beaten senseless in short order; it was truly an old-fashioned ass-whipping. But beating the crap out of a Pagan legend is almost certain to trigger retribution, and death. Larry and his family disappeared. There were rumors that he had moved to South Carolina.

In truth, I was intimidated by Jake. Still, I never showed him any fear. I actually went out of my way to demonstrate a willingness to engage in a fight with him rather than hanging back. My time came at the Pagan farm in the Allegheny Mountains near Pittsburgh, Pennsylvania.

Under club law, every Pagan owned a share of the Pagan farm, a wooded and surprisingly bucolic piece of hilly property with a trout stream coursing through the middle, one small structure and a

Getting ready for a run with the Pagans MC, *during the summer of 1977. That's me on the left.*

motorcycle track for those who dared. There was no sign out front, just a dirt road leading off into the wilderness. Members were allowed to camp out there anytime they wanted to. Pagans were expected to haul in whatever they needed and leave the property in pretty much the same condition they found it in.

We rode in with Pagans from throughout the Northeast one hot summer weekend. It was a long, tough ride for us, on custom bikes with rigid frames that telegraphed each and every vibration and bump in the road.

As we cruised south into the Allegheny Mountains, my mind wandered and I started thinking about "Self-Reliance," a Ralph Waldo Emerson essay that was one of my favorite pieces of writing at the time. Even during my years with the Pagans, I had continued my reading—quietly, of course, and when there was no chance that any other members of the club were around. I could only imagine the look of bewilderment, segueing into suspicion, that would accompany any sort of philosophic discussion. The simple fact that Emerson was loved by a lot of Special Forces types would have no bearing on the matter. Pagans don't dance, and they don't sit around reading old books. I didn't hide my passion for reading, but I certainly didn't flaunt it, either. The author's words had real life in my head especially during protracted rides. I clearly remember passages such as: "I hope in these days we have heard the last of conformance and consistency. Let these words be gazette and ridiculous henceforward. Instead of the Gong for dinner, let us hear a whistle from the Spartan fife. Let us never bow and apologize more."

There were other phrases that resonated with me as well: "Let us enter into the state of war, and wake Thor and Woden . . . in our Saxon breasts." Also: "And so the reliance on Property, including the reliance on governments who protect it, is the want of self-reliance . . ."

A loud bang suddenly brought me back to reality. The engine on Slater's bike threw a connecting rod and literally blew apart. We were only a few miles away from the farm. Jake, who surprisingly wasn't hurt in the incident, helped some of the guys push and lift the bike into the back of someone's van. He rode the last few miles in a cage.

I was exhausted when we arrived and had a hard time just getting off my bike and walking around. None of us brought much along with us—a sleeping bag at best. Everyone was doing meth. Most people stayed awake, partying with a combination of drugs and alcohol. On the first night, I tried to catch a couple of hours of sleep on the ground, but someone tossed fireworks next to my head. On the second night, I slept in the trunk of someone's car to get out of the pouring rain—but only after turning my colors inside out and putting them safely aside. You can never be in a cage with your colors on, and that includes in the middle of a rainstorm.

Jake decided to fuck with me during a mandatory club meeting near the trout stream. We were walking along the edge of the stream, bullshitting about something, when he gave me a violent shove. I turned my body sideways and slightly backward as I fell, and he, too, lost balance. I crashed down into the waist-deep water and put two hands down onto the rocks to steady myself. Slater swung at my head with his powerful right hand, but his balance was off and he missed. I lowered my body into a football lineman's crouch and drove him sideways into the water.

Suddenly, Slater didn't have the upper hand, and it was obvious that things weren't going as planned. A nearby group of Pagans were intently watching the fight. I could have attacked and either beaten or drowned my adversary. Instead, I backed down and stood by his side. He seized on the face-saving gesture, and both of us laughingly got out of the creek. We headed off to the beer wagon, soaking wet and more wary of each other than ever.

CHAPTER TWENTY-THREE

BLOODY FINGERS

Jake and I walked into an upscale bar and restaurant on Ocean Avenue in Sea Bright one Tuesday evening with another Pagan, whose street name was "Jet." Because we were wearing colors, we immediately drew some raised eyebrows from patrons. We ignored the looks and headed for the bar, which was several steps down from the restaurant and offered views of the adjacent Navesink River through floor-to-ceiling windows. Sea Bright had numerous seafood restaurants and was crowded with a mix of tourists and locals throughout the summer.

We were just going to tie the load on, an uneventful evening of polite conversation. You know, our usual banter: Is the theater really dead? Is analysis really worthwhile? Is dark pink the new red? Which film will win Best Musical?

Jet looked like a biker, with long hair and a real thick beard. He was old for a Pagan, maybe 35, slender and about six feet tall. He vowed that he was going to buy a Harley soon (it was a requirement for club members), but I had my doubts. The only time I'd seen him riding a motorcycle, he'd lost his balance and crashed after about 50 feet.

A guy standing next to me at the bar started bullshitting with me about nothing and everything. He tossed some cash down on the bar and treated us to a round of drinks. Almost invariably, men seem to have this innate desire to try to impress bikers with stories of illegal activities or some prior incarceration. They try to paint themselves as "bad guys," as if to gain our admiration. This guy, who called himself "Fingers," told me that he'd boosted a few safes over the years. His tales of nefarious deeds went on from there. He had done time sparingly, but was a master thief—or so he claimed.

It was pretty clear that Fingers was fabricating the stories as he went. If a cat was real, you could see the respect he held for doing time like a solid con. Outlaw bikers were always part of any serious penal institution's population. And outlaw bikers uniformly behaved as solid cons, always high up in any prison's hierarchy. When I went to a prison to visit with Pagans who'd been locked down, I was always struck by the ease with which they assimilated into the prison's way of doing things. Some seemed as happy as jaybirds. They drank, drugged, pumped iron (with the aid of anabolic steroids) and had sex both conjugal and of the kind that brings nightmares to law-abiding citizens. If you got nicked for more than a nickel (a five-year sentence), prison would be your home for a long while. So you learned the jailhouse patois, sharpened your shank, worked on your bench press and covered your body with ink. When you eventually got released, you would look and sound like one of Attila's front line soldiers. A few violent incidents were all that you needed to complete the portrait of the ex-con outlaw biker.

Eventually I grew tired of listening to Fingers's fictional stories. To see how far he'd go, I asked the guy if he happened to know a biker named Jake Slater.

"Yeah, I know Slater," Fingers said, going on to describe how he'd once committed an armed robbery with him.

Somehow, Fingers didn't recognize his former co-conspirator, even though he was standing right next to me and could easily overhear the conversation. I turned to face Jake and quietly asked if he knew our drinking buddy. Slater stared at Fingers the way a Doberman pinscher does before attacking its prey and confirmed that he'd never seen this guy before.

Oblivious to what was happening around him, Fingers then talked about how he'd ridden on the back of Jake's Harley—"riding bitch." I knew that had never happened, and would never happen, because Jake never carried an extra helmet. The only way he'd ever have another guy on the back of his bike was if it were a Pagan who'd been shot and desperately needed to go to the hospital. But Jake seemed willing to give this bullshit artist a pass and not call him on his lies. We decided to call it a night and head for the door. Jet needed to use the men's room and said he'd meet us outside.

As Jake and I waited in the parking lot, we heard an old pickup starting up in the darkness. Its engine revved, and the driver whipped the Chevy Silverado around 90 degrees and started heading in our direction. The truck's rear tires were spitting gravel as it gained speed. It was Fingers—and he was looking for a trifecta, taking out three Pagans in one drive-by.

I glanced over at the bar and saw Jet emerging, carrying an empty half-gallon wine bottle in his right hand. He took a couple of steps toward us and then fired the wine bottle at the driver's side window with near-perfect speed and aim. The window exploded, spraying Fingers's face with broken glass. The truck slid sideways to a halt, with Fingers dazed and bloodied.

Jake walked to the truck, opened the door and beat the shit out of the guy with his fists.

The three of us drove away together in Jake's cage as if we had not a care in the world. We never talked about the incident again.

Now, I look back and wonder if that guy in the parking lot was really me.

It wasn't long afterward that five of us were arrested by the Middletown Police Department on weapons charges.

Around 3:30 a.m. one summer Tuesday, Jake and I walked into the

Sandy Hook Diner on Highway 36 in Middletown along with three other Pagans—Sandy Hook George, Asbury Park George and a prospect. We chowed down on steak, eggs and burgers. There was no doubt that we were loud and boisterous, but we left the handful of other customers alone. Jake picked up the tab for all of us, as usual.

We were just getting into our cages when five marked units from the Middletown Police Department screeched to a halt in the diner's parking lot—all with their emergency lights on. The cops jumped out of their cars and shouted at us to shut the engines off and get out of the cars—immediately. All of us were forcefully tossed up against the cars and patted down. The flashing red lights from the police cars nearby made it hard to see in the early morning light.

The police searched all three cars, even though they didn't have any legal reason to do so. At worst, we'd disrupted the peace inside the diner. But it was highly unlikely that the waitress would have had any problems with us, given the huge tip that Jake left for her. The cops found a hunting knife and a piece of a tree limb in the trunk of my car. In one of the others, they found a front strut off a Harley. They identified yet another "deadly weapon" in the back of the third car.

Soon enough, all five of us were in handcuffs and tossed into the back seat of the waiting police cars for the short trip to the Middletown Police headquarters, where we were fingerprinted and tossed in the small gray cells. Jake placed a call to a bail bondsman that he knew, and we were released before lunch.

Whether the charges were serious or not, the bust put us on the defensive and made it quite apparent that the Middletown Police Department was not going to stand for any activity from the Sandy Hook Pagans. Their tactic was successful, too; we wound up steering clear of Middletown after that incident—even before the charges were adjudicated in the Monmouth County courthouse.

The five of us spent thousands of dollars on attorneys' fees, the bail bondsman and lost work. The trial lasted a full week, in part because five trial attorneys were involved (one for each of the defendants). Fortunately for us, the judge barred the prosecutor from discussing our membership in the Sandy Hook Pagans. The prosecution had to make its case solely on the basis of what happened in that parking lot outside the diner. With the attorney unable to paint us as "dangerous" members of an outlaw motorcycle gang, it was next to impossible to prove that a tree limb or a motorcycle strut was, in fact, "a dangerous weapon." The case quickly fell apart and the charges were ultimately tossed out.

Ironically, before the case went to court, I'd wanted to just plead guilty and be done with the matter. I was willing to pay a fine, or maybe do some community service. But the Monmouth County prosecutor refused to plead the case out without a mandatory jail term, which I was unwilling to accept.

Had I pleaded guilty, I would have had a felony conviction on my record and been barred from ever becoming a police officer. The prosecutor had no idea at the time that he was actually doing me a favor. He might have seen things differently if he'd known that I would become a sworn member of that Middletown Police Department five short years later.

The manner in which the cops handled themselves at the Sandy Hook Diner that night made a lasting impression on me. Those officers were tough guys. Indeed, they were downright nasty to the five of us. But they were professional, and they didn't overstep their bounds. As Pagans, we respected strength and guts in men. Those officers embodied both of those traits. There were equal numbers of officers and Pagans at the diner, and the cops stood tough and took care of business. Nobody was sent to the hospital, and nobody had their colors stolen on the way to the police lockup.

Years later, when I was a patrolman in Middletown, I sat down for coffee with a group of veteran cops in headquarters and listened quietly as two of them told war stories. They described how they'd confronted a large group of hostile Pagans and arrested them, ripping up their colors with buck knives and beating the shit out of a couple of the biggest ones. I was fascinated by the story, and believed it, at first. But then they described how the whole thing had gone down at the Sandy Hook Diner. I suddenly realized that I was one of the Pagans they were talking about. I laughed quietly to myself as the embellished storytelling continued; I never did disclose that I was one of those arrested—though my mug shot was probably still on file somewhere in police headquarters.

Over time, Jake grew increasingly unpredictable—maybe because he'd been drinking more. No doubt he was adding some drugs to the mix as well. He would erupt like an Indonesian volcano for no apparent reason. His mood swings seemed random, and people tended to avoid giving him bad news of any sort.

One night, Jake and I were out at his favorite watering hole—Joey Miles, on First Avenue in Atlantic Highlands. Jake was always in this bucket-of-blood-and-beer joint just a few blocks away from the Sandy Hook Pagans' clubhouse—and down the street from the Atlantic Highlands Police Department. Somehow, it didn't matter that the police department was literally within walking distance. Indeed, Jake was just one of a number of ferocious guys who hung out at Joey Miles. Jake was in rare form this evening, surprising even some of the tough guys by choking and slapping around a couple of the regulars hanging at the bar.

Suddenly, I heard a commotion and turned around to see Jake getting into it with one of the guys at a pool table, Alexi Plotnikova.

Jake grabbed a cue ball off the table and, holding it in the palm of his hand, started pounding Alexi's face with it over and over. I could hear the breaking of soft cartilage and bones in the man's face from where I stood, some 20 feet away at the bar. Women in the bar started screaming as Alexi fell to the floor, his face a bloody mess.

Fearing that Slater would kill the guy, I walked over and shouldered myself between Jake and his victim. Alexi was trying to stand up, and Jake was leaning over him, ready to continue the beating. I grabbed Plotnikova by his arm and hauled him to the bar's back door. He was groggy and could barely see where he was walking as blood poured from his nose and face. I walked him outside and released his arm, letting him slowly drop to the ground.

"Don't fucking come back in," I told him. "Leave now. Leave or that guy will fucking kill you."

Jake was still furious, and I saw him throw a beer mug as I walked back in.

Someone—most likely one of the other bar patrons—had called the cops, and several marked units, red lights flashing, rolled up out front. Rather than come in, the cops stood outside and one of them used a loud hailer to order all of us to come out. It was a bizarre move, and said something about the timidity of the Atlantic Highlands Police, or at least some of its members.

Jake looked at me and motioned for me to join him. It was clear he wanted to fight the cops, which struck me as a profoundly stupid idea. The two of us walked outside, along with about six other tough guys who'd been hanging at the bar. All of us were unarmed.

The Atlantic Highlands police retreated a few steps back toward their cars. One of them shouted to Slater that he couldn't go around beating up people and busting up a bar.

"Fuck you," Slater countered.

The whole scene was ridiculous, like something out of a cheap movie with a horrible screenplay. The cops had no plan to deal with us and seemed unwilling to take us on. While we contemplated our next move, several Middletown Police units rolled up. Someone had called for mutual aid.

The men from Middletown jumped out of their cars with "hats and bats"—wearing helmets and carrying riot batons—and spoiling for a fight. Jake shot me a glance, and we watched as men from both departments gathered between two of the marked units and talked. We couldn't tell what was going on, but we heard raised and angry voices from the Middletown guys. Then the Middletown police returned to their cars, turned their emergency lights off and drove away.

Two of the men from Atlantic Highlands walked over and negotiated with Jake. Eventually he agreed to leave the bar and go into police headquarters the following day to be arrested. The rest of the guys with us quietly dispersed into the darkness.

The next day, I headed over to the Pagans clubhouse to meet up with Jake. On the way, I was stopped by an Atlantic Highlands cop who arrested me for aggravated assault. The same charge was filed against Jake. We were arraigned in night court that evening before a large crowd of locals.

"Take them to the county jail," Judge Norman Peer said. "There will be no overnighters in my jail."

The cops treated us like mass murderers with huge bounties on our heads. We were both trussed up with large leather belts around our waists. Each belt had a big ring on the front, and they threaded the handcuffs through the ring so that we had very restricted motion with our hands. Jake and I also had to loop our arms together, which meant that we had to move in concert. Even a simple action like getting into the back seat of a car was difficult.

None other than the Atlantic Highlands chief of police and a patrolman drove Jake and me to the Monmouth County Correctional Institution in Freehold, a concrete bunker-type building with heavy rolls of concertina wire surrounding it. There, we were processed in— checked for contraband, stripped bare to shower in front of the guards, hosed down with some kind of disinfecting wash. Next, we were given khaki prison garb and thin, plastic-covered foam mattresses.

We were taken to a large dormitory-style area that housed about 60 inmates, all clad in the same khaki shirts and pants. In the corner were one showerhead and tile drain, one sink and one open toilet. Those were the only facilities for use by all 60 of us in that part of the jail. There was a table in the middle of the room that held the remains of a board game and a few copies of *Woman's Day* magazine (there were no women, of course, in the unit). Otherwise, there was absolutely nothing to do, with no TV and no books available to us. The building was a shithole, dark and dank with an unhealthy smell that seemed to emanate from the moisture dripping from the walls. As Pagans, we had nothing to fear from any of the men there. But others would likely have found the place on par with Attica or the Louisiana State Penitentiary, albeit on a much smaller scale.

As soon as I sat down on my bunk to contemplate theorems on quantum turbulence, or when the fuck was I going to eat next, my name was called. I had to go see some jail official about a paperwork question. I was taken to a room and left alone with four African-Americans who were also apparently there to see the same person. Two of the bigger prisoners stared at me with looks of pure malevolence. Would I meet their stare, or avoid it by glancing to the floor? How I reacted would determine how they'd treat me.

Two of the men's names were called, and suddenly I was alone with one of the guys who had been staring at me, and a smaller guy who seemed indifferent to what was going on. I stared back at the larger prisoner, and we locked eyes. He smirked, showing a couple of gold teeth.

Another name was called, and then I was alone with Gold Teeth. He walked up to me and continued trying to stare me down. Without a word, I head-butted him, bringing my full weight onto the bridge of his nose. As he staggered back, I brought my right knee up into his balls.

Stunned, Gold Teeth staggered back and tried to maintain his balance. The guy had been so confident in his ability to intimidate people that he'd allowed himself to be a soft target. I could easily have punched him in the throat and killed him. A guard came to the door and called my name. I never saw Gold Teeth again, and he never ratted me out to the corrections officers.

After a fitful sleep, Jake and I were bailed out the next day.

Plotnikova must have given a more detailed description of what happened at Joey Miles to investigators at some point, because the charges against me were eventually dropped. I can only assume that he realized he would have been dead that night if I hadn't stepped in to stop Slater from beating him. Slater was later found guilty of multiple charges against him in connection with the assault and sentenced to 10 years in prison.

Later that summer, the owners of the Playground nightclub in Long Branch decided that they'd had enough of the Sandy Hook Pagans and kicked us out. From what we heard, one of the investors in the club had gone to see how business was doing and was pissed off to see that there were a bunch of horny, thirsty outlaw bikers hanging out there with their Harleys parked out front.

The owners left it to the club's manager to explain that Pagan colors were no longer allowed. My heart was pretty much covered in leather at that stage of my life, but I can still remember how terrified the man looked as he told Jake and me that we were no longer welcomed there. Neither Jake nor I really gave a shit about the club anymore anyway. Fearful that he'd be beaten or worse, the manager even offered to lock our colors in the club's safe. We declined and left without incident. There were plenty of other bars on the Jersey Shore.

Soon afterwards, the Orchid Lounge in Asbury Park also became off-limits to us. For a while, members of the Kingsmen Motorcycle Club had been able to serve as peacekeepers between us and the bar's 100 percent African-American patrons. But many of those patrons were armed and had done time; they were tough guys, too, and knew how to play this game.

One night, about 10 of us roared up to the Orchid on our Harleys, bent on an evening of hard drinking. As soon as we got off our bikes, the club's bouncers told us to fuck off. Jake and I stood by our bikes, playing it cool and considering our next moves. Some of the other guys casually walked around the parking lot and picked up bottles and other make-shift weapons.

Seconds later, an alcohol-fueled group of men who clearly weren't intimidated by our colors emerged from the bar. They were hot and ready for a fight. Some of them carried bottles, too, and I was certain that some were armed with knives. I couldn't see any guns, at least not from where I stood.

Both sides started shouting obscenities at each other, and a large piece of cement ricocheted off one of our bikes. Police sirens ripped through the air—lots of them, and from different directions. Weapons immediately clattered to the ground, and the angry mob we faced quickly melted away. Some went back into the bar, while others disappeared down the street. The bouncers shouted at us to get the fuck out of town before the cops arrived. The sirens were growing louder by the second, and we knew that it wouldn't be long before the first officers got there. We hopped on our bikes, kick-started them and took off.

As I rode north along the waterfront, a cool breeze blew through my hair. There was still a piece of me that enjoyed being out with the guys, riding where and when we wanted. I had no responsibilities in life and liked it that way. But the steady diet of violence was eating away at me; I knew that I had to either make a change or accept that this was my life.

CHAPTER TWENTY-FOUR
BURNED BUT NOT BROKEN

Jake Slater and I, along with some other members of the club, had started hanging out at an Asbury Park club called the Alamo, where a new blues-rock vocalist and guitarist from Wilmington, Delaware, was playing—George Thorogood. Located in a converted two-story residence, the Alamo was about a quarter mile from the city's oceanfront boardwalk. Two bouncers flanked the front door, and a long bar ran down the right-hand side of the first floor. There was a stage at the far end of the bar for live acts, and a TV over the counter that was used for showing old boxing films. We tried to keep a somewhat low-key presence there, so we seldom wore our Pagan colors when the Alamo was our destination. But, colors or no colors, Jake drew attention wherever he went.

One night, we got word that another outlaw motorcycle gang was going to the same club incognito. Hells Angels, Outlaws, Bandidos and other outlaw biker gangs were not welcome in any of Asbury Park's clubs. Asbury Park was Pagan territory, and it was rare for another club to challenge us. When another gang came into Pagan territory, it was up to the local club's members to take care of business. It was a simple, and oftentimes brutal, gang rule that left some bikers with permanent scars, or worse.

Three of us—Jake, another biker I knew only as Vinnie and

I—decided to go to the Alamo to see if the rumor about outsiders coming into town was true. Short in stature, Vinnie didn't look particularly threatening. But the well-used buck knife that hung from his thick leather belt told another story of frequent combat with other men; Vinnie was a skillful knife fighter. His arms were covered with spiderweb tattoos, and his bug eyes gave him a rather odd appearance, like that of a malevolent lemur. Oddly, Vinnie was also known for always showing up on time; he kept his watch 10 minutes ahead of the actual time.

Soon after we walked through the door to the Alamo, we noticed five legit-looking bikers giving us the once-over. I couldn't tell if they were Hells Angels, Warlocks or Breed. But they weren't weekend warriors; they were real. Both sides kept it peaceful inside the club. Since things were quiet, at least for the moment, I began chatting up a blonde at the bar. Shortly before closing time, the five mystery bikers quietly walked out. Jake and Vinnie followed them. I walked out a few seconds later, after saying goodnight to the woman.

By the time I cleared the door, a full-scale street brawl was already underway as Vinnie and Jake fought with the gang of five. There was diagonal parking out in front of the Alamo that was normally packed with cars and people. But at this late hour, the parking spots and tree-lined street were empty—and that's where the fight was happening.

Vinnie pulled his buck knife from its sheath and slashed one of the mystery bikers across the face. Jake grabbed a piece of a wooden barricade—the kind used by police for crowd control—and fiercely swung it at two of the others, taking them both down. Though unarmed, I ran into the fight, intent on taking out one of the two bikers still standing. Dressed in a black T-shirt and jeans, this dude wasn't particularly big. But he looked like a tough guy, a thug, and I got the sense that he knew how to use the long buck knife in his right hand. Calm and focused, he stood staring at me.

As soon as I came within striking distance, he lunged at me with the knife, aiming for my face. I jerked my body back to avoid the thrust, just as one of the other bikers careened into my shoulder and fell to the side. I threw an adrenaline-laced overhand right that caught my attacker on the bridge of his nose. The impact caused his nose to virtually explode, shattering the soft cartilage and sending blood everywhere.

My attacker lunged at me again, but his move was slow and off-balance—he was disoriented and in pain after my blow to his nose. I grabbed his right wrist and yanked the knife away from him as he wobbled on unsteady legs. Shifting my grip on the knife handle, I slashed backward across his upper chest and to my left. The biker was now bleeding profusely from both his nose and his chest. He lifted his arm to wipe at the blood dripping from his chin before dropping into a crouch. Suddenly, he got knocked into me as Jake and another bloodied combatant continued fighting nearby.

The stunned biker and I grappled, tripped and fell to the street. He landed on top of me, and I could feel the warm blood from his nose running onto my face and chest. I frantically bucked and pushed him off me. The man had no fight left at this point, and he collapsed onto his side. He tried to get up but fell. Slowly, he staggered to his feet, still bleeding profusely from his nose and torso, and backed away from me. His fight was over. I glanced over at Vinnie and saw that his opponent was lying on the street and also bleeding heavily.

Jake, Vinnie and I scanned the scene and shared quick looks at each other. The fight was over. The five mystery bikers were either lying in the street or quietly skulking away from the scene. We knew it was time to leave before the boys in blue arrived and started asking questions.

The three of us hopped into a car Jake had "borrowed" from one of his customers; we knew it would need some serious cleaning to get all the blood out. From what I'd been told, Jake never got complaints from clients about blood stained-interiors or other issues.

There was no joyous celebration of our decisive victory. We were spent and coming down from a high that only people in certain lifestyles and occupations experience. This was grim stuff, and any loud bravado about it would have been unwise.

We drove north along the Jersey Shore, passing through Long Branch and Monmouth Beach before finally arriving back at our club's headquarters in Atlantic Highlands about 45 minutes later. Only the three of us were there that night. I grabbed a hose and used it to get all the blood and bodily fluids off my face, arms and clothes. When I finally went to sleep that night, it was as if I had slipped into a coma.

At one time, I had found that sort of street fight truly exhilarating. Now it left me feeling cold and empty. There could be no real reason for this shit. I knew that the hard-core older members of the club still thrived on fighting. But I felt like my fighting days were done. It didn't feel like another night on the other side of life. It felt like *muerte*, death.

Later that week, four of us got together on the street outside that club in Asbury Park—Jake, me and a couple of guys who'd ridden down from Pennsylvania—to talk about dealing with the offending club's trespass into Pagan territory. We'd heard that a bunch of guys from the same gang, a war party, had gone back to the Alamo the very next night, looking for trouble. No question, the Sandy Hook Pagans needed to do something to kick the mystery bikers' asses out of town. The hard-core cats we met for this meeting were old-school: three guys who were likely in their 30s but looked at least a decade older. I was just 22 at the time. The men had no apparent sense of compassion for anyone or anything not connected to the Pagan Nation. Their gap-toothed smiles seemed devoid of mirth. They were killers, pure and simple.

Since we'd received no assistance in the brawl from the staff and regulars in the nightclub, no one felt that we owed them anything. The discussion turned ugly real quick. Someone brought up the idea of shooting a grenade into the club. There was no real concern for any collateral damage that might occur—like, say, the death of the blond woman I'd been chatting with. But this wasn't the time for polite conversation. For the Sandy Hook Pagans, this was a time to get the job done. I wondered if they were really serious about the rocket-propelled grenade.

"Are we talking about some Chi-Com shit, like an RPG, M203, LAWS rocket or what? Maybe an M79?" I asked.

The looks I got were, in a word, withering.

"If you know so fucking much, you can be the shooter," one of the guys said.

This was no place for arguing the pros and cons of this attack on a nightclub in the heart of New Jersey. Not only were these guys serious, but they actually wanted me to be the one with my finger on the trigger. I'd trained with some of those weapons in the army, and I knew what they could do. There wouldn't be much left of the nightclub, or the people in it.

I said nothing, and we rode our Harleys out of town that night without taking any immediate action. But I'd already made up my mind. I wasn't going to do this, regardless of the personal consequences. I had drawn a mental line in the sand and would go no further. It was time for me to end my involvement with the Pagans. I just couldn't get past the idea of the collateral damage in the nightclub, of killing nameless and faceless people that I didn't know. To continue wearing my colors meant either an extended stay in prison or death.

I had no compunction whatsoever about taking down another biker. That was just part of the life. But the people at the Alamo were just ordinary people. They were the innocents.

I knew that continuing down the road as a Pagan was certain to end very badly. If I could survive leaving, the possibilities were not so bad. I had no criminal convictions, though some charges were still pending. Simply disappearing from New Jersey wasn't an option; I didn't have the money to leave. I was seriously alone, with no allies save my own stubbornness. I felt like the nation state of Israel—surrounded and dwarfed by enemies who would revel in my death. I had no doubt that if I left, a Pagan war party would be coming for me. If that was the case, I would be in either the emergency room or the morgue.

At the time, I didn't really fear an extended stay in jail, either. I knew how to take care of myself, and I figured that I'd probably be with some other Pagans anyway. My decision to leave, which meant turning in my colors to Jake, wasn't all that courageous, but it was necessary. I knew full well that you couldn't just leave the Pagans without some penalty. I had heard tales of quitters receiving a goodbye beating accompanied by a RICO-like property confiscation. The beatings were severe and victims would often wear the results on their faces and bodies forever. To make matters worse, I wasn't just a soldier in the Pagans, I was the Sandy Hook chapter's sergeant-at-arms, responsible for enforcing the club's rules.

I wondered if Jake would send "Tennessee" and some other Pagans to visit me.

Tennessee was an enigmatic Pagan. I have no idea which chapter he rode with, and I rarely saw him, even on a motorcycle. Clean-cut, medium height and weight, the guy looked like a school teacher. He wore his blond hair straight and long and had a neatly trimmed beard. He was, in fact, an assassin for the Pagans—and someone who had completed many hits over the years. I had no idea how the guy amassed sufficient piles of cash to buy chromed choppers, oversized pickup trucks and a very comfortable house—and didn't dare ask. People who knew this cat's personal information usually died of lead poisoning.

Several months earlier, Tennessee had introduced me to another occupation that outlaw bikers were overqualified for: ripping off drug dealers. If you play for the legion of the damned, it can be an easy way to make spending money and have some laughs along the way. It all depends on who you target. If you rip off a Colombian cartel's courier or mule, your family could be spending thousands on a funeral. But ripping off jerks who have no clue what they're doing and see themselves as the stars in some TV crime drama is not so tough.

Absent the chance for one big score, we went for the soft targets. Odd as it sounds, my time in the Pagans spent ripping off drug dealers was actually good training for my later work in undercover narcotics. I damned sure had the right instructor. Tennessee and I didn't talk about it much at all. We just did it for pocket money and kicks.

Often it started with a stripper calling Tennessee and tipping him off with the information needed to do the rip. The pole dancers were always heavily compensated for their work with him. My partner was adamant about treating them politely and fairly. He reasoned, and I agreed completely, that most dancers were not drug addicts or wanton sluts; most were very good company and knew how to enjoy life. The ones who stuck around were a cunning lot indeed. They were quite capable of extracting information from the well-lubricated gangster wannabes.

A small cadre of them genuinely liked Tennessee. He was clean, wealthy, handsome and most importantly, generous. He was a paragon of confidentiality. Meanwhile, the knuckle draggers feared him; he was the consummate bad boy.

Armed with the proper dancer-gleaned intelligence, we rarely broke a sweat. Typically we would visit the dealer like any narcotics user. We would take possession of the drugs, about $600 worth (usually a couple of eightballs). When it was time to pass over the payment, we would pocket the flash roll (wad of money) and threaten his life or the lives of anyone else present. The question the dealer needed to answer was: Is it worth going to war with the Pagan Nation over a couple of eightballs? Not once was the answer yes. Mainly because Tennessee was crafty and able to smell a rat with astonishing accuracy. Also, we scared the shit out of people. They wrote off the loss as shrinkage.

One day Tennessee called me for a meet. We had a much more lucrative score set up. This would likely net about two kilos of Colombian cocaine. That's four and a half pounds of the precious powder, which sold at around $100 a gram at the time. This was an amount of product worth battling over, which was an anomaly for us—we usually ripped off amounts that gave our victims an out. This was different. I could have quit my day job, if I'd had one. Like Oscar Wilde said, "Work is the bane of the drinking class." But if I had learned any lesson at all from this line of work, it was that there is no free ride in the drug business.

I met Tennessee at a shot-and-beer joint in Long Branch. The guy radiated poise. His face and demeanor betrayed no emotion. His eyes held as much compassion as a tiger shark's; you had to look more closely to see the danger signals. I strutted in, all biceps, black boots and motorcycle helmet, wearing the face of doom. We sat at the bar, away from the craven drinkers, who seemed pickled and very much at home in this dreary, smoke-filled pub. The bartender knew to give certain customers a wide berth.

Tennessee explained the situation of the score, which was much like a military operation. A dancer named Nadine had positioned herself to overhear a cocaine dealer spill his secrets. Tennessee made a circle with his thumb and forefinger. "This cat is an asshole, a big asshole. His name is Miguel Vargas. Must have made a couple mid-level scores. Now he thinks he's a player. We are doing the planet Earth a real favor, taking this shithead off the board. Anyone stupid enough to allow some split tail to overhear his play deserves to get clipped. We ought to send a bill for services rendered to the State Police."

"Nadine, huh? Place outside Camden?" I asked.

"Yeah, the very one. Known her for years. Solid and fearless. This bitch knows how to keep a secret. Never let me down, not once," he said.

Tennessee looked straight at me. "She's special. Some drunken cat stepped over the line with her recently. Even threatened her husband, a man I respect. I heard the drunk took a terrific beating. Some biker types took axe-handle swinging practice on him. I'm told he may never experience sexual gratification again. Sad thing, that."

"I can see the compassion dripping off you, brother. Maybe you can wash it back with some beer."

"I have yet to recon the location, so this plan, limited as it is, is in play in all directions," he said. "Clearly this rip deviates from the nickel-and-dime shit we play on occasion. The only reason I would consider this play is because of the target. Vargas is a soft target who thinks he's hard as a rock. His confidence makes him vulnerable. He likes to brag about no one having the *cajones* to take him off. He's a nail sticking up that needs hammering down. I don't like the way he treats the girls, either. I ain't no cop, and those girls got to fend for themselves, but this shitbird just rubs me the wrong way."

I thought about it for a couple of seconds. It seemed unusual for Tennessee to go after someone in this fashion—and that made it all the more intriguing for me. "Okay, I'm in," I said.

"Why did I know you would feel that way? Onward. Asshole is set to meet a couple of Colombians at a set location. It's a sprawling and isolated horse farm in Colts Neck. What's unique is the exit/egress. There's a one-mile dirt road that is the only way in or out. Unless you know about the feeder road. The entrance and exit to this drivable track is obstructed by brush. If you don't know it's there, it's all but hidden. Asshole thinks he's the only person on earth who knows about it. Probably right, if he could shut the fuck up. Now we know. We watch the Colombians make the deal, then watch them split. If we can get to the asshole with the Colombians gone, we do the rip. We abort if we cannot spend alone time with Vargas. We can solid this up when we recon the area of operations. So, tough guy, is this your cup of poison?"

"Pass me the hemlock."

The night we set up for the rip, it was summertime warm. Nadine learned not just the location but the time the sale was to be made. She was in her own car, and Tennessee and I were using his pickup truck. We were parked on the feeder road, safely away from the shotgun shack where the deal was going down. We needed Nadine to help us. She was going to drive to a pay phone after the Colombians left via the main road, and—using a disguised voice—tell Vargas that the cops were headed his way. Tennessee and I would take him down when he went for his wheels. If he had the blow with him, we would rip him on the spot. If he secreted it in the shack, we could be reasonably assured no real surprises awaited us inside.

Tennessee was a real believer in the concept that you can never gain enough intelligence when doing a job. He would rather wait and risk losing a takedown than go in hoping everything would be okay. He must have given the Viet Cong some real headaches during his tour of duty. It was as if he'd never left southern Asia.

I was armed with a 12-gauge street sweeper. Tennessee had a .44-caliber pistol like the one Dirty Harry carried, complete with a shoulder holster, and a razor-sharp bowie knife. He explained that if the location of the drugs became an issue and Vargas was going to play it tough and not give it up, we had to get the info right away. He was going to make Vargas sing castrato if necessary. Tennessee felt that every second we spent dealing with the job brought us closer to a bust or the arrival of unforeseen circumstances.

There were plenty of things to hide behind out near the shack, and we had both found good cubbyholes from which to view the targeted area and stay well concealed. We arrived an hour before the meet time and settled in. The Colombians, who were about 15 minutes late, cruised up in a freshly waxed El Camino. Two swarthy middle-aged men wearing casual clothes sauntered up to the shack and knocked politely. One held what looked like a bowling ball bag. The door opened and they walked inside. Five minutes later, they exited the building, walked back to their vehicle and drove off.

Though we couldn't see her, we were confident that Nadine would have seen the two men exit and gone to make her call from the pay phone. At the same time, Tennessee crouched down and started moving low and fast like a jungle cat toward Vargas's pimp-mobile. Pulling his bowie knife from its sleeve, he shredded the front and rear tires on his side of the vehicle. He then crept off toward his hiding spot close by.

All we had to do was wait for Vargas to split after Nadine's tip—or so we thought. Tennessee suddenly stopped mid-stride and went prone and pressed his ear to the ground. He then lifted his head and looked over at me. He shot his arm straight up with his fist clenched, telegraphing that he wanted me to stay absolutely still. I signaled back. He pointed to his ear with his forefinger, then pointed to the dirt road. We could hear the approach of a vehicle way in the distance.

The vehicle emerged. It was a late-model beige ragtop Cadillac. It stopped nose-to-nose with Vargas's pride and joy. All four doors opened and out popped four very heavily armed African-American men looking very serious indeed. Tennessee and I didn't need a scorecard. Our rip was getting ripped! Two gangsters went to the front door, two went around back. I ran and dove into Tennessee's hiding spot.

Tennessee was grinning and shaking his head. "Can you believe this shit?"

"What do we do, rip the rippers?"

He was quick to reply: "No. Fuck no. Those cats are fucking stone cold. We have to write it the fuck off."

"Should we just make a dash for the feeder road?" I asked.

"Yeah, but first I have to kick the tiger's balls. Head for the road, I need a couple seconds more."

There was a lot of shouting going on in the shack. As I ran, I kept an eye on Tennessee. That son of a bitch. He ran over to the Cadillac and ripped all four tires with the bowie knife. Now no one at the party could drive away. It was sure to make for some very interesting conversation. We split before the festivities began.

Later at the bar with Nadine, we did some shots and beers and laughed like hell about the whole thing. We were all disappointed about the money, but as Tennessee said, "Sometimes you eat the bear and sometimes the bear eats you."

There was another time, one warm day in Shark River Hills, some three miles southwest of Asbury Park, that I had a chance to speak with Tennessee. We were there for a meeting between my chapter of the Pagans and the North Jersey guys. Quiet and soft-spoken, he seemed to never display anger or toughness. The others seemed enemies of the strength he drew from deep within. We were standing apart from the group when I asked him a question about some mundane club matter. He ignored it.

"Did you know some people think you might be a Fed?" Tennessee asked.

"Some people aren't exactly friendly, but I never thought anyone would think that," I said.

"I know you're not."

"Good, because I'm not," I shot back.

"If you were, I would know," Tennessee said. "There's no Feds in this club, yet."

"I seriously doubt anyone with a badge is going to prospect. I know I didn't, and it may look bad. But a cop prospecting, I don't see it."

"You will," Tennessee continued. "The federal government is not going to put up with barbarians howling through the streets."

I backed up a step and shifted my stance a bit. I looked at him and asked, "Why are you telling me this?"

"Because I see a person who has no idea how deep the pit is that you jumped into," he said, looking off into the distance. "Listen closely. There are two things that fuck you up good around here. One is you getting all filled up with yourself. You start believing in your own myths. A Pagan gets his ass kissed all the time out there. Getting your ass kissed leads to blindness. Do not run afoul of club business, and pay your debts inside the club. In this club there is a machine within the machine. Understand?"

"Yeah, I think so," I said.

"Two, a lot of people conduct business and let club people know all about it. They will only work with club people. Me? I never deal with club people in business. I do what I am asked by the right people. But no one, I mean no one, knows how I operate. Lucky you, bro, I am going to do some business with you. But today let's just enjoy some cold beer."

I'd gotten into the habit of calling people "bro" during my years with the Pagans, and for good reason: it meant that you didn't need to learn a fellow Pagan's name. Club members often used the term, and only another Pagan was a bro. No one else was ever referred to in that manner. Not getting familiar with, or close to, others in the club was part of my personal strategy to survive. I'd decided that the less I knew about my associates, the better. Some guys in the club had nicknames sewn onto their colors. Nicknames ran the gamut from amusing to not-so-amusing. You didn't choose your nickname, nor did you have to have one. No one in my chapter used one. Still, the nicknames of Pagans I knew included "Sir Lancelot," "Terrible Ted," "Boob" and "Boo." A couple of other guys went by "Grizzly" and "Dogman." But generally Pagans generally referred to other club members simply as "bro." There was one Pagan I never got along with, for reasons that I could never figure out; his name was "Bandit." He was tall, heavyset and had a bad attitude. Every time the two of us got together, he was on my case. Maybe it was because I'd never prospected and he resented me for it.

I had one question for Tennessee. "Bro, I been looking to straighten things out between me and Bandit, but I can't seem to find him. Can you reach out for this cat?"

"If you want to talk to him, you need to conduct a séance," Tennessee said. "He had a really hot night a few days back. His fucking house burned straight to the ground. Aren't you glad you asked?"

We walked over to a van that was playing some Pink Floyd and had a cooler filled with beer. We each grabbed one, and Tennessee gestured for me to follow him. When we were out of earshot he said, "I am going to tell you something. If you ask me how I know what happened, we will never talk business of any kind again. Got it?"

"I read you lima charlie," I said. Loud and clear.

"Good. When I was in Vietnam I kept a fragmentation grenade on the top strap of my web gear. If capture seemed likely, I was going to pull the pin on the motherfucker. I don't do cages, not in Asia and not here. You need to hear this in case you feel like just quitting this club or cutting a deal with the cops some day.

"Bandit didn't have problems with just you," Tennessee continued. "He had problems period. Too much hitting the green. He owed money all over the club, and when anyone asked him about it, the response was the same: 'Go Fuck Yourself.' Bandit was big and bad and had a nasty temper. But that describes most everybody around here. But he stood out, and not in a good way. The guys made one last attempt at reason that resulted in another string of F-bombs. So one night just after dark a group of Pagans showed up at Bandit's house. They kicked in the back door and walked in. Bandit was married, but he was alone that night. They started the party without her."

Tennessee described how Bandit was overpowered and then smashed to the floor face-first, screaming and cursing. One of the guys pulled Bandit's belt off and used it to bind the man's hands behind his back. Another grabbed a kitchen towel and shoved it into his mouth, muffling his screams. Someone grabbed a large glass Pepsi bottle off the kitchen counter.

"Two of the guys pulled Bandit's pants down to his knees while his upper body was still pinned to the floor," Tennessee said. "The guy with the glass bottle starts screaming at Bandit. '"Fuck me, huh? Fuck me? No. Fuck YOU! Now let's see who is getting fucked here.'"

The Pagan slammed the top of the bottle into the biker's ass. Then he stepped a couple of feet away and kicked the bottle in even deeper with the heel of his boot.

"Bandit started shrieking, but the towel absorbed most of the noise," Tennessee said. The bottle-wielding Pagan then lifted his right leg high and slammed his boot down onto Bandit's tailbone, causing the bottle to shatter in his rectum. A puddle of blood began to form beneath the prone figure, who was writhing in agony.

"Hey, Bandit, a pain in the ass for a pain in the ass," Tennessee recalled. "We are going to give your wife a pain in the ass, too. We'll save the bitch for dessert."

Tennessee continued: "The group doused the first floor of the house with gasoline and torched the place, with Bandit still on the kitchen floor.

"So, you still happy to be part of the band?" he asked.

I stood silent, and Tennessee and I finished our beers.

Months had passed, but Tennessee's story about Bandit remained permanently etched in my memory. As I considered my decision to leave the Pagans, I thought about Bandit's fate and hoped that I wouldn't meet a similar end.

If my decision to leave the Pagans cost me my life, well, I only had myself to blame.

The next day, I called Jake and told him only that I needed to see him. We arranged a meeting at his girlfriend Jean's house in Atlantic Highlands, where he'd been staying. Jean's place was only a few blocks from our clubhouse. It was a big, comfortable home with a wraparound porch, on a sloping piece of property just minutes off the busy Highway 36. Jake was still the unofficial sheriff in that town; the local cops were afraid of him and didn't dare tread where they weren't wanted. It was a warm Indian summer day in the fall of 1978.

A buddy of mine who knew Jake, Jon Friedman, had agreed to give me a ride over there, at great risk to himself. Jon wasn't a big guy, perhaps five foot 10 and 200 pounds, but he was very tough—and handsome, too. He'd never had enough money to buy himself a Harley, and he tended to hang on the fringes of the Pagans. I confided in Jon a lot because he knew all the guys I was riding with but was quiet and knew how to play the game. He was also a fighter, and he always had my back.

Jon was the one guy I knew who had the fucking balls to drive me to Jake's place. No one else would do that. No one.

★　　★　　★

I barely acknowledged Jon as I hopped into his Chevy for the ride over. I held the colors in my hand for the entire ride, never once putting them down. I was in my own world, scripting the details of my upcoming meeting with Jake.

My colors, nothing more than a sleeveless denim vest with the Pagan logo sewn on the back, were perhaps the most valuable thing I owned, and I was ready to give them up. I'd only had my colors for about two years. But we tended to wear them a lot, and so mine were already looking faded. There was nothing all that unusual or special about them; they were virtually identical to those worn by the other members of the Sandy Hook Pagans, though mine had picked up a few bloodstains over time.

I knew I'd be dead if I showed Jake even a hint of fear; he could sense it even at a distance. I had to put my game face on and quickly get in and out. Would I be fighting a life-and-death brawl the second I handed him my denim colors? Would he be armed? Would anyone else be there—Tennessee or some other assassin? Would Jean's blue Volkswagen Beetle be in the driveway, or would she be at work? I liked her, and she would no doubt see me as a betrayer. Would she be there, giving me snake eyes?

If I'd had the money and the wherewithal, I would have sent the colors to Jake by FedEx, insured, along with a handwritten note saying "Suck on this"—and caught the very next flight to Phuket, Thailand. There were no known Pagans in Thailand at the time. But I had no funds and no skills outside those needed to be a mercenary.

I wondered, too, what life would be like for me after I handed over my colors. Certainly I expected retribution of the violent sort. I had made one firm decision that was etched in stone: I would not involve anyone else. No enlisting others to shield me from the storm coming, regardless of how it shook out.

Unlike most of the guys I rode with, I never felt myself drunk with power because of my club status. If people felt less inclined to deal with me because I was no longer this revered motorcycle thug, so be it. No doubt I would make associations with worthier people, as I was no longer a Pagan. For certain, it was going to be entertaining to see how some people who had been my "friends" would react to my clubless status.

We passed the flagpole that stood in the center island between the four lanes of traffic on Highway 36. A couple minutes later, we arrived at Jean's house. Jon pulled up in front, shut off the car and tossed an arm over the back of the seat. He knew enough to stay put.

Wearing a pair of jeans and white T-shirt, Jake was sitting on the wooden front porch when we arrived, his black engineer boots resting on the red brick stoop. There was no one else around. His eyes narrowed and focused on me as I got out of the car, carrying my colors, and strode across the small front yard and up the steps. He stood up but otherwise made no move and offered no greeting.

The two of us stood toe to toe on the front porch. "I ain't into this shit anymore," I said, looking straight at him while handing over my colors.

Jake's stare burned into me; he was silent as a cobra. He took my Pagan vest but otherwise stood rock solid.

I turned around and walked back to Jon's car, not knowing what to expect and not knowing if I'd still be alive the next morning. The two of us drove away without saying a word.

CHAPTER TWENTY-FIVE
THE WARRIOR'S SPIRIT

Slater never did come after me, nor did he send Tennessee. I can only speculate why there was no effort to retaliate. Perhaps it was because Jake's sentencing in the Plotnikova case came soon after I left the Pagans. Being in prison would certainly have been a diversion, though he could easily have gotten word out to other club members if he'd wanted to.

There may have been other factors at play, too. For one, I didn't have any knowledge of murders or major drug transactions that would have made me a liability. I'd also learned that Jake opted not to tell other club members for some time that I'd left the Pagans. Maybe he was reluctant to make my departure known because he'd vouched for me and was loath to explain his miscalculation to those higher up the chain of command. I knew, too, that he genuinely liked me. Perhaps he thought that I'd reconsider and ultimately rejoin the Pagans.

Jake knew that I could defend myself, too, and that might have been a factor, though that seems unlikely. The Pagans had certainly killed others more dangerous than me. If the club's leadership truly wanted me dead, I'd be six feet under. For whatever reason, no one came after me, and for that I am thankful.

My decision to leave the Pagans was an obvious turning point in my life—but danger and numerous tests of character were still ahead.

My brother, Mike, and me at his karate school in Red Bank
with three of his Jamaican connection fighters.

In many ways, my years in the army and riding with the Pagans proved an extraordinary training ground for my subsequent 20 years as a police officer.

I had done my time in hell and was eager to put things right.

No longer being a notorious outlaw biker changes your social calendar, and your life. Your aura is weaker; you simply are not hot shit anymore. I embraced this newfound anonymity. There was a freedom to not having to be the nastiest lion in the pack. But there was a void as well. And nature abhors a vacuum. I filled the void with something that was challenging and required a strong sense of focus—the martial arts.

I spent more time training with the Jamaicans, karate star Tadashi Nakamura's elite, at Mike's school in Red Bank. These men were first-class gentlemen and ferocious fighters who seemed impervious to pain and fatigue. Clearly the group's leader was Leroy Bennett. He was a taciturn gentleman with a compelling edge to his voice when he spoke. I can still hear his Jamaican accent as he uttered commands in Japanese. Bennett, his brothers and his friends rocked my world, as well as pushing my spiritual and physical envelope. They were an inspiration to me and reminded me of the words of a Van Morrison song, "Tupelo Honey," which talks about having insight and being unstoppable on the road to freedom.

My time in the army brought me from a place of innocence to a feeling that life was a battleground, a place where only the strong survived without any real sense of what it was to really even be alive. I wasn't too far off, but my concept of what constitutes strength was where I was wrong. My time with the Pagan Nation was a completely different situation. I willingly and knowingly walked into the wolf's lair and ran with the wolf pack. I did that of my own free will. I could not shake the idea that I had so easily adopted the ways of those so brutal and in so many ways decadent and destructive. I can console myself with the notion that I was thrown to the wolves during my military experience and that the ways of brutal survival are not so easily shed. But, and it's a big but, a lot of people went through a similar experience and didn't wind up on the dark side. And I do not believe that people can lie to themselves with any tangible success.

In my mind, the scales had to be evened. I wasn't a contributor to anything positive or in any way enduringly good. This was serious spiritual baggage; it gnawed at me, and it leapt out at me in the wee hours of the morning, when I struggled to sleep. I could train Korean Karate and lift weights until complete exhaustion, as I often did, but my journey to wholeness was incomplete.

One of the people I trained karate with was Dan Horkelor, a CPA by training and a superb fighter in his spare time, who lived in nearby Tinton Falls.

Dan was lean, maybe 175 pounds, and about six foot two. He spoke with a very educated, polite flair and would likely appear ripe for a beating in the wrong environment; he looked like a geek. But Dan had the most powerful kicks and punches that I've ever seen. He had mentally broken down the kinesiology of martial arts movement and was able to attack with devastating efficiency. He had a side kick, reverse punch combination that crushed the toughest and most skilled opponents. To me, Dan was an iconic figure. He had real credibility among the leaders in East Coast martial arts.

The combination of his very meek appearance and deadly martial skills fascinated me, so periodically I'd try to strike up a conversation with him in the gym, to no avail. At first I think he saw me as uninteresting, an uneducated knuckle dragger. Then things changed.

One evening after a spirited karate session, Dan and I went out for a couple of beers. I was excited to get some face time with the guy, whom I saw as a true living legend. But I wasn't looking to talk fighting techniques with him. I wanted to pick his brain on literature germane to oriental spiritual philosophy. I told Dan of my thirst for books that could help me grow philosophically and emotionally from the field of oriental spiritual discipline.

"I have been really into Castenada," I told Dan. "I recently saw a book by a Buddhist scholar named Suzuki who thinks Castenada is really writing about oriental philosophy using a divergent background."

Dan just smiled. "I am familiar with Suzuki. But not that subject. Are you serious about understanding oriental spiritual discipline?"

"More serious than you can imagine. What's the point of training so diligently and not understanding the concepts that drove the creators who put their lives on the line to spread their message? There is no doubt there are deep underlying principles at play here."

"Not understanding is akin to driving a car, but only in circles. I would strongly recommend Nitobe's *Bushido*. This is the code of the Japanese warrior. It's almost poetic. Then the *Hagakure*, the bible for samurai. It was written in parables—like the Western Bible—about the year 1590."

Dan also recommended I reread *Journey to Ixtlan: The Lessons of Don Juan*, by Carlos Castaneda. It had nothing to do with the Code of the Bushido or anything oriental, but it had everything to do with the Toltec's concept of the warrior. Find the nexus between the first two books and the third, Dan urged.

"Drink in the contents and apply them to your life," he encouraged. "You have to expand your consciousness. The world may not at all be what you currently feel it to be. More importantly there is a way of life, a way of personal conduct that you can embrace. It can make you whole."

Dan had given me the key to the door of oriental wisdom. It was a gift more important than anything he could have taught me in Mike's school. I attacked Dan's recommended books with a zeal I had never felt before. I sensed I was on the cusp of something truly cathartic and at the same time life-enriching. As I searched to find the nexus between the books, a new way of being unfolded in front of me.

I realized that all of the trials I'd been through, both in the military and with the Pagans, were trials that I could use as a foundation for a new, more deeply insightful way of living. I would never even attempt to explain it to another living person. It wasn't the sort of thing that one explained anyway. It was too intensely personal and important. I had the building blocks, three books that burned deep inside me. Not only did they set in motion a new and exciting view of life, they also helped drive an unquenchable love for the written word that continues to this day. I began to devour books and see the past and present world in a crescendo of different voices.

I identified three key concepts from the books Dan recommended:

The *Bushido:* "A man can weep tears from the beauty of watching a cherry blossom fall from the branch of its origin. That same man could cut another man in half with his Katana and feel only the touch of justice."

The *Hagakure:* "A samurai is in need of but three qualities. All things are extensions of these qualities: Compassion—One must merely compare themselves to others and put them ahead of you. Courage—One must view danger and death and move forward. Wisdom—One must listen to others, truly listen."

Journey To Ixtlan: "We have inherited but two and only two choices from the creator: strength or misery. Choose."

CHAPTER TWENTY-SIX
SHOOTING AT THE WRONG CLUB

With my Pagan connections and colors gone, I needed to find another way to make a living. I wasn't even a qualified laborer on a construction site. If I used a hammer and nail, my thumb was constantly at risk. I had no mechanical skills whatsoever and didn't even own any tools. I doubted the army was looking for me to re-enlist. I was still a tough guy, though, and knew I had the look and skills to be a bar bouncer.

I began work in October 1978 at what can best be described as a fight club on Route 35 in Sayreville, New Jersey, called Loose Encounters. It was quiet on weeknights and a drunken and drugged free-for-all on the weekends. The music was by New Wave bands like the Cars and the B-52s. Across the traffic barrier and on the other side of Route 35 was another club that played different music but was identical in outward appearance.

Forget what you may think of tough guys dispatching drunken scoundrels to the delight of sexy young women. The reality for bouncers is far different. The pay sucks, the fair maidens are usually not that "fair" and if things go bad and some drunken loser gets hurt, the club manager will blame you. I worked weekday nights alone, my only "backup" the club manager, who was of absolutely no use in a fight. He was good-looking and cocky, and had plenty of "nose candy"—cocaine—if any of the Jersey girls caught his eye. I generally had little to do with him and hung out in the nightclub's outer lobby, where there was a small TV and a pay phone. As people walked through the front door, I checked for IDs and forbidden intoxicants.

One evening, while the manager and I were watching TV in the lobby, the ultimate big-haired Jersey girl strutted in, wearing a short, ass-hugging skirt and stiletto heels, and noisily chewing gum. When I asked her for ID, she fed me a line of bullshit. Good looks or not, she wasn't getting in. But the horny manager saw things differently and escorted her in. A few minutes later, the manager was back in the front lobby, looking glum. His best pickup lines had apparently failed him.

"That drunken bitch is trouble," I said.

Seconds later, the chick was back and headed straight for the pay phone. "This fucking club fucking sucks," she said, looking disdainfully at both the manager and me. "I wouldn't come to this fucking shithole if it was the last place on earth. Fuck this fucking place."

She was right: the club *was* something of a shithole. Still, no one had dragged this woman in. She'd walked in of her own accord. The club manager was apoplectic. He grabbed her by the back of her neck, quick-marched her through the lobby door and smashed her with real force face-first into the pavement. Damn! Her face was bleeding, she was crying hysterically and she was kicking her high-heeled stilettos. She really got whacked.

The manager retreated to the sanctity of his office. Even though I truly disliked the woman, I went to help her. She pushed me away and screamed that her brothers and the cops would retaliate. I watched as she stormed over to her car, got in and took off down Route 35.

Sometime later, the woman came back trailed by two cops who seemed quite anxious to help her. The police told her that all she needed to do was identify her assailant, and they would make an arrest.

She looked angrily at me but said nothing. All I could think of was the scene at Joey Miles, where I'd gone to the aid of Plotnikova and ended up getting arrested for aggravated assault. The cops went inside with Big Hair and looked around. But the woman was unable to identify her assailant, perhaps because the manager had retreated to his office, as he often did when trouble broke out. With no one to arrest, the woman left, and so did the cops.

While working as a bouncer, I also found the time to get married to my girlfriend, Jane. We stayed married for 19 years before calling it quits in 1999; we never had any kids together. In the classic movie *Network*, Peter Finch says, "I was married to 30 years of shrill, shrieking fraud." My marriage wasn't shrill or shrieking. It also wasn't a fraud. But it wasn't a great and passionate love affair, either. It just *was*.

Jane was always around when I was a biker. She didn't demand leading-lady status. But she had my back. When I was released from the county lockup, she was there with a mug of gin and tonic that would make a rhino stutter.

She proved a theory I had and still firmly believe in: if you treat the right woman honorably, there exists on this earth no creature with greater loyalty. This trait that I so highly value was alive and well in Jane's persona. So if infidelity wasn't an issue and neither of us wanted children, why then did we get divorced? Because life is complex, and people are true creatures of change.

We shared a love of travel to lush, secluded and sometimes dangerous locales. Her father was an executive at Exxon Oil and an accomplished sailor who took his family to tropical destinations. Jane could do serious travel, and never complained about canceled flights, venomous snakes, rabid monkeys or *banditos*.

There exists no shortage of material on movies and TV shows concerning the reasons why divorce is so prevalent in police marriages. The paradigm is usually a cop whose heart has turned to leather because of the horrors he is a part of. He frequently misses spending time with the Mrs. and winds up working to the neglect of wife and family. To be sure, that is probably accurate in some cases. More often it's the increased attention he gets from women after getting the uniform, badge and gun. I didn't "run bimbos" like some of my cop buddies. I had friends who literally had two and three wives—one legal and two more very close relationships. Each woman was supposedly unaware of the others.

In our case, it was just a mutual agreement that we were both still young enough to start new relationships and put sexual and emotional passion back on the table—with new partners. We simply didn't have the spark any more. Although I haven't communicated with Jane for many years, I'm certain she's doing well.

Working at the club gave me time to continue reading the *Bushido* and the *Hagakure*, as well as keep training at my brother's gym. I wound up staying for almost two years, doing a good deal of training and reading during the period. Still, I had a nagging, uneasy feeling about the job. Somewhere deep down, my gut was telling me that this place was trouble and that I should be thinking of another career change, even if it meant working at McDonald's.

I was the lone bouncer one evening when a short and very drunk white guy, about 30 years old and wearing a leather jacket, walked through the door. He didn't need to be asked for his identification. He needed a cab ride home to sleep it off. He was also very angry, and being told that he couldn't enter the club because he was too drunk didn't go over well, either.

The guy tried to walk around me, but I blocked his path, gave him a push toward the door and told him to leave. I even offered to call him a cab. But he went ballistic and let out a stream of obscenities. I opened the door and shoved him outside.

"Fuck you," he said. "I'm coming back with a gun. You are a dead man."

It certainly wasn't the first time that I'd been threatened. The odd thing was that I hadn't done anything all that bad this time. I didn't think much about it and went back to watching TV. About 45 minutes later, the lobby door burst open.

"Call the cops," a man frantically screamed. "Someone's shooting up the club across the street. He must be killing people. Someone call the cops now! Oh my God, oh my God."

I dialed the phone, got the Sayreville Police on the line and handed it to the guy, who looked like he was going to pee on himself.

"It was a short guy with a leather jacket," he told the police dispatcher. "He pulled up to the door of the club and just went crazy. He emptied the gun. He just kept shooting into the lobby. Then he got back in his car and drove away like nothing happened."

I immediately recognized the description and realized it was the guy who had threatened me earlier that evening. I'd narrowly missed getting blown away by the nut because he got confused and went to the similar-looking club on the other side of Route 35. The only outward difference between the clubs was that one sat on the northbound side of the divider and the other on the southbound side. That cat had made good on his threat; he was just too drunk to realize that he was on the wrong side of the highway. The next day, I went to a job recruitment center. I never went back to the club.

Still without any skills, I worried what the woman in the job center would be able to find for me. After a brief chat, she mentioned that the Department of Defense was looking for security personnel for Fort Monmouth, in Eatontown. I had a chance to get the job because I was an army vet. I worried that a background check might turn up my time in the Pagans; I knew that the FBI was aware I'd been a member.

Surprisingly, my application went through, and I was soon wearing a navy blue DOD uniform and working alongside mostly World War II veterans. I was ecstatic and realized that I suddenly had a chance to set a radically new course for myself. I vowed to put it all on the line for the good guys. Somehow I'd lived through my time as a Pagan and emerged unscathed, with no felonies on my record. I'd been spared for reasons that I didn't even know. I was one of the lucky ones, and now I wanted to right the scales of justice, where I felt a real debt was owed.

I went to work at Fort Monmouth in September 1980 and spent three years there as a DOD guard. I worked night shifts and enjoyed hearing a mix of war stories from the veterans there. Eventually, I was promoted to sergeant. During the day, I took classes in everything from computer science to creative writing at Brookdale Community College. And I continued to work out every evening at my brother's gym, further honing my martial arts skills.

I knew that I'd never make any real money as a security guard—there was no opportunity for advancement—so I looked for job opportunities. I wanted more than a 10-year-old car in the driveway and a Naugahyde couch in my living room. Then I heard there were openings for police officers. Ironically, I was perfectly positioned for the job because of my status as a veteran and my experience as a DOD security guard. I took the state civil service exam and—thanks to my veteran status—rose to the top of the list of job applicants. I had my choice of where I wanted to go to work. I could go to the Middletown Police Department or somewhere else in Monmouth County if they didn't want me. I was number five on the county list.

To be sure, the Middletown PD had just cause to reject me, given my arrest at the diner while wearing Pagan colors. But the money and benefits were very good in Middletown, and they had the reputation of being the toughest department in the state, ranking just below the New Jersey State Police. Working for a department that seemed fair in dealing with people, kept order and didn't put up with shit from bad guys appealed to me.

Moreover, my father was the town administrator in Middletown and a close friend of its police chief, Joe McCarthy. Some people thought the fix was in because of the relationship between my dad and McCarthy. But my father had a strict personal policy about favoritism, and I knew there was no way that he was going to get involved on my behalf. He'd told me that quite clearly. My father hated my involvement with the Pagans; if I suffered a career setback because of it, so be it. I'd have to take it as a life lesson and move on. I respected both his judgment and candor, and realized that Joe McCarthy would have to decide.

The Middletown police chief was something of a legend. He was street-smart, loved to fight and was that rarest of creatures, a sober Irishman. The guy seemed to thrive on controversy and stress. Maybe he'd even entertain the idea of having a former member of the Sandy Hook Pagans on his force.

CHAPTER TWENTY-SEVEN

THE MAN IN THE DUSTER

Chief McCarthy called me in for a sit-down meeting in his office before deciding if he'd hire me or not. The chief was sky-high on adrenaline. Gentleman Gerry Cooney had just knocked out Ken Norton, and McCarthy was thrilled by the prospect of a future Irish heavyweight champion. He seemed to admire two qualities above all others in men: toughness and loyalty. The two of us bonded almost instantly. He liked the fighter in me and sensed that I'd be loyal. His street instincts were sharp, and I knew I'd get a shot at balancing my inner scale of justice.

McCarthy told me to find an attorney who could get the arrest in the Sandy Hook Diner incident expunged, and he'd hire me. Just remember to stay loyal, he admonished me. I thanked him, got the charges expunged and joined the department a few weeks later. I spent a few days working in headquarters before entering the police academy in Freehold.

One day, McCarthy told me to hang out in the dispatch area, where dispatchers took the emergency calls and assigned patrol cars. A shift lieutenant ran the show. About an hour after I got there, a police officer came in with a prisoner in handcuffs, a big, burly white guy about 40 years old. It was alleged that the guy had repeatedly raped his 12-year-old daughter.

The arresting officer walked the prisoner in, and I watched as the two disappeared down a long, steep flight of stairs to the basement for processing—which included the customary mug shot and fingerprinting.

Chief McCarthy was in the dispatch area, talking to the shift lieutenant, when the officer came back upstairs and reported that the prisoner refused to have his fingerprints taken. McCarthy asked what the man was being charged with, and the officer described the rape charge.

"Bradshaw and I will fingerprint him," the chief bellowed, motioning for me to follow him downstairs. I recalled the time I'd been fingerprinted with Jake after the diner arrest some six years earlier.

McCarthy grabbed the prisoner and tried to guide the man's fingers over the print card. The prisoner wrenched his hand to the side, smudging the card. The chief told the man not to do that again. McCarthy then repeated his move, and the prisoner smudged a second card. Without saying a word, the chief slammed his elbow back into the prisoner's head. The bad guy crumpled to the ground.

"See him try to hit me, Bradshaw?"

"Yes, Chief," I said.

The two of us reached down and grabbed the prisoner by his arms and dragged him up the flight of stairs and into the area holding three jail cells. On the count of three, we tossed him into the cell and left him there in a heap.

"Thanks for the help," Chief McCarthy said before heading back to his office.

A few days later, I reported to the Monmouth County Police Academy on Highway 33 East in Freehold for training. The county facility did double duty, functioning as both a police and fire training facility. The head drill instructor there reminded me of Louis Gossett Jr.'s character, Marine Gunnery Sergeant Emil Foley, in the 1982 movie *An Officer and a Gentleman*. He certainly had all the vernacular of the movie down.

The class was co-ed and included several Vietnam and military vets who weren't worried in the least about a DI at a police academy; all of us with military training had seen, and learned to deal with, men who were a good deal fiercer than this dude. Week after week of the academy passed by. In many ways, the training was all politically correct and felt good. But I wondered if the training would really be of much help when we were out on the street, trying to catch the bad guys. Like everyone else, I just wanted to complete my training and go to work.

In mid-December 1983, I graduated from the academy and headed off to work in the Middletown PD. Suddenly I was going to be working along-side the very same men who had arrested me that night at the diner. A handful of them had been involved with the actual arrest and knew what had gone down. Others had simply heard stories, embellished by the officers in much the same way that fishermen exaggerate theirs. The local newspaper had unwittingly complicated things by describing me as a black belt in a piece about some of the new officers joining the force.

Donning the uniform and reporting to work in the very building I was once jailed in is difficult to describe. I was excited and wanted to give it hell. But clearly some of my workmates were far less enthusiastic about my arrival. Behind my back, there were mutterings from some of the officers that I was "just a Pagan with a badge."

In truth, I just wanted to fit in. I was very well aware that I was under a microscope and that anything I did wrong would get plenty of attention. I was also aware that I needed these guys to have my back. You cannot survive on the street alone in this business unless you have a lot of experience, savvy and just a bit of old-fashioned luck. Even then, it's tough. So I kept to myself and showed deference to the experienced and respect to supervisors.

I reported for my first tour, which was the midnight shift. My superior officers and squad mates were cordial. Most had lengthy careers under their belts, and my first briefing was without excitement. I was given the keys to a patrol car, assigned a sector to cover and sent off into the chill night air. I didn't even have time to familiarize myself with the controls for the emergency lights and siren or figure out how to detach the shotgun from its mount before responding to my first radio call—a woman dying from a drug overdose.

I made it to the call and pretended to know what I was doing, checking for a pulse and finding none. Other officers and an ambulance were also on the way, and it wasn't more than a couple of minutes before they were on scene. One of the other officers explained to me how I should write up the incident report, which I did. Then I headed off and found a quiet park, where I sat and figured out how the car worked. Most police academies include a whole section on learning how to operate a police car in an emergency situation, including high-speed driving techniques. But that wasn't the case at the bare-bones Monmouth County Academy.

Maybe it was fortunate that local residents had no idea what we learned, or didn't learn, before graduating from the academy. A couple of years later, Middletown and other Monmouth police departments implemented the radical concept of sending new officers out with a training partner to better learn the ropes.

Several days later, I was in the downstairs locker room at headquarters with some of the other uniformed officers when Jim Wladyco walked over to me. This guy was massive and covered with tattoos. I knew that he had been a hang-around with the Breed but not a member of the club. At one point, he'd supposedly stolen the colors from the vice president of the Sandy Hook Pagans. Another time, he'd put his pistol in Slater's face, no doubt because Jake was doing something crazy and dangerous. I was curious how this impromptu meeting was going to play out and thought it had the potential to get really ugly because of my history.

Wladyco reached out, shook my hand and introduced himself. "Welcome to the force," he said. "I used to ride with the Breed. I made a killing running guns for them. But those days are long over."

I shook his hand, we talked a little about the department and that was it—no disparaging remarks about my time as a Pagan, no crude jokes. There was nothing but small talk between us. Still, I wondered if he'd be willing to support me out on the street if I ever ended up in some bad situation. I got the answer to that question some weeks later, when the two of us were out on the pistol range, which was in a large, wooded area adjacent to the police academy. Wladyco was the range supervisor.

After shooting a course with the rest of the squad, I walked over to the table where Wladyco was seated to give him my score. I bent down and grabbed a pencil to jot my numbers down on his clipboard.

"Look," he said.

I glanced up and saw a cocked and locked .45-caliber pistol in his hands, pointed at my family jewels. Before I could react, he pulled the trigger and the handgun went off. The sound was deafening—but I was still standing, and in one piece. Wladyco started laughing hysterically as the patrolmen around me glanced at each other awkwardly and tried not to react.

The round was a blank.

Wladyco wouldn't have pulled a crazy stunt like that in front of the guys if he had any ulterior motives about taking me out some day; this guy would have my back, if I ever needed it. I took his action in stride and tried to joke with him—though deep inside I was still reeling.

Over time, I came to know Jim Wladyco as a quiet guy with a great sense of humor—at least most of the time. He tended not to hang out with cops when he was off duty, though I seemed to be an exception to that rule. He also tended to carry exotic weapons (including an AK-47 with a folding stock) while on the job, which was fine with me. I'd been comfortable around guns for years, and having a little extra firepower in the field could never hurt.

I enjoyed my first week on the job, and it felt like I might be able to fit in with the men, most of whom I had little if anything in common with.

On Christmas Day, roughly two weeks after I left the academy, I responded to a call that could have had a serious impact on my tenure with the department. It was a bitterly cold and windy day. Right after the shift change, at about 3:15 p.m., I was dispatched to a wealthy neighborhood in the southern part of town; there was an intruder—a "dangerous-looking" African-American man who was trying to enter someone's house. Another officer was riding with me that day.

Just as we pulled up to the large house, the dispatcher radioed us again, reporting that she'd received a second call from the homeowner, this one more frantic, saying that the man was again trying to get in. The two of us agreed to split up—I took the front door, and the second officer headed around the left side toward the one in back. As I walked toward the home, I turned to see an African-American male, about 40 years old and wearing a long coat, reminiscent of the duster coats once used by ranchers. He walked straight toward me without saying a word.

I stopped dead in my tracks, identified myself as a police officer and ordered the man to halt. As I did so, I reached down, put my right hand on top of my gun and unclipped the leather strap that held it in the holster.

He ignored my order and continued walking. At the same time, he reached into his coat and pulled out something that glinted in the waning afternoon sun. I cleared leather, aimed at center of mass, applied light pressure to the trigger—but held fire.

It wasn't a gun but a wallet that he'd been reaching for. A metal chain on the side of the wallet is what caught the light.

The man explained that his car had broken down on the nearby Garden State Parkway and that he'd left it to get help. This was in the days before cell phones. Freezing cold and unable to find anyone to give him a hand, he'd tried to get inside.

I called to the other responding officer, and we assured the frantic homeowner that there was no problem. I took the man to headquarters, where he was able to warm up and make some phone calls. A tow truck was dispatched to pick up the broken-down car.

As I drove to my apartment that day, I thought about how easily I could have made the wrong call and shot an innocent and unarmed man who was simply trying to drive somewhere to share Christmas dinner with family. I'd taken a chance when I opted not to pull the trigger. A man's life hung in the balance as I made a split-second decision. Polite and respectful, that man in a duster coat taught me an invaluable lesson on pulling the trigger.

For two years, I continued to patrol. The long hours that I'd spent with my dad delivering milk as a kid came in handy because I'd already learned most of the street names in town. I grew closer to the other guys on the force and continued to demonstrate loyalty to the always-colorful Chief Joe McCarthy. I made some small busts, responded to numerous calls about heart attacks and other health emergencies, and improved my marksmanship at the range. I continued training Korean Karate and working out with weights as well.

Underneath, I was desperate to do something more to prove my worth. Undercover narcotics was what I needed. That was where I could balance the inner spreadsheet against my years in the Pagans. I was young, too, and needed the adrenalin rush that came with living life on the edge.

Looking back on my initial two years in uniform, I know I learned the basic methods of patrolling. But I failed in terms of doing *effective* police work. I didn't really get it, I suppose, until after I'd worked undercover. My attitude changed. After two wild years undercover, I no longer had any desire to impress people or to prove my loyalty and bravery in any way. I had worked with so many solid cops from all over—agents from the federal Drug Enforcement Administration and the State Police, and all the city officers who did the real dirty work—and managed to earn their respect, as they earned mine.

I realized after the Christmas Day incident that I was a touch too authoritative, too black-and-white and by-the-book. I hadn't yet learned that good police work is usually done in more of a gray area. Over time, I learned that most people respond better to honey than to vinegar. I could bull my way through a situation using my gun, badge and strength, or I could take a kinder and more thoughtful approach that resulted in fewer conflicts and better results.

As a patrolman, I responded to plenty of calls about loud parties lasting late into the night and pissing off the neighbors—for good reason. In the early days, I'd demand to see the homeowner and officiously order him to turn down the music "NOW." But that put the homeowner in an awkward position, and they'd often try to save face with their party guests by defying me. Ultimately, I'd win the confrontation, but not before some kind of verbal conflict or a fight. My "in your face" style got the job done, but not without a lot of conflict. Later on, I learned to handle the call in an entirely different way that rarely failed. I would find the homeowner and ask to see them privately, away from the other partygoers.

"Look, man, I need a favor from you," I'd tell the homeowner. "Do this for me and maybe someday I can help you out with a problem or a ticket. Listen, it's your neighbors complaining, and if the shoe was on the other foot, you would be pissed if someone screwed up your Saturday night. So please, I am asking for your help. Kill the music, and you and I are friends."

The response from my new method usually yielded amazing results. I could quietly stand back and watch as the homeowner would start berating the partiers, demand the music be turned off and comply with whatever I may have requested. Not only were the results better, my new policing method wasn't as stressful. The conflicts were gone, and I made solid connections in the community.

In time, I truly started to feel that I was a force for good. I stood for the weak and defenseless and punished the truly deserving. I broke out of the rock-hard shell I'd created during my years in the army and with the Pagans and engaged the compassionate and fair-minded part of me that had been extinguished by that sea of violence.

My new method was to be the muscular, hard-looking "bad" cop in appearance, but kind and understanding in action. Coming on strong and then being kind seemed to put people in a better space. Being a good guy was now my true persona.

One of the younger guys on the job was finishing a tour with the Monmouth County Narcotics Task Force. This cat was a friend of mine and filled me in on undercover work. I wanted in badly, made my request and waited. I'd been on the job less than two years, but I was older than most of the other guys when I joined and anxious to get more bad guys. The MCNTF had jurisdiction in some of the roughest neighborhoods in the state, the same ones that I'd hung out in as a Pagan. Perhaps more important, I knew how to blend in with the people there, because I'd been one of them. I didn't need to assume some undercover persona; I simply needed to adopt the same persona that I'd had only a few years earlier.

The trouble was that the MCNTF had a very tenuous relationship with the Middletown PD. The task force prosecuted the big cases and also prosecuted cops—some with zeal. There was real bad blood brewing, and it was only fitting that I should be in the middle of it. In the end, it was Chief Joseph McCarthy who would decide who went undercover. He chose me, and dissent be damned. My time at the MCNTF was the precursor to my hell ride at the Bayshore Narcotics Task Force.

I have seen cops try to do undercover work and admit they were too spooked to continue. It takes a certain type of person to walk unarmed into enemy territory, with no real backup and no trimmings of authority. No gun, no badge. Just your wits and balls.

I believed that I could fit in and pull off undercover work because

I had been a criminal, at least for the two years I ran with the Pagans. Now, running with the righteous, I was given the extraordinary chance to redeem myself. Not for the affirmation of others, but for me personally. Where I stood morally mattered to me intensely. It was the fuel that pushed me to take down drug dealers like Big John and so many others who treat the world as if they are predators picking off sheep.

CHAPTER TWENTY-EIGHT

COCAINE & CADILLACS

"What the fuck are you doing, trying to take someone down for a fucking eightball? That's fucking ridiculous," the confidential informant said. "I can set up a buy for a *pound* of coke."

I'd already given a nickname to this CI. His name was Rocky LoPresti, but I called him Rocky the Lying Squirrel. I didn't believe Rocky had the connections that he claimed. He laughed in my face when I talked to him about buying eightballs on the street, and told me that that quantity was so small it wasn't even worth bothering with. I had serious doubts at the start whether I'd be able to work with this fuckhead, much less have any success. But I was wrong.

Rocky proved to be a very hot CI, one of the best that I ever dealt with. We worked around the clock for three days straight during the fall of 1985 and scored some major buys from some very bad people.

This white kid looked like you'd plucked him out of a college class at Rutgers. He was an innocuous-looking 22-year-old with shaggy, curly black hair. He lived with his mommy and daddy in a mansion near the Superior Court building in Freehold and constantly talked big. I thought he was full of shit. First impressions can be deceiving, and this kid proved to have a very agile mind and truly amazing connections.

The usual way for undercover narcs to get to the big dealers was to tag a lesser target who was more vulnerable and then use them to roll the network up from the bottom. Sometimes we got to arrest the big guys at the top, and sometimes those major arrests went to other agencies. You couldn't allow it to matter to you if another group of dealers moved in to fill the void. That's just the way it was. You just kept doing your work. In the end, the vast majority of people in the game are pawns—the low-level dealers on one side, and some of us narcs on the other. But sometimes things went in a different direction indeed.

Rocky ID'd a guy named Larry Gaines as a high-value, and dangerous, target. A skilled martial arts figure, he'd been operating out of Middletown and had partnered with a Pagan, my old "friend" Tennessee, the quiet and slightly-built cat who had engineered the Pepsi bottle enema and subsequent murder of our fellow Pagan. Gaines had a guy named Robert Williams on his payroll, a chubby five-foot-10 guy in his early 30s, with a wispy beard and fairly long hair. Working as Gaines's mule seemed to be a second job for Williams, a way for him to pick up extra money, and it ultimately proved both dangerous and stupid.

Rocky arranged for me to buy a pound of coke from Williams. The deal would go down in the parking lot of an A&P supermarket in Port Monmouth, where I'd meet Williams at his car in the early evening. I was supposed to walk over to Williams's car and show him the buy money, and he would hand me the package. Another cop, Alton Bennett, was going to back me up on site, observing the deal from his undercover vehicle. We had multiple marked units stationed nearby but staying out of sight.

As people walked by with their shopping carts full of groceries, Bennett watched Gaines pull into the parking lot in his Cadillac Seville, get out of the car and walk over to Williams's car. The two of them talked briefly before Gaines walked back to the Seville.

I pulled into the lot a few minutes later, parked at the end of the lot by the street and walked over to the vehicle Rocky had described to me a few hours earlier. Williams was sitting in the car, just as planned. I showed him a wad of cash, and he pulled out the brick of coke and handed it to me.

"You're under arrest, fuckhead. I'm a cop with the Bayshore Task Force," I said, sticking my Smith & Wesson in his face.

Bennett radioed to the marked units, and four of them descended on the parking lot from different directions. They picked up Gaines and assumed custody of my handcuffed prisoner, Williams. We ordered tow trucks in and put both Gaines's Cadillac and Williams's cars on the hook; they would be searched later, back at headquarters.

We also executed a search warrant on Williams's house, where we found a half pound of coke, a scale and other drug paraphernalia. Bennett and I hoped to turn Williams and get him to talk about Gaines. But Williams was too afraid and immediately lawyered up. Gaines spent the evening practicing karate kicks and punches in his cell, successfully freaking out the cops guarding him.

We knew going in that the case against Gaines was weak. Bennett and I were pretty confident that he'd dropped the coke off with Williams in the parking lot right before the buy went down. But Bennett wasn't able to see Gaines carrying anything, and our evidence against him was mostly circumstantial. Charged as Williams's co-conspirator on felony drug sale charges, Gaines had lawyered up with an expensive defense attorney who'd gotten a bunch of dealers off in the past. In court, the case would weigh heavily on Bennett's testimony.

The case went to trial months later, with both Williams and Gaines represented by tough attorneys. As the prosecutor built his case, he ordered Bennett to get the pound of cocaine out of the evidence vault and bring it into the courtroom to show to the jurors. The prosecutor displayed the drugs on his table in the front of the courtroom and had Bennett testify at length. The defense attorney then grilled Bennett on the stand. This process continued for hours. When the judge called a brief recess, everyone left the courtroom. Bennett, who seriously needed a break, walked out along with the attorneys.

No one thought about guarding the evidence that was sitting there in plain sight—not Bennett, who had signed for the contraband, or the prosecutor, the judge or the court guards. Somehow they all thought that everything was going to be fine because we were in the Monmouth County Courthouse. Gaines's hot sister, who'd been in the courtroom to observe the proceedings, thought differently. During the break, she walked up front, snagged the pound of coke and casually walked out of the courtroom without anyone noticing. When the recess ended and people returned, someone noticed that the drugs were missing and the entire courthouse was immediately placed under lockdown.

Bennett, who technically had possession of the drugs because he'd signed for them, was surrounded by sheriff's deputies and the prosecutor, who promptly read him his Miranda rights. No action was taken against the court guard who'd been in the room, and of course the prosecutor didn't think that he was at all responsible—even though he was the one who'd directed Bennett to bring the drugs into the courtroom and had the drugs on the table in front of him. The courthouse guards, police and other law enforcement personnel launched a massive search of the building. Bennett's ex-wife, who happened to be a security officer in the courthouse, was among those engaged in the search.

"How are you, dear?" Bennett said as he saw her approaching him in a corridor.

"You really fucked up again, didn't you?" she asked before continuing the search.

A sheriff's deputy subsequently found Gaines's sister, along with the drugs, in a courtroom phone booth. The woman was arrested, and the drugs were placed back in the vault, where they stayed under lock and key for the remainder of the trial. Ironically, she could have flushed the drugs down a toilet and destroyed the case against her brother. But she was greedy and wanted to keep the coke.

No one ever apologized to Bennett about what happened that day.

Gaines was subsequently found not guilty and released. He'd lost his Cadillac to the county and had been forced to shell out tens of thousands for a defense attorney, but he was free. Williams was sentenced to 10 years in prison for the drug sales.

Later, I found out that Tennessee had been at the A&P the night the drug deal with Williams went down. Bennett and I hadn't seen him.

CHAPTER TWENTY-NINE

PASS THE FUCKING PEAS

In 1986, after working undercover for more than a year, I was sent to a
week-long training class on advanced narcotics work at the State Police
training facility in Sea Girt, New Jersey. Sometimes truth seems odder
than fiction, and this was one of those moments.

One of the classes was run by a veteran New Jersey State Police
detective who'd done some very heavy undercover work inside an organized crime family. I knew he'd taken an enormous risk doing that work,
so this dude was a hero to me. Like many who put their lives on the line
for real, he was quite humble.

"How many of you have done undercover work?" asked the tall, lean
detective.

I raised my hand, the only one to do so in a room of about 40 cops,
young and old.

"You have the look of someone who's been there a while," he said,
staring me straight in the eye. "We try to keep assignments like that to
six months. How long you been under?"

"About 13 months. I figure two years to close it out."

"Yeah, I get it," he said. "Big cases to clean up, huh?"

I knew the guy was being friendly, not sarcastic, and nodded my
head.

"Well, you think about it, 'cause you're a serious candidate for burnout. This is how you're going to know you need out. You will be at a family dinner. Your family will be there, mother and father. Your grandparents and aunts. Without even a thought you will look at your mother and say, 'Mom, pass me the fucking peas.'"

It was good for a laugh. But it stuck with me. And some months down the road, when I was still undercover and having dinner with my mother and father, my brother's family and his kids, I looked at my mother and said, "Mom, can you pass the fucking carrots?"

The kids laughed; the adults, not so much.

It's the little things that you notice when you're doing undercover work. When you're a cop, the community generally opens its arms to you—especially the merchants. But if you're working undercover, you are lucky if you get the *worst* table in the restaurant. You look like a thug, because that is the role you're playing as if your life depended on it. And the universe conspires to remind you of who you are. If you have a hot informant, you might run with them for days, with little sleep. You feel like crap, but you soldier on. You get pulled over by cops who bust your balls.

The New Jersey State Police pulled me over once during my years undercover: two State bulls together. I told them that I was working undercover and that my ID and weapon were in a briefcase on the back seat. They let me show them my ID—at gunpoint. Then they relaxed but got sarcastic.

"Man, you really look like shit," one said.

"Thanks. I'm supposed to. It's easier to keep breathing this way," I replied.

"Man, you *do* look like a piece of shit," the other one chimed in. "You really do look like shit. He's not kidding, ya know."

"Are you done?" I asked. "Or do you want to go issue some tickets to the taxpayers?"

They left, after delivering some other snide comments.

Months after my "pass the peas" moment, I started to wonder if I *was* getting close to burning out. The doubts began when Jack Mullins and I set up a six-pound marijuana buy with a Jamaican cat and saw the meet go down in flames because we were drunk.

The two of us were supposed to meet the Jamaican at a construction site off Route 35 in Hazlet. Workers had just completed the foundation, and the site was a mess, full of piles of dirt, construction equipment and pieces of lumber and debris. A big strip shopping center was adjacent to the property. The plan was that I would play the big-shot construction supervisor and Mullins would be one of the guys working for me.

We intended to meet the target late in the afternoon, after the regular workers had gone home, and take him down with his haul of weed. The rip was set to go down at about 4 p.m., right after the site had closed down. In this case, we didn't have to worry about burning an informant, and it was going to be an out-and-out rip. But we fucked it up and our target got away. We had no one to blame but ourselves.

Mullins, Alton Bennett and I were all scheduled to testify before a grand jury at the Monmouth County Courthouse on some of our drug cases late that morning. Normally, grand jury presentations are quite routine—a prosecutor tells the 23 grand jurors what the proposed charges are and then presents a bare-bones case, usually with just an arresting officer or victim. The prosecutor doesn't have to prove the case beyond a reasonable doubt—that happens later, in a court of law. The grand jury process merely assures that the prosecution has sufficient evidence to present a case; the legal standard is lower. Most of the time, grand juries issue "true bills of indictment," with few if any questions. Serving on a grand jury can almost be fun for citizens, because it's a window into a world they don't often see. It's less fun for those whose paychecks get interrupted. Grand jury presentations were a piece of cake for me.

After we testified under oath, the three of us decided to go out to get lunch together. We headed to a fancy restaurant for food and drinks.

We always carried cash for a number of reasons. We never knew when we were going to make an undercover drug buy. And our superiors understood that some of the money we had would be used on food and drink—all as part of our work undercover. The more successful undercovers had access to larger amounts of cash; it was a results-oriented system. The tuxedoed bartender and maître d' thought they had the Oakland chapter of the Hells Angels entering their sophisticated establishment. We walked to the bar, looking every bit a one-percent biker crew in search of whiskey. The bartender looked blankly at us while drying some glasses, and we each ordered white wine. Looking a bit bewildered, he poured a chardonnay for the three of us.

Wanting to be friendly, I asked a well-dressed older gentleman next to me what he was drinking. "Gin martini," he said. "But never more than two at any given time. They will sneak up on you. By God, they can bite."

Oddly, none of us had ever had a martini, and it seemed like a nice idea to try one, or maybe two. Mullins ordered gin martinis for all of us. Bennett, who rarely drank, gagged on his and declared it "turpentine." He went back to his wine. Mullins and I were heavier drinkers, and we decided to stick with the martinis. We drank them down as fast as the bartender could make them, even as the older guy sat there, shaking his head.

As we walked outside, the combination of the fresh air and the heavy alcohol content of multiple martinis hit us; Mullins and I were plastered. Bennett dropped us off at headquarters, but not before urging us to call off the buy from the Jamaican. But neither of us could find a phone number for the target. We hopped into our undercover car and headed for the construction site.

Mullins and I were both able to get out of our car without difficulty. But we found it incredibly hard to maintain our footing as we walked across the construction site, stumbling on each and every pile of dirt and bit of debris along the way.

The dealer pulled up and we both turned to meet him. It didn't take him more than a couple of seconds to realize that we were sloshed. When Mullins got closer to the dealer, the guy also caught a whiff of the alcohol on his breath. That was it. He told us both to fuck off, hopped back into his car and drove away. He was gone before we even had a chance to object.

Then we saw our supervisor, Lieutenant John McCabe, pull up in his unmarked vehicle. It seems he'd been parked in the shopping center next door and managed to observe the entire sad sequence of events. Mullins and I both hung our heads in shame, ready for a well-earned dressing-down and feeling like two busted school kids.

McCabe smiled at us and said, "You guys have been under real pressure for a long time. It's okay if you blow one. As long as it's just one. I'll drive you home. No problem."

To say we would jump through a wall of fire for that man is not saying enough. Sometimes leadership is about action *not* taken.

Middletown Detective Captain Frank Gleason, a highly placed, venerated and anachronistic commander, walked into the detective bureau one day and tasked me with taking down a man in Highlands, a borough of Monmouth County, who allegedly had 50 pounds of marijuana in his apartment.

"Take care of it, ASAP," Gleason told me. "Make me proud. Get it done, old boy."

Several hurdles stood between me and bringing this supposed criminal to justice: none of the cops I knew had ever heard of the guy; we had no informant; we had no one who even had a clue about any big marijuana shipment in the county; the Bill of Rights strongly suggests that we have a very good reason before asking a judge for a search warrant; and, lastly, the commander who gave us the name had no absolutely no other information about him.

Absent any intelligence and without any informants, Mullins and I decided to try something outlandish. The first stop was a local pizza joint to pick up a cheese pie. The idea was that Alton Bennett, a sort of demented-looking mountain man, would attempt to deliver pizza to our target and try to either gain access to the apartment or see something that we could then use to get a search warrant or otherwise make some progress. Mullins and I would do the surveillance from our undercover vehicle.

"I didn't order a pizza," the suspected dealer said, staring at the odd-looking delivery guy holding a cheese pie.

"But aren't you Jimmy Healey?" Bennett asked.

"Yes, but I didn't order any pizza."

"Well, can you let me in so I can show you this, maybe someone else here ordered it?" Bennett continued.

The two men started arguing at the door to the apartment, as Bennett did his best to get inside, and the suspect continued to state—accurately—that he didn't order any pizza and didn't want any.

Bennett was so upset about not making any headway that he absent-mindedly started gesturing with his hands—and wound up with the pizza box being held vertically, so that the pizza slid to one end of the box. Mullins and I started laughing hysterically as we observed from the car. Bennett seemed increasingly infuriated by his inability to get inside.

Suddenly, Healey threw his arms up in the air, yelled something and slammed the door shut. Bennett stormed back to his car, opened the door and threw the pizza in like a Frisbee. The three of us wrote up a report about our creative, but ultimately failed, effort and moved on.

In the late spring of 1987, Mullins and I began working with an informant to set up an undercover drug buy in Keyport, a bedroom community overlooking Raritan Bay, just west of Hazlet and Union Beach. The informant, an African-American in his late 20s who worked on a garbage truck, had a sheet with some violent crimes on it, including assaults. He'd been picked up on drug charges and was trying to work them off by serving as an informant for us. He was way too slick for my taste. From my days riding with the Pagans, I knew that the assaults on his record were just the ones that he'd been *caught* for doing; I was sure there were plenty more.

The buy was supposed to go down in a run-down part of Keyport where a tightly packed cluster of two-story residential buildings covered several blocks. Mullins and I checked it out early one morning and realized that it was something of a labyrinth. It would be virtually impossible to do surveillance on anyone inside the complex. The area also happened to be predominantly African-American, meaning that the white undercover members of the task force would immediately stand out. There was no way anyone on the surveillance team could remain stationary; they'd have to be in a car and mobile.

I would be going in alone, with only the informant at my side.

As usual, I intended to wear my biker stuff—blue jeans, a ratty T-shirt, a baseball cap with the Harley-Davidson logo and a pair of work boots. I ignored the black engineer boots that I usually wore and instead grabbed a pair of tall, tan-colored construction boots with laces. I didn't tell Mullins, but I'd also decided to carry my five-shot Charter Arms snub nose in an ankle holster. Normally I didn't go into a buy carrying a gun, but this time was different.

I drove down to Keyport in my undercover car late one Tuesday afternoon and parked adjacent to the residential complex. I met the informant outside, and he walked me through a maze of narrow alleys and corridors. We went down one corridor, then another and then a turn down a third. Finally, we walked to the end of a hallway where there were three doors. The informant opened one of them, and we went down a flight of stairs into a dingy and dimly lit basement.

I immediately had the sense that something was wrong. There was no furniture around—no chairs, no couches. This wasn't a location for a drug buy but for a robbery. I always carried at least $200 or $300 in cash, and sometimes much more. An eightball was going for around $225; a quarter ounce went for around $450.

I heard voices and then footsteps as a half dozen men came down the basement stairs and stood facing me. They were street-hardened thugs, intimidating just by their presence. There were six of them, and only five shots in my Charter Arms. They stood there, playing it cool, smiling and joking and looking at me the way the jaguar looks at the bush pig; the hunter was being hunted.

"Shit, these motherfucking laces," I said, casually dropping onto a knee and reaching for my boot with both hands. I pulled the Charter Arms out of the holster and brought it up on the men, cocking the trigger as I stood.

"I know at least one of you fuckers is packing," I said. "I ain't going down in this place."

They all held their ground and let me move past them, my finger never moving off the trigger. All of them had the pleasure of being aimed at for at least a full second.

I backed out of the basement and up the stairs and made my way outside. None of them attempted to follow me. Mullins spotted me soon after I emerged. I hopped into his car, and we took off. I never saw, or talked to, the informant again.

Later that day, I put in a call to the county prosecutor's office and told the attorney that the informant was full of shit—and might have just tried to get me killed. Any chance the guy had of working off his charges disappeared after my call. That afternoon probably wound up costing him a couple of years in prison.

One thing seemed certain that day: The cats that came down into the basement were for real. I knew just by their demeanor. They knew, too, that I had a hair-trigger pistol, cocked and locked. No one seemed alarmed or tried to play cocky, either. Nope. They were players.

Closing in on two years undercover, I knew I had used up my share of luck. Besides, I really wanted to get a decent table at a restaurant.

CHAPTER THIRTY

RENZO COMES TO TOWN

I went back in the bag for two years, working as a uniformed officer, before I was made a detective again in September 1988 and got assigned to the youth crimes unit. I was okay with being a uniformed patrolman, pulling cars over for vehicle and traffic code violations and responding to various emergencies. But I preferred being a detective and was happy to be out of the marked unit. I had more freedom to pursue the cases and causes that interested me most, and that sense of personal freedom was important to me, too. In the youth crimes unit, I worked primarily with the administrations of the two big high schools in town. I had steady eight-to-four hours Monday through Friday, and an unmarked unit. It was a pretty nice gig that allowed me to feel I was making a decent contribution to my community.

I said goodbye to our Chief Joe McCarthy, who was forced to retire due to mandatory civil service age requirements. That gave the politicians in town a rare opportunity to hand-select his replacement—someone who'd be loyal to them.

Over time, I started to believe that the cops in town needed stronger union representation, and I thought about running for an elected position in the Middletown Patrolmen's Benevolent Association. I knew that becoming a PBA leader could hamper my career, but I cared about the men and liked the independent, no-nonsense manner in which the

274 ★ JERSEY TOUGH

department had been run for many years.

Then, in 1993, I saw Middletown Police Officer Mike Hoydis come under attack for an incident involving a fleeing murder suspect, and I decided that it was time to become active in the union. Police in Connecticut had put out an all-points-bulletin (BOLO) advising officers to be on the lookout for a man who had murdered his wife with a pair of scissors and was believed to be fleeing south in his car. From what we heard, he was still believed to be wearing his blood-stained clothes.

Hoydis spotted the guy's car, radioed for backup and gave chase. The suspect led Hoydis on a wild car chase through town, and the cop was finally able to stop him, with help from Red Bank Police, on the border between Red Bank and Middletown. Adrenalin pumping, Hoydis yanked the guy from his car and punched him several times before backing off and putting the man in cuffs. The suspect was put in the back of a squad car and taken into police headquarters, where he was processed in.

Under interrogation by a Middletown detective, the suspect provided a full statement admitting to his wife's brutal murder. "Have I or anyone else associated with your arrest mistreated you in any way?" the detective asked, following departmental protocol.

The suspect said that the detective hadn't mistreated him, but that one of the cops who arrested him—Hoydis—had slugged him a few times.

The Monmouth County prosecutor was outraged and ordered his office to investigate. But the investigation stalled because none of the cops on the scene would testify against Hoydis, and it was just the suspect's word against the officer's.

The prosecutor refused to let the matter die. He had his investigators call the Red Bank Police officers into an office, where they were shown copies of their financial records and warned that they could be suspended or indicted for interfering with an investigation if they didn't tell the truth about what happened. They folded and, under duress,

Outside the Middletown Police Department headquarters with one of the agency's marked vehicles. (Photo by Douglas P. Love)

admitted that the alleged killer was hit a few times but didn't sustain any injuries.

"We have the goods for assault and official misconduct. Plead him out. He gets fired, no pension, health benefits and no honorable release, just no jail," the prosecutor told Hoydis's attorney. Official misconduct is a second-degree felony, on par with non-aggravated rape or selling heroin. It's punishable by five to 10 years in jail and up to $100,000 in fines.

Hoydis pleaded out to avoid the roll of the dice in the courtroom. Most of the cops thought he should have gone to trial, since all that he did was throw a few punches at someone who was fleeing police after a murder. They figured jurors would side with the cop.

Highlands Police Chief Howard Brey publicly declared that he wanted to hire Hoydis—that he thought the cop was a hero for bringing in a dangerous, fleeing felon. But the prosecutor squelched the hiring, too. Hoydis eventually got a job in the private sector as a financial advisor.

I'd seen enough and decided to get actively involved with the union, with an eye toward becoming president. Soon enough, I was elected the union's sergeant-at-arms (yes, the same position I'd held in the Pagans) and made head of its board of trustees.

Not long afterward, I was transferred back to patrol division, in November 1993. I worked in patrol for another four years before getting transferred back to detective division in 1997. My assignments seemed to change based on my responsibilities with the union. I was a detective from 1997 to 2002 and then transferred back to patrol. I finished out my last year with the department, 2002–03, as a beat cop—which was okay because it kept me close to the action.

My transfer out of the youth crimes bureau in 1993 outraged the administrations of the two high schools I was working with—perhaps because I was leading the department in arrests on a monthly average. I was visible and doing my job, and that seemed to matter to the high school principals. Both sent letters to the press objecting to the move— and one newspaper even wrote an editorial objecting to the transfer.

But none of it made a difference to the police department's administration. I had been doing some serious weight training along with my continued Korean Karate, and that was where my energies would now go, along with my union work.

The world-famous Brazilian Jiu Jitsu expert Renzo Gracie has a great saying about BJJ: "Look at the lions, the most dangerous of beasts. The lion is savagely adept at killing animals even much larger. A pure killing machine. Now take the lion out onto the ocean, where sharks hang out. Drop him into the water. The lion is just another meal."

At its simplest, BJJ is applied kinesiology. The practitioner attacks

*Renzo Gracie, me, and Carlos Gracie Jr. at Renzo's home in Holmdel,
New Jersey, around 2004.* (Photo by Barbara Bradshaw)

the joints or spine of his opponent by placing his body in a position to
leverage its entire weight, often using his hips to bend one part of his
adversary's body in a particular direction, causing the joint or spine to
break. So the fight becomes one man versus just one of his opponent's
appendages.

Though simple enough in theory, it can take years to become an
expert in BJJ—and not everyone is ready to take that trip. I was ready,
and I started training with Renzo Gracie in 1993, when a business
opportunity brought him to the Jersey Shore, and we met and became
close friends.

Today, I'm one of the senior practitioners of Renzo Gracie's Brazilian
Jiu Jitsu family—and one of the first six people in the United States
to train with him. I often train others in the skills that I've patiently
acquired from Renzo and other experts, including Karl Pravec, the

"Silver Fox"—a second-degree black belt in BJJ who also happens to have a master's degree in finance from Columbia University.

Renzo and I walked in different circles, and when I met him, I didn't expect him to be interested in becoming my friend. But he seemed eager to pursue the relationship, and he became my "Mr. Miyagi" (the mentor in the movie *The Karate Kid*). He was, and still is, my personal consigliere and the greatest positive influence both in terms of hand-to-hand combat and dealing with the challenges that life throws at all of us.

When Renzo arrived, few people outside the martial arts world had any clue who he was. Only hard-core martial arts types in New Jersey had heard of the Gracie family from Rio de Janeiro, or Renzo in particular. It was like suddenly having immediate and personal access to a great sporting figure whom you'd never even dreamt of meeting, like baseball's Ty Cobb, football's Jim Brown, or hockey's Wayne Gretzky.

This gregarious and outgoing yet supremely confident fighter immediately earned the complete respect of all who came to train. Since the only people who knew who Renzo was were Special Forces types and ranking martial artists, he had classes filled with people who theoretically should have been able to hold their own in a fight with him, or perhaps win. I was a ranking black belt who weighed in at 240 pounds, while Renzo weighed just 178. We had Navy SEALs in the group, too, as well as some of the hardest street fighters around.

Renzo smiled while he destroyed us all so quickly and so efficiently that we were in total awe. This was a guy who was a legendary street fighter in Brazil, where no-rules, no-size-category fighting had gone on for years. Yet he stood undefeated. A shatteringly adept killer, Renzo was and continues to be highly sought after by Special Forces troops around the globe for his instruction.

Perhaps more important to me, Renzo is also one of the (if not the) most caring, decent and honorable people I have ever known. I value his close friendship now as I did then—way more valuable than gold.

We share a passion for books and literature, too—though most people who train at one of Renzo's academies probably wouldn't think of him as a learned man who enjoys reading.

Renzo's charisma and skills in fighting were earned on the very violent and mean streets of Rio de Janeiro, where on one occasion he was shot three times with a handgun by a drug-dealing thug. The gunshots didn't stop him, and he used his BJJ skills to beat the shooter to near-death. His brutal and bloody no-rules defeat of the legendary Oleg Taktarov in the U.S. prompted Senator John McCain to call for, and subsequently see enacted, a ban on no-rules fighting.

In Brazil, Renzo fought a grudge match against a notorious fighter backed by powerful drug cartels. Renzo dominated the fight—despite getting stabbed by a spectator during the actual match. Ultimately, Renzo laid a beating on his opponent with his bare fists, and an all-out riot began. Rio de Janeiro, too, banned no-rules fights. That made Renzo responsible for the banning of real, true-to-life no-rules fighting both in the United States and Brazil. He has never lost a fight where rules are exempted, whether on the streets of New York or the beaches of Rio, or in the ring.

I had a detached garage at my home in North Middletown where I would often train with some of the guys from the Middletown PD. It had electricity, so we could continue using it late into the evening. And it was large enough for the hard-core weightlifting equipment I had as well as an open area for practicing Korean Karate. When BJJ came to town, I overhauled the space and put in thick rubber mats more suitable for grappling. I had the perfect spot and location to practice with my friends when not attending classes. It was our sanctuary, and on any given day, a world-renowned BJJ expert such as Renzo Gracie, Ricardo Almeida or Craig Kukuk could be working out with us.

It was during one of our countless training sessions that Renzo started to call me "Big Chuck," a nickname that stuck. In BJJ circles, I am known simply by Renzo's nickname. No one calls me anything else.

Jiu Jitsu is never forced. The adept practitioner merely attacks whatever appendage presents itself. It is practiced full-speed, and the person having his joint manipulated must signal submission by "tapping out" (smacking the mat or tapping the opponent) quickly before his body part snaps. Many of the moves are taught and used on the ground. Here, only the skilled practitioner has the advantage, as few people have a clue about how to fight from the ground or their back. A BJJ fighter is lethal even while lying on his back. We say: Take your opponent to the ground, where you can swim and he drowns.

One of the principal moves is called the triangle. Lying on his back, the practitioner wraps his legs around his opponent's neck, cutting off the carotid arteries on each side. The opponent loses consciousness in three to five seconds. The closing of the carotid arteries by arms or legs is a safe way to finish the combat. If the hold is released quickly, no permanent damage is done.

Another move is the figure four, in which you grab the opponent's wrist, reach under your opponent's arm with your other hand, circle around and grab your own wrist and then—slowly—begin to apply pressure to your opponent. Do it too quickly and your opponent's shoulder will be forever damaged. Do it slowly and you gain control of your opponent, no matter how big he or she may be.

The sessions with Renzo created a fierce comradery born from shared risk and brutally difficult training. In BJJ you have to trust your training partner with your life and health. The moves we practiced were designed to break bones, break necks and destroy your opponent's knees. We went full force, and tapping submission quickly was the only way to save yourself from injury. It was training on the edge. Everyone suffered injuries, and no one placed blame.

Often, after weekend sessions, we would grab our wives and girlfriends and feast in the local restaurants. Anyone was welcome to train with us. We had just one rule that could not be broken: you had to conduct yourself in a humble manner and treat your training partners with real respect. Violate that rule, and you risk a beating before banishment.

In this environment, in front of no judges other than ourselves, we became warriors of Renzo Gracie Brazilian Jiu Jitsu. To a man, we would have happily caught a bullet for our leader, Renzo. Honor and loyalty were not token concepts to us. Death before dishonor was not a cliché. We lived it.

At that time, only a rarefied few had knowledge of Gracie Jiu Jitsu— and anyone hoping to learn the art had to go through brutal training that few would even entertain. We literally sacrificed body parts to learn the skill. But if you knew the techniques and the other guy didn't, well, the fight was pretty much over before it started. Gracie Jiu Jitsu gave me an ability to subdue virtually any bad guy that I came across—without resorting to weapons. I brought people into the Middletown Police Department cells in handcuffs, which seemed far preferable to sending them to the hospital or the morgue.

The patrol squad I was assigned to was okay, and I liked my co-workers for the most part. But I could never understand why so few of them opted to train with Renzo. Maybe they were scared of getting hurt. But somehow it made more sense to me to train in a controlled environment with experts and not have to worry so much about getting hurt when I was out in the field, confronting a violent felon.

The few who trained with Renzo became remarkable fighters who were very adept on the street.

CHAPTER THIRTY-ONE

DENNIS THE MAD DOG

"Where the fuck is Mad Dog?" Dave Lentz shouted as he slammed down the phone.

The two of us were standing inside Dave's office at his Red Bank fighting academy. I'd gone there after my shift one evening in late 1993 to work out with Dave and a few other guys, including my longtime buddy George Sammett, who owned a successful tree-trimming company in town. None of the guys had arrived yet, and I'd wandered into Dave's office to say hi.

I'd just walked past "Mad Dog" outside the school seconds earlier. That was the nickname Dennis Downey had adopted in his on-again, off-again career as a professional kickboxer. A career sadist and convict who'd been in and out of jail for assaults and thefts, he managed to fit in a couple of paid fights in Atlantic City when he wasn't behind bars. Mad Dog stood about six foot two, weighed 210 pounds and was a natural heavyweight, with very solid leg kicks. His long hair, demonic eyes and thick beard created a sinister appearance that he positively reveled in.

Dave and I checked the school's classroom and then ran to the front door. Mad Dog had bolted. Dave told me he'd just gotten off the phone with George Sammett's wife, Kathy, a pretty, petite brunette who didn't have a single enemy in town. Kathy was crying and absolutely beside herself, he explained. She'd found George beaten to a pulp and barely conscious in the gym they had in a massive, two-story garage behind their house. The structure also served as the base of operations for George's business. She knew that Mad Dog had been there earlier in the day and believed he was responsible for the assault, but she had no proof.

Kathy told Dave that she'd gotten George into the house but that he was in really bad shape and she wanted to take him to the hospital. He'd refused.

The next morning, I met George and Kathy in the emergency room at Riverview Hospital. She'd finally convinced her husband, who had uncannily good boxing and Jiu Jitsu skills and would be a tough opponent for anyone, to get treatment.

George was usually a witty and gregarious guy. The man I saw in the ER was obviously in bad shape, groggy and barely able to move. He'd clearly been subject to a severe beating. In the gym, George and I had fought dozens of times, and I'd won maybe twice. Most of the time I tried to end the bouts in a stalemate. Whoever had done this to him was either incredibly powerful or had gotten the drop on him.

George thought nothing of allowing people who were broke to come to his house and spend the day chopping firewood or doing other menial work to make $100. He'd always be around, and was confident that he could maintain control no matter what the circumstances.

Kathy explained that Mad Dog had come by the house early in the day, and that he and George had gone out to the garage, which was tucked into the woods behind the house, to work out. George didn't need to be at a job site until later in the morning, and he rarely missed an opportunity to improve his fighting skills. Kathy said that she got worried about her husband after she didn't see or hear from him for a couple of hours, and she went back to the garage to see what was going on. She found George on the floor in the training area, barely conscious and moaning in pain—the first time she'd ever seen him that way.

George groggily said that Mad Dog had suggested that they do some sparring, and he had agreed. The fighter asked George to put up a 75-pound heavy bag so he could warm up his legs before the fight.

While George was hanging the bag, Mad Dog whipped a near-lethal round kick to George's temporal lobe that knocked him to the floor. George said he couldn't remember much of what happened next but that he did recall Mad Dog throwing a weighted barbell onto him while he was lying prone. He also dimly remembered a series of kicks and punches raining down on him.

The incident didn't make a lot of sense unless something had been taken while George was down or the beat-down was part of some larger plan that Mad Dog had in mind. George was my friend, but I was also a cop, so I did what made sense: I filed an assault report that day and began an investigation. In the course of talking to George and Kathy, I also learned that Bob Smith, a local plumbing contractor, was supposed to have come by that day but, as far as George and Kathy knew, had never shown up.

As I drove away from Riverview Hospital, I thought back to the time in about 1991 when I ran into Mad Dog deep in Hartshorne Woods, a hilly and wooded 787-acre Monmouth County park. Located just south of Sandy Hook, the park overlooked the Atlantic Ocean and the Navesink River. It contained miles and miles of hiking trails and the remains of World War II–era concrete bunkers that once housed heavy artillery to protect the entrance to New York Harbor.

My Akita, Bushi, was a handful, and I had to keep him on a short leash at all times; letting him run untethered was not safe, for either animal or man. As we meandered through the trails, I heard an odd thumping sound coming from a deeply wooded area. Bushi started to growl with real malice as we walked closer, and almost ripped my shoulder socket out trying to attack something.

When I turned a corner, I saw Mad Dog standing in karate pants and wearing 16-ounce boxing gloves, kicking and punching a tree. He looked deranged. Mad Dog took a couple of steps toward the dog, but then thought twice and stopped in his tracks. Bushi seemed anxious to eat him for dinner.

"Hey, that's a nice dog," he said, keeping both eyes on the Akita.

"Yeah. Looks like he wants a piece of you."

Mad Dog had the distinction of serving in a Florida chain gang during one of his many arrests. He'd been caught hanging around local Veterans of Foreign Wars halls and stealing money off aging combat veterans. The guy could be charming. But most of the time he affected a wild persona, exuded true menace and was more than willing to fight the police.

In addition to holding the leash on Bushi, I was carrying my Smith & Wesson that day. I had nothing to fear from Mad Dog. But I wondered about the safety of the young women who jogged these trails alone. I yanked on Bushi's leash and we continued on our way. I couldn't help but think that this guy was a danger to everyone who lived in the area. It was just a matter of time until something bad, really bad, happened involving Mad Dog.

Following a series of interviews, I learned that Smith, the plumbing contractor, had indeed gone to the Sammetts' house that morning. He'd pulled into the driveway, saw Mad Dog by George's house and rolled down the window to say hello. Without saying a word, Mad Dog kicked the driver's-side rearview mirror off the truck and punched Smith in the face. Smith put the truck in reverse and left. He could meet up with George some other time, when Mad Dog wasn't around.

My guess is that Mad Dog had planned to knock out George and enter the house, where he would have raped Kathy, who weighed maybe 110 pounds and would never have been able to fight him off. It was only the plumber's arrival that stopped Mad Dog from entering the residence and carrying out his plan. Mad Dog also knew that Smith could have placed him at the residence, which was not at all what he wanted.

I'd known Kathy for years and would have been horrified if something had happened to her. I needed more than an aggravated assault case to put Mad Dog behind bars—and keep him away from Kathy for years to come. So I went back and talked to George and the plumber again.

George searched his memories and recalled that he'd had two $50 bills in his pocket when Mad Dog arrived that morning—the money that he was going to use to pay the man for his labor. But the two bills went missing. I obtained sworn statements from both George and Bob Smith, and used them to get an arrest warrant for Dennis "Mad Dog" Downey on charges of aggravated assault and strong-arm robbery. The combination, along with Mad Dog's long criminal history, would have serious repercussions in a court of law.

Now all I had to do was arrest a very violent guy who was likely to become desperate when he was made aware of the robbery charge. Mad Dog was living in a shotgun shack in Highlands, much of which was blue collar and depressed. It had five times as many bars as churches.

Detective Lieutenant Timothy Lake, Detective Sergeant Richard Dieckmann and I decided to pick up Downey around 6 a.m., when we expected him to still be sleeping—and hence less volatile. There was some tension between the three of us, in part because of my union activities, and in part because I didn't much care for the way the other two handled themselves.

Lake and Dieckmann wanted me to sit in the car while they made the actual arrest. But there was a jurisdictional issue at play here, too. The Borough of Highlands had its own police force, and we would be on its turf. When we arrived at the scene, a patrolman from Highlands decided that the bungalow was too small for five men, and that no more than two men should do the takedown. The cop knew me because of my martial arts training and wanted me at his side. Lake and Dieckmann had no choice but to cool their heels outside.

Mad Dog was already up and wearing work clothes when we knocked on the door. He saw the Highlands cop first and smiled as he opened the door. He asked about the officer's health, and then turned to me, asking how I was doing. I told him I had paper on him for the George Sammett beating.

"I know you and George are tight, Detective," Mad Dog said. "But me and him, we just had a rough sparring session. You know. I have a fight lined up with Dennis Alexio, man. I needed the training; George is like one of the only people that can hang with me. He just, you know, came up short. Walked into a kick. He's alright, isn't he?"

Dennis "the Terminator" Alexio is a former world kickboxing champion, and I had no doubt that Mad Dog was scheduled to fight him.

"Dennis, George is hurt, but he's going to make it. But between you and me, bro? I don't think you could beat Sammett in a straight fight even if you had a hatchet in each hand. But that's not what this about. You're thinking it's all bullshit. A he-said/she-said about a sparring match. Think the fuck again. I am taking you for strong-arm robbery. You know, bro—the two U.S. Grants you stole from his pocket after you suckered him." I suggested that I had also figured out his plan to take Kathy that day.

"Fuck that shit, fuck it. This is bullshit. I never stole nothing from that man," Mad Dog said. "I got nothing going on with Kathy, and that cunt knows it."

"Yeah, well, tell it to the jury," I said. "With these charges and your record, getting close to any women will be a distant thought. You can sit with your Aryan Brotherhood inmate friends and lie about pussy all you want. You sure as shit will have plenty of time to discuss it. By the time you max out, you will forget what to do with pussy. One more thing, hope you ate steak last night. They don't serve that kind of food where you will be hanging your dick."

Mad Dog bladed on me, turning perpendicular and positioning himself for an attack. I could feel the tension in his body. The patrolman and I bladed as well. We expected this fight was going to get bloody and dirty, real quick.

But Dennis Downey decided to fight another day. He turned his back to me, put his hands together for the cuffs and offered no resistance. He went to jail without incident.

Processing Mad Dog back at the Middletown Police Department was a trip. He had a big audience, as men from the incoming and outgoing shifts were coming through. He started some rambling dissertation about wanting to go out west and live with the grizzly bears after clearing his name. After we got Mad Dog's photos and fingerprints, I locked him into the Gray Bar Hotel.

"Dennis, I really hope you do go out west, if you survive the jail time," I said. "You take your act out to Wyoming, and some sheriff's officer is going to put a rifled deer slug right between your eyes. He will get a huge medal for it. Your act won't play so well out there."

Mad Dog pleaded out the charges and accepted 10 years in the Trenton State Prison, New Jersey's only maximum security facility and a real shithole. Dennis Downey failed every parole hearing he had and wound up doing every day of his dime sentence, with not one day off for good behavior. I guess that shouldn't have come as a surprise.

CHAPTER THIRTY-TWO

A CLASSIC HOT CALL

The dispatcher's voice telegraphed urgency and danger. She directed me to a bungalow in a gritty, blue-collar area of Port Monmouth, where a 25-year-old steroid user had taken an unknown quantity of LSD and was completely out of control and howling like a wolfman. The guy's 19-year-old girlfriend—the one who placed the call—was screaming for her life.

I flicked on lights and siren in the patrol car and jabbed the throttle hard. It was just after 2 a.m. one summer night in 1998, and the location was only a few minutes away from me. Other cars were also being dispatched, but I was the closest responding officer.

This was a classic hot call. On the way there, I went through different scenarios of how the incident could go down, and my adrenaline was pumping. I didn't want to hurt this guy, but I had no problem taking him down if his girlfriend was in imminent danger. My gut told me this was going to turn into a cage fight—my strength and Brazilian Jiu Jitsu skills against this Muscle Juice maniac high on LSD.

No matter how skilled one gets in handling confrontations, one thing is certain: anything can happen, and often does. If God stays out of it, the better fighter will usually win. In this case, there would be no referee to stop the fight. Wolfman could easily be armed with a butcher knife or worse, anything the mind snakes of LSD may prompt. This was going to be either a decided victory for me or a real disaster.

Lights were on inside the house, and I heard howling as soon as I pulled up. I hopped out and saw Dieckmann's car screeching to a halt. The shrill sound of sirens told me that a couple of other marked units were closing on our location fast.

The shouting and howls got louder when we pounded on the door. The house looked really small, and I realized that the space inside would likely be tight and cluttered. The chances of someone getting hurt would be high if three or four of us walked in together. I asked Dieckmann for permission to try to take the guy down by myself—one on one—and he agreed.

I threw the bungalow's front door open and stepped into a 12-by-12-foot room serving as living room, dining room and kitchen combined. The young brunette who had called the Middletown Police Department was crouched in a corner of the room, crying hysterically, shaking, her arms over her head. Wolfman, a big, muscle-bound guy, stood in the middle of the room, wearing only a pair of gym shorts. He was sleeved up, with tattoos on both arms.

"Hey buddy, what's going on here? Your girlfriend is freakin' out," I said. "How about if you and me talk this one out."

Wolfman squared off in front of me and started howling again, louder than before. His girlfriend shrieked and crouched tighter into a fetal position in the corner. I shifted my stance, and he squared up to me again so that we stood parallel to each other. Every time I moved, he squared up and kept an eye on me. The seconds were ticking by, and I knew he was going to attack if I didn't make a move—and now.

Wolfman started throwing his arms up in the air and stomping his feet on the floor.

I maneuvered around just a bit so that my opponent was standing in front of a low wooden coffee table. A quick shove was all it took to make him tumble backward over it. When Wolfman fell, he landed on his back. He immediately rolled over so that he could get back to his feet—and that gave me the opportunity I was waiting for. As soon as he was on his knees, I dropped my full weight onto him, forcing him to fall face-first to the floor.

I immediately brought my right shin across his lower back and leaned all of my weight onto this controlling knee. I then drove my left arm through his right shoulder/armpit area. Now my left arm was through, and I brought it toward my right arm. My right fist was gripping Wolf's right wrist. I used a thumbless grip, with my left hand grabbing my right wrist.

Next, I switched knees and placed my left shin across the back of his neck and straightened my right leg, putting all my body weight on the back of his neck. I then slowly began pulling his right wrist toward his spine and upward.

Wolfman's entire body went stiff as a plank; his shoulder was a fraction of a movement away from being ripped from its socket. I was in control, and I could have easily crippled him for life with a hard pull inward and upward—but I held my position. His eyes were bulging but he was in too much distress to yell or howl.

"Yo, Sarge! Get in here," I yelled.

Dieckmann and the guys were in the door before the words left my mouth. I kept the pressure on while they shackled Wolfman's arms and legs.

Wolfman was arrested for disorderly conduct, a misdemeanor. I could also have charged him with assault for his menacing behavior—but I decided to give him a break. We transported him to Riverview Hospital, where he was given a drug to negate the effects of the LSD. He sustained no injuries from the takedown and was served with a summons at the hospital and released.

The next day, the Wolfman and his girlfriend walked into the Middletown Police Department to thank us for the way he'd been taken down, without a beating and without weapons.

I had a choice that night, and I could easily have gone into that bungalow with a side-handled baton, a PR-24, and beaten the shit out of the guy. That's what some of the guys on the force may have felt compelled to do. But that wasn't my style. My days of hurting people for no reason were over.

"Car 41, Car 43, Car 47, Car 48, Car 49, respond to a report of a fire at King's Row assisted living, 1800 Route 35," the male dispatcher said in a no-nonsense manner that telegraphed urgency.

Detective Mike Rubino and I, who'd been out working as part of the street crime unit, were just a couple of minutes away in an unmarked unit. We hit lights and siren and headed toward the complex, which was home to dozens of elderly residents, some of them infirm. The dispatcher had just sent five of Middletown's seven sector cars to the fire scene, leaving just two available for patrols. It was rare for that many cars to be sent to one location.

Rubino and I were the first officers who pulled up in front of the sprawling two-story complex on the south side of Route 35. We saw smoke rising from the rear of the facility. There were some people milling about out front, and we ran to the entrance closest to where we'd seen the smoke. A maintenance worker directed us to the residential corridors, and we started working the doors.

Some doors were open. But in other cases, residents had locked themselves inside and we had to kick in doors to get them. The doors were strong and resisted. I was able to get through them by using kicks I'd learned doing martial arts. But even then, it was tough work and took rigorous effort.

My partner and others wrapped wet towels around their faces so they didn't take so much smoke into their lungs. But I couldn't keep the towel in place and work the doors, so I just continued without a towel. I was able to get a couple dozen residents out before needing a break.

I headed for the front lobby, where some firemen and EMTs had gathered. As I walked there, I grew light-headed, and my legs felt like rubber. The EMTs grabbed me, gave me oxygen and placed me on a gurney for a ride to the hospital. I spent two nights there, recovering from smoke inhalation. Later, I was given a proclamation from the New Jersey State Legislature for heroism.

The impact of the Columbine school massacre in April 1999 was felt across the U.S., including the two high schools in Middletown, where bomb threats were starting to occur—much to my dismay and that of school administrators and parents. Every couple of days, someone would call in a bomb threat, and the high school would be closed down for the rest of the day as a precaution. The students may have thought it was funny the first couple of times, but everyone else was getting increasingly frustrated. It had gotten so bad that the principals had my personal cell phone number, and we were meeting on a regular basis.

One sunny morning in May, the principal called and said that he'd received another bomb threat, this one written on the wall in the boys' room. It read, "There is a bomb hidden near the cafeteria. It will go off at 11:00 a.m. You have been warned."

"Are you worried about this?" I asked the principal. "Do you believe it, even a little bit?"

"No. I think it's pure crap," he said. "But what if I'm wrong? Can't we bring in a bomb dog?"

"The reality is that the County Sheriff's Department has about three of them, for the entire county," I said. "To really do a credible check would take about three days, covering the entire place. But . . . I have a dog."

"What, like a dachshund?" The principal chuckled.

"No. An Akita. He's real scary-looking, but he wouldn't harm a soul," I said, thinking out loud and hoping my somewhat harebrained plan wouldn't get me in serious trouble. The one thing I was sure of was that my new Akita, Mujo, had the perfect temperament for this job.

On protective detail for President George Bush Sr. during a campaign run in 1992. The propane tanks in the background were an obvious danger— and gave me grave concern about POTUS's safety.

He was huge and looked ferocious—but the worst he was going to do was slobber on someone. "If we keep this between you and me, I'll walk him in, scare the crap out of everyone, walk him right back out. I don't tell my people, you don't tell yours. This bomb scare stuff is getting old, fast."

"Okay, every kid in this place knows when you show up—the grapevine in school is real fast. Let's go for it," the principal said.

I went home, changed into black jeans and a shirt, put the leash on Mujo and asked him if he wanted to go for a ride in the car. He bounded into the back seat of my unmarked unit and promptly stuck his big head out the window. When I got to the school, I cruised slowly in front of the place, still with Mujo staring out the back window. I parked, hauled Mujo out of the car and headed inside the high school. It was about a

50-yard walk to the administration office, but the bell had just rung and the hallways were packed with kids trying to make their way to their next class. The oversized black dog sauntered down the hallway as students flattened themselves against the lockers to the left and right. Mujo seemed interested in sniffing out a treat or two from the students.

"Nice doggie," one girl said as she extended her hand to Mujo.

"Freeze," I said. "This is a bomb dog; he will rip off your hand."

The girl's face went white with fear, and she flattened herself against the lockers with some of the other kids.

One of the older female staffers seemed ecstatic as I walked into the administration office with Mujo. "Praise the Lord for a miracle. I have been so worried. That door over there has been open, and it's not supposed to be. I am so worried the bomb is in there," the woman said.

"Not to worry, ma'am, my trained bomb dog will clear the area." Mujo all but pulled me into the oversized closet, used to store brooms, cleaning supplies and a three-foot-tall stuffed lion—the school's mascot. Suddenly Mujo had something to play with—and destroy. I yanked the stuffed animal from his mouth as he sat there, tail wagging.

"Thanks be to the Lord, we are safe," the staffer said as we continued to check out the administration area with my "bomb dog."

"As I said, ma'am, not to worry."

We headed out of the office and back down the hallway. A 16-year-old girl walked up to Mujo, carrying a backpack in her hands. Mujo immediately tugged at his leash and headed toward the girl, sticking his nose in her bag—and no doubt smelling her lunch.

I theatrically yanked the knapsack away from Mujo and his new-found friend. "Are there any explosive materials in this?" I asked.

"No, please, no," she said trembling.

"The bomb dog was hitting on something, young lady. Were there any fireworks in there recently?"

"Oh my god, no. Please, my boyfriend, he didn't mean to do anything. I was just carrying them," the girl said, now on the verge of tears.

"No problem, young lady, just give it a nice cleaning and be more careful in the future."

I noticed the principal standing nearby, and giving me the sign to bring this visit to an end. I took the hint and announced that I would walk the dog down the main corridor as a safety check.

I walked Mujo down the hallway while classes were in session. He was clearly enjoying himself and had no interest in leaving. I, on the other hand, was anxious to wrap up the visit and get the hell out unscathed. We exited a few minutes later, and I walked Mujo back to the car. I could feel hundreds of eyes on us from inside the classroom.

I brought Mujo back home, gave him a treat, changed back to my original attire and went back to my normal activities. For the rest of the school year, until the third week of June, when school ended, not one bomb threat was issued from that high school. Mujo was batting a thousand for bomb searches. He retired that day from his bomb dog life, secure in the knowledge that he had done some good.

A few days later, I casually mentioned to my supervisor, Lieutenant Rubino, that I'd used Mujo to help bring the bomb threats under control. "Oh, I almost forgot to tell you," I said before describing what happened.

"Are you fucking nuts?" he asked before shaking his head and walking away. He'd already heard more than he wanted to know.

CHAPTER THIRTY-THREE

TOO LATE

"Hey, Chuck, the phone's for you," one of the guys in headquarters shouted. It was the principal of the Middletown High School, and he was calling to tell me about a sexual predator.

A 15-year-old had walked into the principal's office earlier that day to say that Guy Marganti, the father of one of her classmates, had sexually abused her during a booze-filled party in his house the previous evening. The principal said he had no reason to question the girl's story and that he wanted it investigated.

Later that day, I met with the teen and her mom to take the girl's sworn statement. She tearfully described how she and a bunch of her friends often went to the house because Mr. Marganti would give them booze and let them party in his finished basement without complaints. Some of them had even started to bring their own liquid refreshments with them. She explained that Marganti, who had a teenage daughter himself, would often hang out with the kids in the basement, and that he knew all of the girls on a first-name basis. They ranged in age from 13 to 17.

Apparently the parties had been going on for quite some time. The teens liked having what they thought was a "safe" place to hang out and drink, and they'd kept quiet about it. Mrs. Marganti, who was apparently addicted to some kind of painkiller, generally hung out upstairs in the kitchen and didn't care about the parties that were going on literally beneath her feet.

I wasn't all that surprised to hear about the scene; I'd noticed a drop in juvenile alcohol offenses in that part of town, around Port Monmouth, and had been wondering what was going on.

Over the next few days, I tracked down numerous other teens who'd been seen at the Marganti parties and took statements from each of them. A bunch of the girls made a point of telling me that I should talk to a 15-year-old named Michelle Dooley. They said that she seemed to have an especially close relationship with the 40-year-old, five-foot-eight Marganti.

Dooley came into police headquarters one morning, accompanied by her mother, who wore fancy clothes and drove a fancy car—but stank of booze and seemed pissed off to be anywhere near cops. I wasn't surprised; I knew this family from its previous run-ins with the law. Michelle Dooley's brothers were known thieves, and her father seemed perfectly okay with fencing anything that his two boys brought home. The father hated police in general—and me in particular, because I'd arrested the boys in the past.

With tears and nervous glances at her mother, Michelle eventually admitted to me that Marganti had been wining and dining her for months; that he'd taken her to New York on more than one occasion and even bought her a diamond ring; and that they were lovers. She seemed reluctant to give up any incriminating information about her "boyfriend," who was some 25 years her senior.

Michelle Dooley was a pretty, post-pubescent teen who had the maturity of a 12-year-old. She was different from the rest of her family—naïve in a way and still a little girl at heart. I really liked her a lot, and it broke my heart to hear what she'd gone through. Rarely have I been so motivated to bring down a criminal. Maybe Marganti gave her the love and respect that she couldn't find at home. I could only guess at what prompted her to give in to his advances. I wasn't a psychologist or social worker, and it didn't really make a difference in the end. My role was to pursue the sexual predator who had preyed on this young girl and try to bring him to justice.

All the statements that I'd gathered in the case, including the one from Michelle, painted a picture of a middle-aged sexual preda-tor who took advantage of the fact that he had a teenage daughter to attract other teens to his house. The finished basement had a separate entrance so that the teens could come and go as they pleased. There were wood-paneled walls, a large refrigerator and several couches where they would hang out.

At one point in the investigation, Michelle's dad called me and tried to start ordering me around, admonishing me to get all the paperwork done properly in the case. His attitude, and the fact that he'd somehow missed the fact that his teen daughter was having a months-long affair with someone his age, infuriated me—and I told him as much. It was the last time I heard from the guy.

One of the parents I interviewed described to me how she'd seen Marganti and the Dooley teen making out on a beach in Port Monmouth one night. The woman made it clear that she didn't want to "get involved" and most certainly didn't want to testify in any courtroom.

Girls were coming out of the woodwork to accuse Marganti. But those cases only involved improper sexual touching—nothing that would have put the guy behind bars for any length of time. I wanted him to do some heavy time in a state prison for what he'd done to the Dooley kid. But a social worker on the case had already warned me that the girl was going to be a reluctant, and ultimately awful, witness on the stand.

The Monmouth County Prosecutor's Office agreed to take the case but cautioned me going in that it would be a hard one to get a convic-tion on because there was no physical evidence and everything hinged on Michelle Dooley's testimony.

The case went to trial the following year. Marganti had hired an expensive and highly skilled defense attorney whom I knew. I testified at length for the prosecution. In a stunning twist, the defense opted not to cross-examine me, and I was dismissed from the courtroom. I was shocked that he let me go and wondered why. The only thing I could guess was that he was worried about additional damage to his defense if he kept me on the stand for even a minute. I'd never seen that happen before in my entire career. Michelle Dooley's testimony, which had been shaky going in, fell apart on the stand, and the jury delivered a not-guilty verdict. Marganti went back to living his life as if nothing ever happened.

Another year passed. I got a call from one of my buddies in the department with some devastating news: Michelle Dooley was dead. The teen had gotten her hands on a gun and used it to shoot herself in the head. That poor, vulnerable girl was gone.

Michelle couldn't handle explaining her conduct in a public forum. It broke her.

What cuts me so deep is this: she didn't see her own beauty, her own niceness. And she had it. She was a nice, young girl. She didn't hurt people, she didn't act cruelly. She got used for base reasons. She was a throwaway, until the day she took a handgun and shot herself in the head. Women rarely use a gun to end it. Pills or razored wrists, that's the female way. Men take a shooting iron and blast a bullet to their heads.

How tortured inside was Michelle? Many believe that there is justice in the hereafter, that the scales are evened. They had better be. If this teenage girl isn't set free of torment when she is in the hereafter, then this entire world is a meaningless playground for too many people worth less than shit.

What is it like to be a cop, a detective, a patrolman?

You are in a profession where ever admitting to being wrong, even when you commit the most human of mistakes, can cause you to be publicly placed in stocks. If you are involved in any sort of contro-versy, expect to be Monday-morning quarterbacked in a uniquely nasty fashion.

Cops are the lowest part of the criminal justice system. They must face the inequities of society as a sort of whipping post. If your life is turning to shit, and you have run out of elements to lay into, they are your last stop. People speak to cops and make demands of them that these same people would find unspeakable if they later saw the vid-eotape. Wearing the badge, I have been spat on, slapped, called every disgusting adjective known to man—all for the high crime of being sent there to help.

At times, the badge was the only thing that held me back from administering my own type of justice, using the skills that I'd honed with the Pagans. I arrested one guy for taking his eight-year-old son's arm and holding it over an open flame on the stove as a way of disciplin-ing the child. He held his son's arm there until the roasted meat started to melt onto the stove top. Hours later, that same man asked me what I could do about getting him a reduced bail. I wanted to turn his face into hamburger. But I didn't.

The badge stopped me from crushing the face of a gentleman who told me that he fucked his 12-year-old daughter because she "was asking for it." The badge stopped me from slapping the face of a motorist who smoked a red light simply because he drove an expensive Mercedes-Benz and felt he was entitled.

I have worked with too many cops to lie about the nobility of it. It is noble only if you make it so. The job is a unique method of making a difference in the world every day, in real time, no bullshit.

But I hate the cliché of "making a difference." I despise the touchy-feely, politically correct jargon of this disappointingly non-enlightened age. All too often, cops conform to the images they are molded into by mass media. But if you are a mid-level business professional, a sanitation worker, a small-business owner or a supermarket cashier, you can easily be as noble as any of the "brave police officers" called to the profession.

Follow the words from the *Hagakure*: make compassion, courage and wisdom your everyday goal. Weep at nature's beauty and cut down those who spit on justice. And, like the Toltec warrior, understand that the Creator really did give us two choices, strength or misery, and choose strength. I do not follow these precepts as I should. I am often too weak, but I will never end my trying. It remains the only task worthy of my manhood.

CHAPTER THIRTY-FOUR

WORKING THE PILE
AT GROUND ZERO

The gray dust that covered lower Manhattan when the Twin Towers fell still sits deep within my lungs—just as it does in the lungs of the thousands of other volunteers who raced to the site that day. None of us got too hung up about safe breathing apparatuses. We just wanted to help.

I was hanging out in the Middletown Police Department's detective bureau, complaining about how the New York Giants had let themselves get hammered by the Denver Broncos on *Monday Night Football*, when the first TV broadcast hit about a plane striking one of the towers. When the second plane hit, the NFL, like so many other things, became as trivial as old dreams.

Detective Jerry Wiemer and I hopped in a car and raced to Mount Mitchell, a scenic promontory in Atlantic Highlands with clear views of lower Manhattan. We watched the towers fall from there. It seemed as if all of Manhattan was covered with a grayish-brown smoke. We stood in stunned silence, unable to comprehend the disaster that was taking place miles away. Jerry and I both knew that countless residents from Middletown and nearby areas worked in the Twin Towers and the Financial District, commuting daily by train or via the ferry that ran from the Atlantic Highlands Marina to either Jersey City or Hoboken. The ferry terminal was only two miles from our hilltop location.

On the ferry on September 11, 2001, heading to lower Manhattan.

Back at headquarters, all of the detectives were ordered to change from street clothes into uniforms and await orders. The department's leadership had no idea how we would be used that day, but one thing was clear: we'd be needed.

The Federal Bureau of Investigation had information—which ultimately proved false—that some of the ferries used to transport commuters to the Wall Street area were going to be targeted by passengers with bombs. I volunteered, along with Jerry, Mike Rubino, Cliff O'Hara and a few other guys, to go to New York and help secure the ferry lines. We were given the green light, and we headed out to the ferry terminal at the marina.

Shell-shocked commuters were fleeing New York in droves, and the ferries coming into Atlantic Highlands were packed. We checked on the ferry passengers for a while and then started hearing that police volunteers were needed for the work at Ground Zero. Early information was spotty at best, and rumors and facts were blended. The best information seemed to be coming from the workers themselves, while senior leaders back at Middletown Police headquarters were relying on other sources that appeared way off the mark.

Around 4 p.m. on Tuesday, September 11, we headed back into New York along with members of the department's Special Weapons Assault Team to render any assistance that we could. There was a Catholic priest on the ferry who was going over to help. "Father, what should we do to the people who did this to us?" I asked.

"Nuclear war. Exterminate them," he said. "They are burning and killing innocent civilians. They . . ." He couldn't continue.

Lower Manhattan was a frightening chiaroscuro of twisted metal, in places where it couldn't be, yet was. Smokey and desolate, with bits of paper flying everywhere and tossed about in the acrid smoke. The ash was several inches deep, and we were covered with gray soot that invaded our being.

We stopped at a fire station to use the bathroom and found a small group of firefighters with a thousand-yard stare in their eyes; they were the only survivors from their house.

Ground Zero, lit with klieg lights powered by generators, was a thick pall of smoke and ruin. We assembled at nearby Stuyvesant High School to prepare to work in rescue teams. Cops and other people who had already been working on the pile filtered in, soot-covered and exhausted. Nothing seemed to work. Even the toilets were backed up. The air became fetid.

Our small volunteer group separated from the SWAT team. Rather than sit and wait for some organizer to put us to work, we headed off to Ground Zero, intent on doing what we could. There, a New York City Police Department supervisor thanked us heartily for our efforts but said that we should stand down until daylight. "We have to assess how to even proceed with the start of a rescue," he told us. "It's too risky in the dark.

"Our guys are exhausted," he continued. "Please come back. I'll get you a ride to Jersey City. I'm told there's one train on your line that's still running. You can get out while it's still possible tonight."

Seven of us hopped onto the back of an NYPD pickup truck and sat in the cargo area, atop jerry jugs full of gasoline used to keep the generators going. The sergeant jumped in and drove us through the eerily empty Holland Tunnel. We were literally the only vehicle going through the tunnel in either direction. He dropped us off near the train terminal in Jersey City, waved goodbye and headed back to Ground Zero.

We had an hour to kill before the train left and decided to look for a bar; all of us were in dire need of a beer or two. Though we had our uniforms on, technically we were off duty. We noticed a couple of young guys with long hair who were clearly pipe heads—drug users. Normally, the guys would have deliberately steered clear of us. But this was 9/11, and everything was different. One of them walked over to us.

"Just back from the towers?" the guy asked.

"Yeah. Any place to get a beer around here?" Rubino said.

"Yeah, man, one place open that will be cool for you. I'll walk you there." The man took us to an upscale pub in a newly gentrified section of Jersey City.

"Hey guys, thanks," he said. "You know. For going over there to help."

For that moment, the guy wasn't a pipe head, he was one of us, an American. The whole nation seemed to come together that day. I wonder if that's what it felt like for Americans the day Japan bombed Pearl Harbor.

When the seven of us walked into the bar, we got a standing ovation from a room full of complete strangers. We hadn't said anything, but they immediately knew where we'd been from the gray dust that so thoroughly caked our uniforms. People started buying us drinks, far more than we could consume. Women kissed us, men shook our hands and many said, "God bless you." The owner gave us a case of beer and refused to even consider taking money.

Me with Detective Barry Grimm and Detective Lieutenant Michael Rubino in the Holland Tunnel on September 11, 2001. The tunnel was completely empty and eerily silent as we headed back to New Jersey.

A short while later, we headed back to the train station and boarded the one headed for Middletown. Somehow, the conductor arranged for us to have our own car. I got home about 4:30 a.m. and was back to work with the rest of the guys at 8 a.m.

The mood was somber in headquarters that day. The chief was manic and determined to micromanage everything that we did. Our task that day was to check all the ferry and train stations for anything that looked out of the ordinary. Nothing was running to New York City, and any car left overnight in one of the parking lots likely belonged to someone who'd died in the World Trade Center. We took down the plate numbers and passed the information along to a group back at headquarters that was working on victim identification and notification of families. Middletown was the hardest-hit single community in the country in terms of deaths on 9/11. The brokerage house Cantor Fitzgerald, with offices in the World Trade Center, had a number of employees who lived in Middletown; some died, and others survived. We were tasked with notifying the survivors' families that they had been located.

It was a very strange aura that hung over the land anywhere in the tri-state area. Crime had come to a standstill. People appeared to be moving at a much slower pace, and it seemed many were reaching deep within to try to cope.

Amid the devastation, the words of the stoic philosopher Epictetus on our mortality comforted my soul:

> What God/Zeus would say to Epictetus if he but could. My son and servant whom I love, I wish I could provide for you a body that would not so easily be shattered. But mortals possess bodies like clay vessels, and easily broken. I would love to give to you, Epictetus, a home never destroyed by the storms. But alas I cannot. But I can give you something much better, a treasure, a piece of the Gods. The faculty of using the appearances of things, the faculty of desire and aversion. If you take care of this faculty and consider it your only possession, you will never be hindered, never meet any impediments, you will not lament, you will not blame, you will not flatter any person.

Rubino was in contact with relief workers actually moving debris on the pile. He told me the guys were exhausted and happy to have cops from anywhere relieve them. The chief, meanwhile, was towing the bureaucratic line that the relief effort was going smoothly, and that only those who were trained for rescue efforts should be there. Having seen the actual site, I was stunned. How many people could there be who are trained to deal with mass-casualty disasters in which skyscrapers are brought down by jet aircraft?

My experience, as well as Cliff O'Hara's, suggested that no one really

*A view of the lower façade of the World Trade Center
with first responders on September 11th.*

Building 7 comes down right in front of me.

knew how to proceed, and they were winging it using ingenuity, guts and lots of manpower. So, on September 13, Mike Rubino, Cliff O'Hara, Jerry Weimer, Steve Dollinger and I, along with several other men, took personal days and headed back to Ground Zero—despite opposition from the chief, who feared that someone could get hurt and trigger a worker's compensation claim. I couldn't fathom the chief's position and thought I was in some kind of twilight zone. We left police headquarters under the glare of doom from higher-ups.

The Middletown Police Department routinely worked with the team from the nearby coast guard station in Sandy Hook, so our group arranged to hitch a ride on a cutter from Sandy Hook to lower Manhattan. Normally, the waters south of Manhattan would have been a busy hub of activity. But that day, there was nothing moving on the water. There were no recreational boats, no ship traffic and no commercial or private planes overhead. We were on the only boat moving through the area. An occasional air force fighter would fly by high overhead, as well as a few helicopter gunships.

We went straight to Ground Zero and regrouped near a fire engine parked outside a tall building. Some of the other volunteers were trying to figure out the best route onto the rubble pile. One of our guys, Larry Hall, grabbed a seat on a folding metal chair; seats were at a premium.

Suddenly, a chorus of panicked screams came from the nearby building.

"Run, run! It's coming down!"

Hundreds upon hundreds of rescue workers—and anyone else nearby—started running for their lives. Pieces of debris began falling around us, and we all thought we were going to get buried alive or crushed. Hall tripped as he was getting up from the chair. He fell forward, landing face down, and suddenly had shoe and boot marks on his back as people ran over him.

I grabbed the guy under his left arm and hauled him to his feet, just as others smashed me to the ground. I went down hard on my surgically repaired right knee. Afraid of being trampled—or potentially getting killed by a falling building—I stood and began to run with the group of panicked humanity. The pain in my knee caused me to view the world through multicolored dots. The people who trampled others were not cowards or uncaring persons. Hell, they'd volunteered to be there, just like us. What took place was primal, a fear of being buried alive or crushed like an insect.

To this day, I'm not quite sure what happened. I believe that the American Express building suffered some kind of internal structural collapse but remained standing. Some debris cascaded down, and it truly was a close call. We never could have outrun the carnage had that building actually collapsed; we were way too close.

After catching my breath, I realized my knee was stiffening and giving me some real pain. I went to an aid station nearby, and they wanted to take me to a hospital. I refused, saying I wanted to go back on the line, and they relented when I walked away showing more confidence in my knee than I felt inside.

I worked for hours as part of a bucket brigade, removing debris piece by piece from the pile. No one knew if we were standing on something firm or something that would give way under our weight. Somehow, none of us seemed to care about our own safety. It was all about clearing the pile of debris and trying to get to any survivors, or victims, who might be buried there. At one point, I stared down through an opening in the debris and could see the remains of a parking garage far below me. I kept working.

I was there when members of the city's sanitation department raised a symbolic American flag on the site.

The sights, sounds and smells will stay with me forever. It was at once a terribly sad day and yet an awesome one, too, as strangers got together and did what they could. I watched as well-coiffed women in expensive clothes lugged drinking water from trucks to the pile for the thirsty, dust-caked volunteers. No one yelled, no one barked orders.

I worked the bucket brigade until my knee became so sore I was a liability. I then secured the gear for the rest of our group and guarded the perimeter as heavy construction equipment, including backhoes and cranes, was brought in.

At one point, soldiers turned over two Middle Eastern males to me. They looked every bit like jihadists, had no ID and claimed they were Armenians. But they were unable to explain why they needed to be so close to the rubble pile. I turned them over to a very tough-looking and decisive sergeant from the NYPD. I never learned what became of those two men, but I am pretty confident that they cooperated with the cop.

A white stretch limousine slowly made its way through the rubble and heavy machinery, looking very out of place. It had no front license plate but carried a special plate bearing the New York Yankees logo—the one in red, white and blue, with the baseball, bat and top hat. When it got closer, I walked over, stopped the vehicle and asked the driver what he was doing at Ground Zero.

The driver popped out and said, "Mr. Steinbrenner wanted to get coffee to the workers. Can you help me?"

The entire vehicle was loaded with tray upon tray of Styrofoam cups, all filled with hot coffee. There must have been hundreds filling the interior and the trunk of the 10-passenger stretch. I hobbled over and started helping the driver unload his cargo. Other volunteers came over and pitched in, too.

CHAPTER THIRTY-FIVE

THE GREAT JAKE SLATER

I pulled into the lot for the Middletown Police Department right around 7:30 a.m., parked my Nissan Altima in one of the spots up by the communications tower and walked down to the sprawling one-story brick headquarters that had been my home base as a cop for the past 20 years. The year was 2003, and it was my last year on the force. I took an exterior stairwell down to a steel basement door reserved for police personnel and headed for the locker room.

Donning my uniform and gear, I headed for a large conference room where one of the sergeants would do the daily briefing before we started our shift at 8 a.m. The meeting was attended by all the officers who would be out on the shift, along with dispatchers, plainclothes detectives and other support personnel. The noise associated with the shift change triggered some shouting from the prisoners in the nearby cell block. All of us were inured to this and generally paid no attention to it. This time, though, one of the voices seemed strangely familiar to me.

"That your boy in there?" Lieutenant Cortland Best, a 30-year veteran of the force, asked.

I didn't recognize the prisoner's bellowing bass voice at first. Then it hit me. The voice belonged to one of the most feared motorcycle outlaws alive, the ferocious and feared former leader of the Sandy Hook chapter of the Pagans Motorcycle Club, Jake Slater.

The lieutenant knew me well—and he was also aware of my history with Slater. I often referred to my superior as "Lou," short for lieutenant.

"Lou, are you telling me that's Slater?" I asked.

Best nodded. "He's being held on a warrant. He isn't very happy about it at all."

"Mind if I have a word?"

"Go ahead," he said.

I nodded at the two uniformed officers guarding the prisoners and headed back to Slater's cell. Like all the other cells, the one Jake was in was equipped with one wooden bench, a cheap blanket and a utilitarian toilet. Its cement-block walls were painted in an institutional yellow.

Slater looked a little older but otherwise just as I'd remembered him. Standing six foot two, with a massive, muscular upper body, he was still a hard-core tough guy. He exuded menace and had a predatory air. He was wearing the same sort of clothes that I remembered: jeans, a sleeveless undershirt and black engineer boots. He had shaved his head and sported a graying Fu Manchu beard with the chin whiskers grown long.

"Remember me?"

"Yeah," he said, leaning on the gray steel bars, a look of doom on his face.

"You want a bottle of spring water, rather than that toilet shit?"

"Yeah. Thanks."

"I'll bring you some," I said casually. "You know, guys like us got to slow down. Getting old. Let the young guys do the heavy lifting."

"You're right, but make sure you watch your back. Some people who you think are your friends, aren't. You can't let them fuck with you."

I nodded and said, "Don't go anywhere. I'll be back with your water."

When I returned, Slater and I talked briefly about some of the guys we'd known and ridden with, and I noticed that his mind wasn't as sharp as his body. Soon I headed back to the briefing.

As the sergeant gave us the rundown—a private detective working a case in town, a car crash at a major intersection, a couple of breaking-and-entering cases and the chief wanting the cars washed—I thought about Jake and my time in the Pagans.

In a way, looking at him was like looking into some crystal ball and seeing what I would have been had I continued to ride with Slater and the Pagans rather than becoming the first man in the U.S. to leave an outlaw motorcycle gang and become a decorated police officer. It was a place I most clearly didn't want to be.

But for the grace of God, it could have been me incarcerated that humid summer day in the Gray Bar Hotel. To be sure, Slater was anything but pathetic; he was still practiced in the art of intimidation. But upon closer inspection, you could sense he was close to rot. The world had passed him by. He was going to have to make a lot of noise to get the attention that had come his way so easily before. Rap gangsters and tattooed white kids with sideways ball caps and pipe-cleaner arms were the "in" bad boys.

I thought back to some of the great Hollywood westerns, like *The Wild Bunch*, the 1969 classic about an aging outlaw gang on the Texas-Mexico border, and about Patrick Floyd "Pat" Garrett, the American lawman, bartender and customs agent who became famous around the turn of the century for killing Billy the Kid. How did aging outlaws deal with getting old and not being very special anymore?

The warrior/sage Tecumseh said, "The hardest thing about growing old is that people don't fear you anymore."

And I no longer feared the great Jake Slater.

EPILOGUE

The warm tropical sun beats down most days in my new home in southwest Florida. When I married Barbara in 2008, I went from single with no children to having a large family, with three grown kids and a slew of grandkids—which is a blast. The number of grandchildren just went up to seven. And I have never even changed a diaper. Renzo Gracie still teases me on that score. Hell, I have never even said no to any grandchild over the age of 10. They must wonder who this far-out old man really is. I hesitate to say read the book. My father, Bud, passed away in 2010, and my mom, Pearl, is in an assisted-living facility in New Jersey. My brother, Mike, is married and still living in New Jersey.

I was recently interviewed by a reporter for the local Fox affiliate here in Florida about the biker massacre in Waco, Texas. She observed during a break that I must have had countless incidents in which I should have wound up dead during my days in the army, biker clubs and undercover narcotics. I realized that a day hasn't gone by during which some situation or another doesn't remind me of how very fortunate I am.

I'm reminded of one of the iconic films of my generation, *Apocalypse Now*. One of the many memorable scenes is the "Charlie don't surf" segment, in which Lieutenant Colonel Kilgore (Robert Duvall) tells one of his soldiers, "What do you know about surfing, Major? You're from goddamn New Jersey."

Discussing women's defensive tactics with the hosts of Fox4 Rising *in Cape Coral, Florida, around 2009. I was a regular on the show for three and a half years.*

The end of that scene hits home for me. Kilgore kneels in the sand on the beach and speaks lovingly of napalm. Then Captain Willard, played by Martin Sheen, narrates: "He [Kilgore] was one of those guys that had a weird light around him. You just knew he wasn't gonna get so much as a scratch here."

When I was traveling toward Ground Zero soon after September 11, 2001, that phrase about coming back without a scratch drifted through my mind and rattled my senses. Detective Jeffrey Barner and I were discussing the risk factors at the devastated site. Suddenly Barner's face went blank for a second.

"That's you, man," he said, referencing the scene in *Apocalypse Now.* "Oh yes, man, that's you. You have that weird light, I've felt it for a long time."

I had no reply. But two days later, when debris was raining down on my head during that partial building collapse at Ground Zero, and I was

Me and my wife, Barbara, during a Mexican vacation in 2006.

running for my life, the thought soothed my mind.

Oddly, retiring to South Florida has not ended the close calls for me. I still find myself in some strange and dangerous situations under the semi-tropical sun. But there's some space between the incidents here and my dangerous past that I'm thankful for. One night, Barbara and I experienced—and then put down—an attempted home invasion at gunpoint. Another time, some gangbangers tried to box in my vehicle in an attempted carjacking on a desolate roadway. That was quickly solved by my constant companions, Mr. Smith and Mr. Wesson. My grown stepson, Bernard, was there with me that day; it was one that he likely won't soon forget.

At another point, I was involved in an alleged kidnapping involving a Russian Muay Thai fighter wanted for crimes in Central Europe and a famous retired member of the New York Yankees—anyone who has followed the team over the last 20 years would be well aware of him. We did not part as friends from our benighted meeting. Too bad; I dig the Yankees. If he reads this: hint—dark sunglasses and backward baseball cap isn't as threatening as you may think.

Like William Holden in *Network* (my favorite movie), I designed to write my memoir and do what one does in the autumn of one's years. Or, as Charmian is told in Robert Stone's *Dog Soldiers*, "I desire to serve God . . . And to grow rich, like all men." I know that I am being dragged into this digital age, no happier about it than a Luddite. Anachronistic to the end, I roar like a lion in defiance at the winds of change, and they ignore me universally. But I will continue to roar until the next phase takes me.

Jerry Garcia nailed it: "What a long strange trip it's been."

ACKNOWLEDGMENTS

As you read through *Jersey Tough*, you may have noticed that there are very few pictures of my Pagan times. Simply put, using a camera would likely have gotten me killed. Some members were wanted felons or on parole and forbidden from associating with other Pagans. Pagan hierarchy considered pictures with a person wearing colors to be club property.

When you attempt to write your first book as you are nearing sixty years of age, it is reasonable to expect a great deal of polite smiles and a good many condescending glances. I got a few of those, but mostly people were very supportive:

My wife Barbara's support was, at times, heroic due to my ongoing scorched earth war with all things computer. The battle lines are drawn, and I am losing; but the war drums always beat.

Renzo Gracie, to whom I owe *Giri* (a debt so steep it is all but unpayable); the gift of your love and friendship has deeply enriched my life.

If there was no Mike DeGiglio, there would be no book. I owe you *Giri* also, my brother.

Charles Varrone, the undisputed heavyweight champion of life and *mero mero* of KB Security Consultants Inc. A book about you would unleash a thousand ships.

My brother, Michael, and his wife, Elaine, both of unflinching belief in this project.

Toni Cariero, who had to hear about this project in triplicate. A sage for our times.

Jonathan Cariero, the first proofreader. I think he still likes me even after removing a layer of the onion.

The four doctors who against all odds keep me straining at the leash of life. Dr. Rocky Seckler, Dr. John Ardesia, Dr. Ronald Gardner and Dr. Brian Arcement. All have gone beyond the call of duty.

My trusted agent and friend, Frank Weimann. If you value your money, do not play poker with this man.

The crew at ECW, indefatigable and creative. Jack David. For his vision. Erin Creasey, Crissy Calhoun and Susannah Ames. For dealing with my Quixotic and often mercurial personality. Emily Schultz, I thought you would cut me with a sword. But with grace, you pointed me to a star.

George Sammet. When this cat has your back, you can sleep very tight.

Karel Pravec and Frank "The Tank" Camiscioli, the warriors of Silver Fox Brazilian Jiu Jitsu Academy. Fighting from your foxhole would be an honor. Josh Madama and Milo Esteves, in the foxhole to our right. Come one, come a thousand.

Douglas P. Love. Welcome to the jungle.

Louis Wesolowsky. Filmmaker extraordinaire. LouisWes.com.

Cliff O'Hara. A rock.

To the countless standup cops, prosecutors, lawyers and selfless citizens, it has been a distinct honor to have shared the same space with you.

To my dear family and many friends, my very humble thanks.

Published by ECW Press
665 Gerrard Street East
Toronto, ON M4M 1Y2
416-694-3348 / info@ecwpress.com

To the best of his abilities, the author has related experiences, places, people, and organizations from his memories of them. In order to protect the privacy of others, he has, in some instances, changed the names of certain people and details of events and places.

LIBRARY AND ARCHIVES CANADA CATALOGUING IN PUBLICATION

Bradshaw, Wayne (Wayne Evans), author
Jersey tough : my wild ride from outlaw biker to undercover cop /
Wayne "Big Chuck" Bradshaw.

Issued in print and electronic formats.
ISBN 978-1-77041-261-3 (paperback)
ISBN 978-1-77090-842-0 (PDF); ISBN 978-1-77090-843-7 (ePub)

1. Bradshaw, Wayne (Wayne Evans). 2. Pagans (Motorcycle club).
3. Motorcycle clubs—United States. 4. Motorcycle gangs—United States.
5. Gang members—United States—Biography. 6. Police—New Jersey—Biography. I. Title.

HV6439.U5B73 2016   364.106'60973   C2015-907281-6
C2015-907282-4

Cover design: Michel Vrana
Interior images: courtesy of the author

Printing: Friesens
3   4   5

Printed and bound in Canada

FSC
www.fsc.org
MIX
Paper from
responsible sources
FSC® C016245